On April 12, 1865, General Robert E. Lee of Virginia surrendered to General Ulysses S. Grant of the Grand Army of the Republic essentially ending the U.S. Civil War. Hundreds of miles away, in a small New England city, the Wooster Square area was in transition. Prior to the war, wealthy Yankee merchants and business owners populated the area. By the 1870's, the neighborhood's population had become archaic. Furthermore, dozens of industries moved into the area.

Larry Pisani, a Yale graduate and long time professor at Southern Connecticut State University, stated that the first Italian to settle in New Haven was William Diodati (Pisani, *The Italian in America*, pp. 143). Diodati was the son of a prosperous family from Tuscany. His grandfather, Giovanni was a theologian in Geneva.

Upon his arrival in the Elm City in 1715, William went into the gold and silver trade. On February 16, 1720, he married Sara Dumbar and they had a child named Elizabeth.

It is believed that Diodati passed away in the winter of 1751. In his will, he instructed Sara to improve their farmland which was located on present day Court Street.

Alberto Cupelli, the author of "*The Italian of Old New Haven*" claimed that Luigi Roberti was the second Italian in New Haven (Cupelli, *The Italian of Old New Haven*, pp. 2). In 1847, Roberti established a preparatory female boarding school at 128 Chapel Street. When Luigi passed away in 1882, his wife Elza retired and moved to 697 State Street.

The 1880 Census revealed that one hundred and two Italians lived in the city. Within a decade, the Italian population in the Elm City would be in the thousands.

The people of southern Italy, Il Mezzogiorno, endured unthinkable suffering after 1861. The northern Italians looked down upon their predominately uneducated countrymen in the south. Furthermore, the southerners experienced natural disasters, soil erosion, and economic bust. Discouraged, but willing to work, southern Italians left for destinations, first in South America, and later America.

Ellis Island, located in New York Harbor, opened in 1892 as an immigration inspection station. Millions of Italian immigrants anxiously made the arduous voyage across the Atlantic Ocean to be processed at Ellis Island. Authorities interrogated each immigrant asking pertinent questions such as the amount of money they had upon arrival and their medical history. Immigrants who were approved generally moved to northern cities where their relatives or Italians from their home village had settled. Thus, neighborhoods such as the North End of Boston or South Philadelphia became small Italian villages in America.

Ellis Island-Early 1900's

The Hill Section

Initially, there were two distinctive Italian enclaves in New Haven. The northern Italians settled in the Hill section along with the Russian Jews and the Irish along Howard Avenue.

The southern Italians settled in the Wooster Square area. The antagonism between the two groups originated in Italy and carried over into the Elm City. Most Italians in the Hill were working poor. Hundreds were employed by the New York-New Haven-Boston Railroad. By 1908, over ten thousand Italians worked for the railroad as the company extended the tracks north (Cupelli, *The Italian of Old New Haven*, pp. 7).

W.R Arms Company (Winchester) also employed numerous Italians from the Hill including Sebastiano Lavorgna of 90 Oak Street who worked there at the end of the 19th Century.

The New Haven Clock Company was incorporated in April of 1856. By the outset of the Civil War, the company was producing close to two hundred thousand clocks a year and had over three hundred employees. In the last decade of the 1800's, Alfonso Maresca of 107 Oak Street worked at the plant.

In 1902, the leadership of the company was under the direction of Walter Camp who played football at Yale. Years later, he was inducted into the Professional Football Hall of Fame. Camp added wristwatches to the line of production in 1915. In 1923, he was succeed by Edwin Root.

The Dilapidated New Haven Clock Factory at 133 Hamilton Street in 2009.

During the Second World War, the company produced war products. In March of 1946, the plant resumed making clocks and watches. The firm continued to be one the largest clock producers in the world until it claimed bankruptcy in 1960.

The Sargent Company, which hired an abundant number of Italians from Wooster Square, also employed Italians from the Hill. The distance from the neighborhood to the plant was not easy to cover on foot, especially during inclement weather. Nevertheless, in the late 1800's, Lorenzo Batto of 88 Oak Street, Francesco and Vincenzo Triano of 12 Minor Street, and Ralph Russo of 91 Oak Street earned a living at the plant.

Le Marche

In 1909, thirty-six men who traced their roots back to the Le Marche region in northeastern Italy created the Marchigiano Club. In 1923, the social club moved to the present location at 226 Cedar Street. The organization provided sick benefits for its members and a place for the men to enjoy homemade wine while playing cards.

At its peak, the Marchegian Club had over four thousand members (Lattanzi, *Oyster Village*, pp. 131.) and was the third largest Italian American organization in America.

There were two churches that offered mass to the Italians of the Hill Section. The oldest, Sacred Heart, located on Columbus Avenue was established in 1896. The second, St. Anthony, was founded in 1904. The first pastor was Scalabrini Father Bartolomeo

Marenchino. "The Beacon on the Hill," is situated at 70 Washington Avenue and after a century still offers mass in Italian.

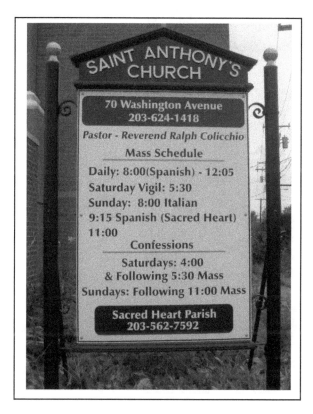

2005-St. Anthony's Church Grounds

Reverend Joseph Moffo was born on December 23, 1930. As a young clergyman, he was working at St. Joseph's Church in New York when screen icon Robert DeNiro approached him about playing the priest during the religious street festival in the film Godfather II. The legendary actor wanted Father Moffo because he was an authentic Italian American priest.

For seventeen years, the congenial and soft spoken priest served at St. Anthony's Church. Idolized by his parishioners, Father Moffo presided over the one hundredth year anniversary of the parish in 2004. Father Joe passed away on August 25, 2007, after making a lasting impression on scores of people.

Father Moffo at Anthony's Ocean View Restaurant.

St. Anthony's
Church

Summer of
2011

New Haven Italian Population

(Source: Michael J. Petriccione, *Immigrant City of New Haven*, pp. 33.)

Year	Population	Number of Italians	Percentage of Population of Italian Descent
1890	85,981	2,332	2.9%
1900	108,027	7,781	7.2%
1910	133,605	14,139	10.6%
1920	162,519	23,000	14.1%
1930	162,650	41,858	26.0%

Religious Procession on Wooster Street-Circa 1940

(Photo Courtesy of Ruby Proto)

Wooster Square

After 1890, Italian immigrants in considerable numbers began to move into the Wooster Square area. The majority of these immigrants were from the villages of Amalfi, Atrani, and Scafati. Mostly unskilled, they were attracted to the neighborhood's cheap housing. In fact, the tenements in Wooster Square were overcrowded and dilapidated. Further drawing the Italians to the area were the nearby factories. These companies, such as the Candee Rubber Company, and the J.B. Sargent Company hired thousands of Italian workers.

By 1905, the Wooster Square area was a self-contained neighborhood. "Little Italy" provided the immigrant with a sense of psychological security. With their old world traditions intact, along with family and friends in the vicinity, there was virtually no need for the Italian immigrant to leave the area.

Wooster Street was dotted with small family operated businesses selling cheeses, meats, vegetables, macaroni, tobacco, and seafood. Also, the neighborhood contained Italian doctors, lawyers, blacksmiths, shoemakers, clothing stores, banks and its own newspapers. The popular weekly journal, La Stella d'Italia was founded in 1892 by Paul Russo. Another favorite publication, Corriere Del Connecticut was established in 1897 and was located at 223 Wooster Street.

In 1906, the immigrants beamed with pride when Antonio Vannacori was elected as city Alderman. Antonio, from Wooster Street, was a Republican. Other pillars of the immigrant community included Dr. B. Macaluso who had his office at 202 Wooster Street, Dr. Pietro DeSantis who cared for his patients at 141 Olive Street and Dr. Biagio Francolini of 541 Chapel Street.

At this time period, very few Italians had the opportunity to graduate from high school or to purchase real estate. Michael Petriccione, in "*The Immigrant City of New Haven 1890-1930*" recorded the history of Pasquale Perrilli. In 1906, Perrilli was an ice cream peddler boarding at 16 Union Street. Five years later, he had acquired enough capital to start his own business. Pasquale owned a confectionary store at 81 Chestnut Street.

Dr. Eugene Fappiano was a highly regarded scholar and Professor of Sociology at Southern Connecticut State University. He has written extensively about the Italian presence in the Elm City. A son of an Italian father and a Swedish mother, Fappiano grew up in the "Goatville" section of the city. Eugene also served as a past president of the Italian American Historical Society of New Haven.

In the winter of 2001, Dr. Fappiano wrote an article for the society's newsletter *La Storia* entitled "*Ethnic Pluralism in the Greater Wooster Neighborhood Circa 1915*."

In his work, he emphasized that although Wooster Square was predominately Italian, there were Jewish and Irish business owners in the area. Nevertheless, Dr. Fappiano highlighted a number of Italian proprietors throughout the area. Including:

Grand Avenue between Olive and Jefferson

Liborio Labate-barber

Triforo and Sons-painters

Matteo Canelli-grocer

Angelo Pietrasimone-grinder

Constantine DeMetrio-confectionary

Jefferson to Bradley

Alfonso Fasano-jeweler

J. Mignone-shoe store

Ferdinand Gentile-barber

James Mongillo-saloon owner

Ruggiero and Vegliante-barbers

Bradley to Franklin

A. Mignone-watchmaker

M. Maresca-undertaker

Franklin to Hamilton

Mrs. M. Iovanne-grocer

Charles Conte-florist

Gaetano Popolozio-real estate

V.D Addio-shoemaker

L. Montanaro-drug store

Newspapers.—Oxydonor.

The Corriere Del Connecticut
ITALIAN WEEKLY.
THE OLDEST IN THE STATE
FOUNDED AUGUST, 1897

The Best Advertising Medium in the New England States; is acknowledged as the most influential and practically the only Republican Newspaper in the State.   Published every Saturday. . . . . .

2 Cents per Copy.   Subscription Price, $1.00 Per Year.
223 WOOSTER STREET.

"L'INDIPENDENTE."

The Most Influential Italian Weekly Newspaper in New England.

FOUNDED SEPTEMBER, 1902.

Office, 153 Franklin Street, New Haven, Conn.

Best Advertising Medium in the States of New England among the Italian People.

TWO CENTS PER COPY.   SUBSCRIPTION PRICE $1.00 PER YEAR.

OXYDONOR CURES DISEASE.

The Connecticut Sales Co.
STATE DISTRIBUTORS.
113 CHURCH STREET,   ROOM 307.
TELEPHONE.

Source-Michael J. Petriccione

PASQUALE FUSCO
Banker and Broker,
STEAMSHIP TICKET AGENT,
Jeweler and Watchmaker.
67 BROAD STREET,   NEW HAVEN, CONN.
TELEPHONE 1781-3.

FRANK DE LUCIA,
Banker and Broker,

Real Estate, Mortgage Loans, Insurance. Steamship Tickets, Notary Public, Building Contractor.

FUNERAL DIRECTOR AND EMBALMER.
382-384 East Street, New Haven, Conn.
TELEPHONE 4702.

FREDERICK C. HULL,
Investment Securities
26 HOWE ST., NEW HAVEN, CONN.
PHONE 4300.
REPRESENTATIVE OF BEHTRON, GRISCOM & JENKS, Bankers,
NEW YORK.   PHILADELPHIA.

Maps of New Haven,
Convenient for the Pocket.

Price 25 Cents Each.

The Price & Lee Co., 206 Meadow Street.

Source-Michael J. Petriccione

Following the Allied victory in World War I, America entered a joyous period of time. During "The Roaring Twenties," Italian Americans became the largest ethnic group in New Haven. In the heart of Little Italy, along Wooster Street, ninety-eight percent of the residents were Italian Americans (Lassonde, *Learning to Forget*, pp. 20.).

Little Italy 1930-1960

In a thirty year period of time, Wooster Square underwent unprecedented changes. Social, cultural, and physical changes disrupted the continuity of the area. Ultimately, inter-marriage, social mobility, mainstreaming into the American society, and Redevelopment transformed Little Italy into a multi-ethnic neighborhood.

Proud and uneducated, the Italian immigrant tended to de-emphasize the importance of education. In Italy, the northern Italians controlled the school system. The immigrants did not value the ability to read and write. What was important were the lessons of manhood and the augmentation of the family income. School was often viewed as an intrusion into the sanctity of the family. However, once the immigrants became committed to the United States as their permanent home, their views on education changed. Education became the vehicle for self-improvement and financial prosperity.

(L to R) Frank Gargano, Congresswoman Rosa DeLauro, Mayor DeStefano, and Alderman Alphonse Paolillo marching in the 2012 St. Andrew's Procession. Rosa's family has been active in the Wooster Square area for nearly a century.

At the conclusion of the Second World War, a jubilant America welcomed home soldiers, sailors, and other military personnel. In 1944, the federal government passed the G.I. Bill of Rights which provided higher education, job training and low interest loans for veterans.

Thousands of Italian Americans who fought heroically in the war were able to attend college. In most cases, these individuals were the first in their family to earn an advanced degree. A college degree made it possible for many Italian Americans to obtain careers in medicine, law, business or in other white collar jobs. Educated and proud, Italian Americans began to ascend "the social ladder."

The G.I Bill of Rights had a tremendous impact on the United States. Families who had lived in Little Italy for decades left to join the more affluent in the suburbs. In short, the G.I. Bill of Rights enabled many Italian Americans to fulfill their dreams of home ownership.

Inter-Marriage

La Famiglia (the family) was the most important institution to the Italian immigrants. The family consisted not only of the father, mother, and children but also the grandparents, aunts, uncles, cousins, and godparents. It was not uncommon for the extended family to live and to work together in a Little Italy such as Wooster Square. These early immigrants were strongly opposed to marriage with members of other nationalities. The customs and morals of the other ethnic groups baffled the Italian immigrants.

In fact, in 1930, foreign born Italians in New Haven had an unusually high inter-marriage rate. Ruby Jo Reeves Kennedy conducted a survey which further illustrated this fact. The data concluded that Italians in New Haven had a higher inter-marriage rate then Jews, Irish, Polish, and Germans (Lassonde, *Learning to Forget*, pp. 119.).

However, by the 1950's, as a result of the G.I. Bill of Rights, Italian Americans were experiencing compelling changes. In pursuit of "something better" many left Italian neighborhoods such as Mulberry Street (Manhattan), Murray Hill (Cleveland), and Wooster Square. As the Italian Americans moved to the suburbs, the closeness of the extended family began to dissolve. Children who had lived with their parents met once or twice a week for dinner. Cousins who had grown up together only saw one another on special occasions. Coinciding with the separation of the extended family, more Italian Americans began to marry members of other ethnic groups.

No longer were Italian American men and women inclined to marry "one of their own." By the early 1960's, seventy percent of Italian Americans married a spouse of another nationality.

Mainstreaming into American Society

The early Italian immigrants were forced to settle into Italian enclaves as a method to protect themselves from an unfamiliar and harsh environment. The "Little Italy's" provided the immigrants with a sense of psychological stability. Along Wooster Street or Arthur Avenue (Bronx), the immigrants were allowed to maintain their language, religion, customs, and culture. The immigrants did not comprehend or desire social interaction with established Americans. However, the children and grandchildren of the immigrants had different wishes. To a certain extent they wanted to become Americanized.

The second generation Italian Americans were not isolated to their neighborhood. These men and women spoke both Italian and English. Unlike their respected elders, many second generation Italian Americans wished to excel in school. In an attempt to break away from their heritage, many left Little Italy, married non-Italians or changed their last names.

The children of immigrants chose to live in two different worlds. They remained affiliated with many of their cultural traits but at the same time they incorporated aspects of the American culture. For example, these second generation Italian Americans spoke Italian at home and English when outside of the home.

Third and fourth generation Americans of Italian descent combine a mixture of American and Italian social and cultural characteristics. Unlike the previous two generations, they were secure with their American identity. More American than Italian, they were curious to learn about their heritage. Many return to Little Italy to investigate the neighborhood that their grandparents had lived in.

Although the vast majority of this group cannot speak Italian, they remain proud of their heritage. The third and fourth generations understand the value of education. As a result, many are college graduates and prominent members of society. This group includes doctors, lawyers, business executives, teachers, professors, and politicians. In essence, Italians Americans have come a long way in a very short period of time.

Wooster Square Today

Stephanie and Christopher Porto in front of the garden at the entrance of Wooster Street in 1994. Their grandparents came from Olive and Chestnut Streets.

Since Redevelopment, the Italian population of Wooster Square has declined. Wooster Street is no longer a predominately Italian enclave. In harsh reality, the population is of mixed ethnic origins and gentrified. Despite Redevelopment, social mobility, assimilation, and mixed marriages, a certain "Italian flavor" has remained in the area.

Today, there still is a contingent of Italian owned businesses in Wooster Square. One can walk down the streets of Little Italy (Wooster, Chapel, Warren, etc.) and experience the aromas of fine Italian cuisine from the neighborhood's eateries. There are also other Italian American owned businesses such as Riccutti Hair Salon, Lincoln Flower, and Scarpellino Reality to go along with the restaurants and funeral homes.

An important component of Wooster Square today are the St. Andrew and Santa Maria Maddalena Societies. Hundreds of men and women, most with ties to the neighborhood, belong to these fraternal organizations. The leaders of these century old institutions orchestrate cultural and religious events to promote Italian pride and to retain the values that their elders installed in them decades ago.

St. Michael Church, the iconic symbol of Wooster Square, has also undergone drastic changes. The school was forced to close due to reduced enrollment. Now, the majority of the parishioners commute to the church for mass. Nevertheless, St. Michael Church has dedicated members determined to see the church thrive well into the future.

What does the future hold for Wooster Square? Only the passage of time can answer this question. Perhaps by the virtue of their nature, Italian Americans are proud, and value based people. Many younger people, in search of their roots, have moved back to the neighborhood of their parents and grandparents. There is hope and evidence that the Italian influence in Wooster Square will thrive well into the future.

Wooster Square Society Presidents Ruby Proto (L) and Julia Nicefaro (R) before the St. Andrew Procession in June of 2012.

Their Stories in Wooster Square

"My parents never assimilated, they could not speak eight words of English. They did not want to learn. They could not help us with our school work but they feed us and kept us clean. They taught us other lessons." Harry Trotta

Harry Trotta   Joseph and Rosalie Derrico   Anna Anastasio

<u>Harry Trotta</u>-was delivered by a mid-wife at 149 Wallace Street in 1928. His parents, Frank and Maria had ten children. Frank owned Trotta's Bakery located at 157 Wallace Street. Unfortunately, he lost his business during the Great Depression. Harry attended Hamilton School, Fair Haven Junior High, and graduated from Hillhouse. For many years, he was the proprietor of Central Grocery located at 272 George Street.

<u>Joseph and Rosalie Derrico</u>- Joe was born on Wooster Street in 1939 to parents named Frank and Mary DeLuca Derrico. Frank worked at Acme Wire in Hamden. Joe was baptized at St. Anthony Church. He married the former Rosalie Cocco of St. John Street in 1959. Her family owned Cocco's Apizza. As a young couple, they left the Hill section and moved to North Haven. The couple has three sons. Their son Joseph Jr. owned Derrico's Restaurant on Washington Avenue in North Haven.

<u>Anna Anastasio</u>-was born on Wooster Street. She has resided at 336 St. John Street for over seventy years. Anna worked at Alba Dress Shop on Hamilton and St. John Streets.

Images From Little Italy

A Young Charles Bove (Standing)

(Photo Courtesy of Charles Bove)

Mayor Biagio DiLieto (Center) at the St. Maria Maddalena Society

(SSMM Archives)

Tony Sacco and his daughter in 1985

127 Wooster Street

(SSMM Archives)

Frankie Lee on Wooster Street

Mid-1990's

(SSMM Archives)

Nicola Incarnato

Nicola Incarnato and his granddaughter Callie on the corner of Chestnut and Wooster Streets in the Spring of 2016.

Nicola Incarnato met his future wife Therese Maiorano while she was vacationing with her parents and a cousin in Calabria. The following year, on November 18, 1969, Nicola immigrated to New Haven. The couple married at St. Michael Church on July 18, 1970. Initially, Nicola found work at a steel shop in North Haven. He then was able to secure a job with the city in the Parking Authority.

Nicola and Therese have three children named David, Nicole, and Danielle. The couple also has five grandchildren. Today, the Incarnato's reside on Wooster Street and they are active members of St. Michael Church and a number of Italian American organizations.

Chapter Two-Wooster Square as an Industrial Center

From the post Civil War period to the Great Depression, New Haven was a bustling industrial center producing thousands of items. Esteemed author, Anthony Riccio (*Farms, Factories, and Families*), noted that from 1900 to 1920, there were eight hundred companies in the Elm City with hundreds of garment and manufacturing facilities. The newly arrived immigrants from Eastern Europe, Ireland, and Italy comprised of much of the labor pool. The major employers of Italians from Wooster Square were:

<u>Sargent</u>-Joseph Bradford (J.B.) Sargent and his two siblings initially operated a wholesale hardware business in New York City. In 1864, they moved the plant from New Britain to New Haven to be situated next to the harbor and railroad. The massive Sargent factory was located at the intersection of Water, Wallace, and Hamilton Streets. Although the corporation produced tens of thousands of items, it was best known for its production of locks. Sargent was credited for being the first company in New Haven to pay its employees weekly. A multi talented individual, J.B. entered the political realm in 1890. He served as the mayor of New Haven for two terms.

In his personal life, J.B. married a lovely Italian woman and he therefore tended to be affable towards his Italian workers. By the 1920's, three quarter of the workers at the plant were Italian. In 1967, the descendants of J.B. sold the company.

In 1890, examples of immigrants that worked at Sargent were: Graziano Altiero and Alfonso Calandrilla. Altiero boarded at 191 Hamilton Street and Calandrilla at 135 Hamilton Street.*

*(Cupelli, *The Italian of Old New Haven*, pp. 5.)

Sargent Company

January-June 1910

(Source-Rae Douglas, *City*, pp. 117-118.)

From 1901 to 1910, over two million Italians arrived to destinations in America.* Thousands settled in the Italian communities in New Haven. During the first six months of 1910, the Sargent Corporation hired close to five hundred new employees. Dozens of these employees lived in the Wooster Square area including:

1. M. Acamfora — 64 Wooster Street
2. Frank Cammira — 47 Collis Street
3. N. Constantinople — 71 Wooster Street
4. James Egan — 486 Chapel Street
5. S. Esposito — 28 Collis Street
6. Lawrence Floyd — 29 Wallace Street
7. A. Gaspino — 174 East Street
8. Antonio Gambarde — 51 Collis Street
9. M. Gradioso — 156 East Street
10. Michael Garlly — 487 Chapel Street
11. Anthony Imperatore — 20 Hamilton Street
12. Joseph Juknit — 180 East Street
13. Angelo Lura — 51 Collis Street
14. F. Ligori — 436 Chapel Street
15. F. Luibello — 45 Collis Street
16. D. Monaco — 29 Collis Street
17. Vincenzo Natale — 29 Collis Street
18. Anthony Piscitelli — 16 Wallace Street
19. Dom Pantero — 25 Collis Street
20. Michael Sleany — 164 East Street
21. Vincent Spinello — 24 Wallace Street
22. A. Vissiccio — 62 Wooster Street
23. E. Vaccino — 19 East Street

* (Kathleen Lee, *Tracing Our Italian Roots*, pp. 2.)

<u>A.C. Gilbert and L. Candee Rubber Company</u>-A.C. Gilbert was a humorous individual who enjoyed a remarkable life. He was born on February 15, 1884, in Salem, Oregon. As a child, he was infatuated with magic. Years later, he helped to pay off his college tuition by performing in magic shows.

Gilbert attended Pacific University for two years. In 1904, he was the Intercollegiate wrestling champion. Prior to his junior year, he transferred to Yale to study medicine. In 1906, A.C. established a new world record in the pole vault by clearing 12'6. Two years later, he captured the gold medal at the Olympic Games held in London. A.C. completed his studies from Yale in 1909.

As an inventor, he had over one hundred and fifty patents to his credit. In 1938, Gilbert purchased American Flyer, a manufacturer of train sets. During the Second World War, A.C. modified his plant to produce war goods. For decades, his factory, which was located in Fair Haven, was profitable. Hundreds of Italian Americans from Wooster Square made the walk from Little Italy to the factory to produce goods that were sold worldwide.

Leverett Candee was born on June 1, 1795, in Oxford, Connecticut. After a few disastrous business ventures, he decided to produce rubber products. His corporation became the pioneer in producing rubber footwear. A victim of the Great Depression, the Candee Rubber Company closed its doors in March of 1929. As a result, eight hundred employees lost their jobs. As with A.C. Gilbert, Candee employed hundreds of Italian Americans.

An example of an immigrant that worked at Candee Rubber Company in 1890 was Andrea Cappala who boarded at 334 East Street.

<u>C. Cowles and Company</u>-The C. Cowles and Company was founded in 1838. Originally, the company made lanterns for horse drawn carriages. Located at 83 Water Street, the corporation had six operating divisions in 2011.

C. Cowles-2011

The C. Cowles Company in July of 2011. This firm was a survivor of Redevelopment. In the photo, on the left, the highway is visible. A few years later, C. Cowles closed the New Haven plant.

Sperry and Barnes-was a slaughterhouse and meat packing plant located on Long Warf. The company was formed in 1870 and hired thousands of Eastern Europeans, Polish, and Italian immigrants. On July 16, 1886, at 5:00 P.M. in the evening, John Torsney, a night watchman discovered a fire in the storehouse. As a result of the facility being saturated with grease, the blaze spread with great rapidity. By 11:00 P.M., the fire was under control. Joel A. Sperry the owner, claimed that the damage was between $275,000 and $300,000. However, fifteen hundred hogs were rescued. Sperry and Barnes was profitable for over half a century before closing its doors.

In the early 1900's, Raffaele Calienno worked at the company and he boarded at 191 Hamilton Street.

New Haven Railroad and H.B. Ives-In the early 1900's, the railroad was expanding their tracks from New York to Boston. Immigrant labor was in demand to lay tracks, dig ditches, and build bridges. By 1908, ten thousand Italians were employed by the railroad (Cupelli, *The Italian of Old New Haven*, pp. 7.).

H.B. Ives-was founded by Hobart B. Ives in 1876. The plant produced household hardware and it was located on Artizan Street.

Strouse and Adler-For many decades, there were dozens of garment companies in Wooster Square. The largest of these companies was Strouse and Adler. In 1860, Isaac Strouse founded a corset firm. Two years later, Max Adler joined him to create their company. The massive plant, located at 78-84 Olive Street, was built in 1876. Strouse and Adler employed hundreds of Italian workers from the area to produce their girdles. The company's most popular product was the "Smoothie."

Other garment companies such as Lerners Dress Factory, Clardi Dress Shop, Ideal Shirt, and Lesnow Brothers were in competition for cheap labor. Luisa DeLauro, a lifelong resident of Olive Street, worked at Lesnow Brothers. She shared her experiences at the sweat shop.

Luisa DeLauro marching (Center) in the St. Andrew Society Procession in June of 1986.

(St. Andrew Society Archives)

Question-How old were you when you started at Lesnow Brothers?

Luisa DeLauro-"At the age of sixteen, I worked at Lesnow Brothers, a shirt factory located on Hamilton Street. I worked at the factory during the Great Depression. After my father died, I worked at our family pastry shop, Canestri Pastry on Wooster Street."

Question-What were the conditions like at Lesnow Brothers?

Luisa-"The machines were very old but safe to operate. The factory did not have smoke alarms, and overcrowding was a problem. We were cheap labor and we were not unionized. The company moved down south instead of becoming unionized."

Question-How much money did you make?

Luisa-"I made six dollars a week."

Question-What percentage of the employees were Italian American?

Luisa-"I would guess that about ninety percent of Lesnow's workers were Italian. Most of these people lived in the area. We were very close, like one big family. We walked together to the rubber factories or the garment shops."

Question-What happened after Lesnow Brothers closed?

Luisa-"Many people lost their jobs. Eventually, the bridge was built and the area was destroyed. Most people were forced out of the area. A few of us remained, but not many. At one time, we had everything. There were schools, a church, fish and chicken markets, and five drug stores. The area was safe. There is a book, "The Shut Down" about what happened to the area."*

*Interview. Luisa DeLauro. May 31, 1993.

The magnificent Max Adler House was built in 1879. The home is located at 311 Greene Street.

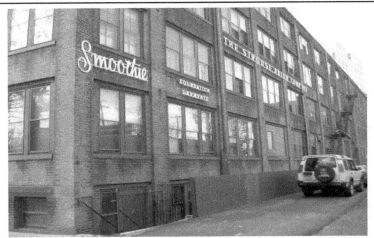

Strouse Adler Company Building-2010

Their Stories in Wooster Square

Rose Fratini

Anthony Notarino

Fay Natale and Jo-Ann Buccetti

<u>Rose Fratini</u>-was born as one of nine children to Francesco and Agnesa Carrano. Francesco and his wife were born in Amalfi. They married at St. Andrew Cathedral in 1919. Five years later, Francesco came to America. His wife joined him the following year and they resided at 51 Greene Street above Gag's Grille. Later, the family moved to 51 Wooster Street. To provide for his family, Francesco worked as a forklift operator on the docks for the railroad. He retired from New Haven Plumbing and Board on East and Greene Streets.

Rose married Anthony Fratini in 1959. Anthony was a butcher by trade and they couple met at Rose's work. They had two sons. Rose has been an active member of the St. Andrew Ladies Society for over forty years. She has returned to Amalfi thirteen times and she has hosted exchange students from Amalfi at her home.

<u>Anthony "Burt" Notarino</u>-was born one of five children to Anthony "Shorty" and Adeline Toscano Notarino. The family resided at 128 Greene Street. "Shorty" worked at Seamless Rubber on Hallock Avenue. Burt married the former Anne Consiglio of Hamilton Street. The couple had three children. Burt earned a living as a truck driver for the city and for the New Haven Register. For over seventy years, he has been picking mushrooms and he is the most accomplished picker in the state.

<u>Fay Natale and Jo-Ann Buccetti</u>-are two of eleven children born to Joseph and Bernice Buccetti. To support his family, Joe worked for the city in the sanitation department. The family lived on Olive Street and later Chestnut Street. Fay and her husband Frank have two children and eight grandchildren. Jo-Ann is very active at the North Haven Senior Center and she enjoys writing poetry.

Images From Little Italy

Theresa Argento (Left) and Ann Marie "Nonnie" Fronte-Circa 1980's

Proudly they served as the Presidents of the St. Andrew and St. Maria Maddalena Female Societies for decades.

(SSMM Archives)

Members of the Bonetti family on Franklin Street early 1940's.

(Photos Courtesy of Andrew Bonetti)

Chapter Three-World War II

Anthony "Flash" Consiglio at 171 Chestnut Street.

Tony Vitolo (R) Camp Lejeune 1943

(Photo Courtesy of the Scarpellino Family)

Gary Garibaldi

(Photo Courtesy of Bernard Garibaldi)

James V. Routolo with his daughters at 251 Greene Street. James was killed during the Battle of the Bulge on November 18, 1944.

(SSMM Archives)

On December 7, 1941, the Imperial Navy of Japan launched a surprise attack on the American Pacific fleet in Pearl Harbor. For the next five years, America sent her young men and women to all stations of the globe to fight the Axis Powers.

According to the National Italian American Foundation (niaf.org), 1.2 million Italian Americans served in the war effort. Remarkably, this number represented one out of every ten individuals in the military. Despite being the children of immigrants, or in many cases, having relatives still in the "old country," Italian Americans earned the reputation of being courageous soldiers. By the end of the conflict, fourteen Italian Americans earned the Congressional Medal of Honor. Two Italians Americans, Dominic Salvatore Gentile, and John Basilone were highly decorated.

Dominic "Don" Gentile was born on December 6, 1920, in Piqua, Ohio to Italian immigrants. During the war, Major Gentile was credited with downing twenty-five German planes. For his efforts, he was awarded the Silver Star and the Distinguished Service Cross. Ironically, Gentile was killed in a plane crash on January 28, 1951. He was survived by his wife Isabella and their sons Don and Pasquale.

John Baslione was born the sixth of ten children on November 4, 1916, in Buffalo, New York. His father Salvatore immigrated from the Naples region to the United States in 1903. His wife, the former Dora Bencivenga Baslione was born in New Jersey in 1889.

Initially, and unknown to most people, John first served in the United States Army. While stationed in the Philippines, he was a military service boxing champion. In July of 1940, Basilone enlisted in the Marines. Within a few years, this Italian American would become a household name.

John Basilone

On October 24, 1942, the Battle of Henderson Field took place on Guadalcanal. Approximately, three thousand Japanese troops from the prominent Sendai Division attacked Basilone's unit. For two days, the fighting was fierce and the carnage was appalling. John demonstrated little regard for his own safety and he was a machine of destruction killing dozens of Japanese soldiers. Following the battle, the war department brought their hero home to help to sell war bonds. John never felt comfortable in this role and he missed being with his fellow "Leathernecks." Consequently, he requested to be sent back to the front lines.

While away from combat, John met and fell in love with Lena Riggi the daughter of Sicilian immigrants from Portland, Oregon. Lena was a sergeant in the Marine Corps Women's Reserve. The couple married on July 7, 1944.

On February 19, 1945, the United States invaded the island of Iwo Jima. John died in combat on that first day. Before the island was secured over five thousand Americans lost their lives. For his valor, Basilone became the only enlisted Marine to win the Purple Heart, Congressional Medal of Honor, and the Navy Cross. He is buried at Arlington National Cemetery. Unlike her husband, Lena lived a long life. She passed away on June 11, 1999, at the age of eighty-six. She never re-married.

New Haven

Men and women from the Nutmeg State were prevalent in all theaters of the war and for a small state suffered staggering causality rates. The website ctcasualmedianara.gov breaks down the causalities as:

956 Dead
12 Died in Prison Camps
61 Missing
1,232 Wounded
43 Released Prisoners
2,303-Total Causalities

According to the same data base, eighty-one soldiers from New Haven were killed during World War II. All sections of the Elm City experienced the pain and sorrow of a soldier's death. Grieving was shared by the family and their neighbors. Fair Haven lost Joseph Abbatello of 279 James Street, Thomas Collins of 310 Lenox Street, Salvatore Carbone of 62 Farren Avenue, and John Perrilli of 84 James Street. Killed in action from the Hill section included John Dest of 163 Columbus Avenue, Ed Cunningham of 724 Washington Avenue, Romolo Luzi of 72 Barclay Street, and John Troy of 178 Kimberly Avenue.

The more spacious neighborhoods of the Annex and Morris Cove lost young men on foreign grounds. Ralph Furino of 851 Woodward Avenue, Leon Robinson of 393 Huntington Avenue, and Joseph Riordan of 56 Woodward Avenue all paid the ultimate price.

Tragically, Mr. and Mrs. John Duffy of 12 Fox Street lost two sons while fighting the Axis Powers. James Edward, Seaman Second Class, and John Francis, a fireman in the Navy, both perished in the war.

Little Italy, a tight knit neighborhood, was especially heartbroken by the loss of its sons. In an neighborhood, where extended families resided and neighbors were as close as family, a battlefield death was traumatic. Wooster Street, the heart of the Italian colony, lost Joseph Liberti, and Biaggio Del Amuro. Nearby, Brown Street lost Gaetano Scaramella and Mike Accurso.

There were also many men from the Tenth and Eleventh Wards who were wounded in battle. Neighbors John Bombace (175 Chestnut Street) and Dominic Biondi (171 Chestnut Street) were both Purple Heart recipients. Other neighborhood boys wounded in battle included Vincent Fragola (49 Warren Street), Peter Ricciuti (16 Brown Street), Attilio Sequino (6 Jefferson Street), Nicolo Annunziata (138 East Street), and Nicholas Fiasconaro (9 Hughes Place).

Today, after seventy years, there are markers in Wooster Square that pay homage to the fallen soldiers. On Wooster Street, at Memorial Playground, there is a beautiful plaque which was dedicated on October 2, 1955.

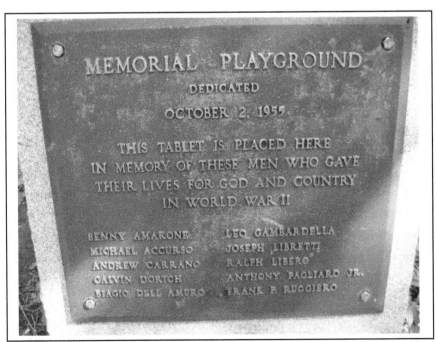

A block away, in Columbus Park, the World War II Veteran's Memorial Monument honors the soldiers from the Eleventh Ward and was erected in 1950.

A hundred yards away, near Greene Street, a marker honors the fallen soldiers from their classmates in the Class of 1928 at Columbus School.

Lastly, on Jefferson Street, a scenic park honors Joe Lenzi who was killed on Iwo Jima.

Brazi's Restaurant in December of 2013

Bill Iovanne (L), Felix Del Guidice (C), and Mike Coppola (R)

Del Guidice (Korea) and Coppola (Battle of Okinawa) were former Marines and war heroes.

Although victorious, the United States suffered over 400,000 military service deaths during the war. Thirty-four members of the Tenth and Eleventh Wards died while serving their nation.

THE HONOR ROLL

ALBERT ACAMPORA	JERRY ESPOSITO	FRANK FISCO	ANTHONY PAGLIARO JR.	GAETANO SCARAMELLA
MICHAEL ACCURSO	ANTHONY D'AMATO	MICHAEL IOVENE	DOMINIC A. MARESCA	PASQUALE ZIMBARDI
ANTHONY ALDIERI	JOSEPH DECUSATI	ANTHONY GAMBERDELLA	ANTHONY A. MARZULLO	
BENNY AMARONE	BIAGIO DELL AMURO	LEO GAMBERDELLA	SALVATORE E. MIGLIARO	
JOHN ARMINIO	JAMES DEPINO	VICTOR D. LAUCELLA	MATTHEW NASTRI	
ANDREW CARRANO	ROSE DI'ADAMO	JOSEPH LENZI	ANTHONY RAIANO	
SAMUEL CELONE	LOUIS D'ONOFRIO	RALPH LIBERO	FRANK P. RUGGIERO	
PETER CORATO	CALVIN DORTCH	JOSEPH LIBRETTI	JAMES V. RUOTOLO	

A Soldier's Story-Biagio Ralph Amarone

Biagio was born on July 11, 1924, at 180 Wooster Street. Similar to many brave Italian Americans from Wooster Square, Biagio proudly served his country by joining the Marines in August of 1944. He was an infantryman in the Fifth Marine Corps Division.

On February 19, 1945, the United States launched a perilous amphibious landing on the volcanic sands of Iwo Jima. The objective was to capture the island to build an air base. In total, six thousand and eight hundred men died during the two month battle, making it one of the deadliest in the Pacific Theater. Over one hundred young men from Connecticut perished during the campaign.

Displaying valor and little regard for his own safety, Biagio jumped on a Japanese hand grenade and sacrificed his life for his buddies (two Italian American boys from New Haven) on March 2, 1945. For his actions, he was posthumously awarded the Silver Star. In 1949, his body was exhumed from a grave on Iwo Jima and brought home to New Haven. His wake was conducted at Lupoli's and the funeral services took place at St. Michael Church.

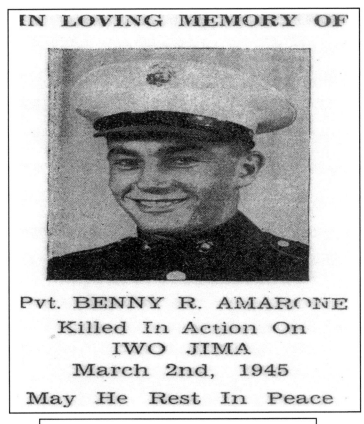

IN LOVING MEMORY OF

Pvt. BENNY R. AMARONE
Killed In Action On
IWO JIMA
March 2nd, 1945
May He Rest In Peace

Photo Courtesy of Pam Amarone Follo

A Soldier's Story-Domenico Antonio Biondi

Domenico Antonio Biondi was born as one of six children on May 29, 1916, on Portsea Street in the Hill section. As with the customs of the time period, he was delivered by a mid-wife named Mrs. Geraci. Dominic's parents Filomino and Felice Parenti Biondi originated from Benevento, Italy. Filomino worked hard as a laborer to support his children; Louis (who eventually moved to California), Salvatore, Theresa, Michael, James, and Dominic. Felice, the typical loving Italian mother, raised her large family without a great deal of money.

Relaxing in the Hill section

Filomino (L) with his sons Jimmy (C) and Dominic (R). Circa-Late 1940's

Dominic was a good-natured kid who enjoyed reading. After a year of high school, he dropped out to go to work.

Maria Leonzo Biondi

Maria Leonzo was born on April 14, 1913, in Clinton, Connecticut to Marcelino and Marrina Ciaburri Leonzo. Marcelino worked as a laborer.

On October 26, 1940, Dominic married Maria at Sacred Heart Church on Columbus Avenue in the Hill. Rev. William P. Loflices performed the ceremony as Dominic Vitale and Pasqualina Camputaro served as best man and maid of honor.

The young couple had a child named Richard Dominic Biondi who was born on January 23, 1943. The family resided at 171 Chestnut Street in Wooster Square.

On November 8, 1943, Dominic entered the United States Army. Eventually, he was sent from Fort Devens, Massachusetts to Camp Seibert, Alabama and then to Manchester, Tennessee. While in the Volunteer State, his unit built sidewalks, fences, culverts, and bridges.

In May of 1944, the unit arrived at Camp Shelby, Mississippi. Dominic was a member of the 245th Combat Engineers. After extensive training, the 245th left New York Harbor on October 30, 1944. The transatlantic voyage was completed on November 10, 1944, when their ship arrived at Avonmouth, England. In England, the men diligently trained for weeks on road maintenance and clearing minefields and booby traps. The engineers were assigned to the Third Army under General Patton.

Dominic returning home to New Haven in 1946.

On Christmas Day 1944, the 245th left Southampton, England and crossed the English Channel for France. While in that country, the men slept in bunkers that were one hundred feet below ground and apart of the Maginot Line. Dominic was in the 2nd Platoon C Company. Vito Melillo, of 88 Bradley Street in East Haven, was also in that company.

On February 8, 1945, Dominic and his squad were on patrol crossing the Saar River near Ripplingen. The group encountered a minefield. Seven American soldiers were injured by shrapnel and received Purple Heart's including P.F.C Biondi. Dominic ended up getting an infection as a result of the wound. Another soldier, Sgt. A.J. Cochran was awarded the Silver Star.

Dominic, an electrician in the service, was a certified rifle marksman. He earned medals for serving in the Battle of the Bulge, and Central Europe. Biondi also received African and Middle Eastern Theater ribbons.

Private First Class Biondi was honorably discharged on February 11, 1946, from Fort Devens, Massachusetts. After the war, he worked in his trade and later for the Post Office. Dominic passed away on November 19, 1982, at the age of sixty-seven. His beloved wife died on September 22, 1992, at the age of seventy-nine.

Dominic and his wife at 171 Chestnut Street-Early 1950's

A Soldier's Story-Mike Coppola

Photo Courtesy of Mike Coppola

Mike Coppola has been a fixture in Wooster Square for over seventy-five years. Polite and respectful, Mike has owned a restaurant on Wooster Street and he has been a long time member of the St. Maria Maddalena and St. Andrew Societies.

Mike was born on April 1, 1926, as one of three sons to Michael Sr. and Maddalena Coppola. In 1943, he was drafted into the Marine Corps. His survival and will to live in one of the bloodiest battles of the war is legendary.

On April 1, 1945, a large invasion force comprising of mostly young Americans hit the beaches of Okinawa. Well disciplined and courageous Japanese forces defended the island to the death. It took the Allies eighty-two days to secure the island. In the end, seventy-seven thousand Japanese troops perished, as well as, fourteen thousand Americans.

On May 5, 1945, Coppola was severely wounded. Mike was shot six times by Japanese fire suffering wounds in his right arm, left leg, and abdomen. Miraculously he recovered from his life threatening wounds. For eighteen months, Mike convalesced in military hospitals in Guam, Hawaii, Oakland, and Chicago.

Two other Coppola brothers also saw heavy combat in the war. Paul was stationed in the Aleutian Islands and fought the Japanese. John was a navigator on a B-24 and he survived twenty-five bombing missions over Axis territories in the European Theater.

The Dellamura's

Francesco Dellamura, and his wife, the former Carmella Infante, originated from Minori, Italy. Frank worked as a laborer to support his eleven children. The family resided in a tenement building at 4 Franklin Street.

Francesco and Carmella along with their son John on Franklin Street.

Dellamura family members and friends on the corner of Franklin and Wooster.

During World War II, the city of New Haven sent hundreds of young men to fight in the European and Pacific Theaters. It was not uncommon for many families to have multiple sons in war zones. Simultaneously, Alphonse, Emilio, John, and Ralph Dellamura served their country. For their parents, these were anxious times dreading the arrival of a government telegraph notifying them of the combat death of one of their boys. During the holiday seasons, the family remained cautious and guarded refusing to put up their Christmas tree.

Brothers Alphonse (L) and John (R) on Franklin Street.

Alphonse was born on October 8, 1922. He graduated from Fair Haven Junior High School in 1938 and attended Commercial High School. After his freshman year, he left school and got a job at Sargent. On January 21, 1943, Alphonse entered the Army at Fort Devens.

He served close to two years in the European Theater as a Power Generator Operator on anti-aircraft guns. Alphonse saw combat in Normandy, northern France, and the Rhineland. Dellamura earned numerous ribbons and medals for good conduct.

On the left, an unknown G.I. is holding Frank Cosenza. To the right, John Dellamurra is holding his niece Marie Crisco Pettola.

Francesco Dellamura and his son John.

John(L) and friends in John's backyard on Franklin St.

Emilio served under General Patton from 1943 to 1946. He fought in the Battle of the Bulge, the last German offensive of the war.

All four of the Dellamura boys safely returned home to the Elm City. Each lived a long and enjoyable life.

*The photographs were from the collection of Andrew Bonetti.

A Sailor's Story-Vincent Donarumo

"During World War II, in my father's two buildings on Wooster Street, there were nine boys that were serving in the military."

Vincent Donarumo

77 Wooster Street

Circa-1930's

(Photo Courtesy of Ann Votto)

Catello Donarumo and his wife Maddalena Camera Donarumo had six sons. To support his family, Catello worked at the Sargent plant. After a few years, he went to work at Van Dyke Printing on Grand Avenue. Unlike, the majority of the residents in Little Italy, Catello owned properties. His tenement building at 77 Wooster Street had twelve flats and his second building at 75 Wooster Street had five apartments. Antonio Danese ran a profitable bakery attached to 77 Wooster Street. The business was open twenty-four hours a day and seven days a week.

Vincent was born on October 19, 1922. He was delivered by Mrs. Gambardella, a mid-wife who resided on Wooster Street. Scholastically, Vincent attended Wooster Street School, Columbus School, and Hillhouse High School.

Despite the tribulations of the Great Depression, Vincent has fond memories of his childhood. Daily, he played with his buddies, "Buck, Buck, Buck" and "Red Rover, I Dare you to Come Over." Both of these games were played on Wooster Street.

Nevertheless, for the Donarumo's and millions of Americans, life was a struggle. Catello, had his hours reduced at Van Dyke to three days a week. Vincent recalled "during the Depression, we ate a lot of macaroni. On Saturday's, my mother would walk to Staino's Market and buy meat. At that time, in our building, the rent for the four room flats were fifteen dollars a month. The three room apartments drew thirteen dollars a month. I can still remember the families in our building. The D'Eugenio's, Fappiano's, Abate's, Proto's, and DePonte's rented from my dad. My father was an affectionate man. He would work with the families that were struggling."*

In August of 1936, the German airship, the Hindenburg flew over New Haven. In advance, the residents of Wooster Street knew of the arrival and anticipated viewing the pride of Nazi, Germany. "Wooster Street was packed with people waiting for the Hindenburg. The ship was flying so low, we could almost see the pilot. I remember it like it was yesterday" stated Vincent.

At the time of the lethal attack on Pearl Harbor, Vincent's brother Catello was in the Navy serving aboard the USS Colorado. The battleship was in the Bremerton (Washington) Naval Yard undergoing repairs as the Japanese torpedoes were decimating battleship row. The vessel rejoined the Pacific fleet and took part in many campaigns.

In 1942, Vincent entered the Navy and he served in aviation. In total, four Donarumo boys fought in World War II. Johnny was stationed aboard the USS Miami, a light cruiser, and Louis on a LSD landing craft. During the conflict, Catello and Johnny saw the most combat while in the Pacific Theater. Another brother, Frankie, joined the Navy in the 1950's. He served aboard the USS Hank, a mine sweeper.

After the Japanese defeat, millions of soldiers returned stateside. Catello established G.I. Cleaners in his father's building. In his free time, he was a skilled saxophone player. Catello played in an Italian band, for the New Haven Register Band, and for the Governor's Foot Guard.

Vincent attended culinary school on the G.I. Bill of Rights. Upon graduation, he worked for a catering company and then in the kitchen at Yale University.

On June 4, 1949, Vincent joined hands in matrimony with Antoinette Anastasio at St. Michael Church. Antoinette grew up at 48 Wooster Street. In May of 1961, he went to work at Blue Hills Farm in Wallingford. Eventually, the couple both found employment at Choate Rosemary Hall. Antoinette worked in the housekeeping division under Headmaster Seymour St. John. Vincent was a driver. He often drove future screen vixen Jamie Lee Curtis to appointments in New Haven. The Donarumo's lived on campus and retired from the prestigious institution.

Vincent and his wife had two children named Matthew and Ann. Antoinette passed away on August 15, 2012.

Now, in his mid-nineties, Vincent was in a reflective mood. " Wooster Street means the world to me. What we did as kids there could never be done again. The people were forced to leave and it was terrible. My family did not know what the hell was going on. It had a great impact on our family. My parents cried when they tore down our buildings. They did not want to leave. For our two buildings, we got forty-five thousand dollars. My parents bought a home on Chatham Street in Fair Haven. I would go back to those days on Wooster Street in a heartbeat," stated Donarumo.*

*Interview. Vincent Donarumo. January 14, 2016.

The Donarumo Family on Wooster Street during World War II.

(Left to Right) Louis, father Catello Sr., mother Anna, and Vincent.

In the back is Joe and in the front Frank.

(Photo Courtesy of Ann Votto)

A Sailor's Story-Michael A. Freda

Michael A. Freda was born on July 2, 1925, on Hamilton Street. His parents, Massimo and Louisa, also had a daughter named Phyllis. Prior to arriving in America, Massimo was a respected judge in the Naples region. Louisa, an educated woman, was a writer for the popular Italian American newspaper, *Il Progresso*.

As a teenager, residing at 174 Wallace Street, Michael earned a reputation for his physical strength and toughness. Thus, his friends gave him the monikers "Tarzan" and "Smash." Scholastically, Freda attended Hillhouse High School.

By 1943, the American industrial prowess was slowly beginning to turn the tide in World War II. Scores of young men in the Wooster Square and Hamilton Street areas were serving. Michael enlisted in the Navy and was stationed aboard the USS Roche (DE-197). The destroyer escort was a vital component in the protection of battleships and aircraft carriers against clandestine enemy submarines.

On March 13, 1945, the USS Roche rescued eleven men from the frigid Atlantic Ocean. The USAT McAndrew, an army transport ship, collided with a French aircraft carrier, the Bearn. Michael was directly involved the in rescue efforts.

In May of 1945, after the German surrender, the vessel was ordered to join the fight against the Empire of Japan. On September 2, 1945, the Japanese surrendered aboard the battleship USS Missouri in Tokyo Bay. Four weeks later, on September 29, the USS Roche was struck by a floating mine. As a result of the blast, three of Freda's friends perished. Sadly, the Americans had been searching for a Japanese submarine that was unaware that the war had ended.

After the war, "Smash" returned to the neighborhood and briefly worked at the New Haven Clock Shop. While employed at the plant, he met the stunning Mary Palumbo. The two married in 1950 and had two sons named Michael and James.

In 1949, Michael found employment at the New Haven Board and Carton Company on East Street. He worked there until 1967. Freda was a valuable member of the company fast pitch softball team playing catcher and third base. He was also a devoted member of the Lincoln Club located at 184 Wallace Street.

In 1967, Freda went to work at Sears and Roebuck in Orange as a salesman in the Automotive Department. He remained there until he passed away in 1975.

New Year's Eve 1950-Nightclub New York City

Michael "Smash" Freda and his wife Mary

(Photo Courtesy of First Selectman Michael J. Freda)

A Sailor's Story-Anthony Gambardella

Anthony Gambardella was born on May 1, 1924. His parents, Luca and Mary Nazario Gambardella, had three other sons named Ralph, Al, and Andy. The family lodged at 814 Grand Avenue.

Growing up in New Haven, Anthony attended Columbus School and Commercial High School. He was a soft spoken and cordial individual who spoke English, Italian, and French. Gambardella's uncles Anthony and Alphonse had served in the Italian Navy.

Seaman First Class Gambardella, a draftee, was assigned to serve aboard the USS Snook (SS-279). The submarine was commissioned on October 24, 1942. The vessel had a crew of six officers and fifty-four men. Lt. Commander C.O Triebel and his crew were credited with sinking seventeen Japanese warships.

Photo Courtesy of Carmen Gambardella

On April 9, 1945, the Snook disappeared in the South China Sea. The entire crew was lost at sea.

Anthony's brothers Al and Andy enjoyed careers as motorcycle policemen in New Haven. Ralph, passed away on February 7, 2015.

A Soldier's Story-Salvatore Gary Garibaldi

Salvatore Gary Garibaldi was delivered by a mid-wife on Christmas Day in 1918 along with his twin sister Theresa. Their parents, Philip and Angelina Castellano Garibaldi originated from southern Italy.

Philip and his beloved wife had six children. In 1928, their son Joseph died in a work related accident at a powerhouse on Grand Avenue. Joseph had been on the job for a day before becoming mortally injured. A decade later, another son Bernie perished in a car accident on Nicoll and Edwards Street. The couple's other two sons Gary and Albert served in World War II. The Garibaldi's also had two daughters named Theresa and Louise.

As a boy, Gary's family lived on Chestnut Street. He enjoyed playing sports and he was very active at the Boy's Club. In high school, at Boardman Trade, Garibaldi was a terrific student and he excelled at basketball and baseball. On the baseball diamond, he played next to Carl Vederame (Red's brother) in the outfield. In 1938, Gary completed the necessary course load to earn his diploma.

On November 20, 1941, Gary married the former Mary Sansone of 38 Collis Street at St. Michael Church. The following year, Garibaldi was drafted into the Army. His unit, the 36th Infantry Division, was based out of Texas. While fighting in southern France and Italy, Gary displayed incredible valor. As a result, he was the recipient of the Bronze Star, Distinguished Service Medal, two Purple Hearts, and the Silver Star. At the end of the conflict, Capt. Garibaldi was stationed in Austria commanding an unit that guarded Nazi leader Hermann Goering as he awaited trial for war crimes.

Captain Gary Garibaldi in Europe

(Photo Courtesy of Bernard Garibaldi)

Gary and his wife had three sons named Bernard, Gary and Joseph. The importance of obtaining an education was emphasized as all three sons earned advanced college degrees.

In 1969, Garibaldi returned back to Wooster Street living in the Columbus Mall. An energetic man, Gary filled his time by being involved in many organizations. Nicknamed "The President of Wooster Street," he served as the President of the Wooster Square Historical Business Association, as well as the Wooster Square Old Times Reunion Committee. He was also engaged in many veterans organizations proudly serving as the Past Commander of the VFW Post 320 and the American Legion Post 47. Furthermore, Gary remained active in the Boys Club.

Gary passed away on December 15, 2009.

Gary on the steps of St. Michael Church with Branford High School teacher Salvatore Zarra and students in June of 2005. Gary spoke at Branford High School each year on Veterans Day.

A Soldier's Story-Joseph Lenzi

Joe Lenzi was born on May 9, 1922, as one of six children to Diamond Lenzi and his wife Lillian. Diamond supported his family by working as a New Haven Police Detective and their home was located at 181 St. John Street.

Tall and good looking, Joe was a gifted athlete. At Hillhouse High School, he earned varsity letters in football, basketball, and baseball. Following graduation in 1941, he attended Staunton Military Academy where he continued to play football. Lenzi's enthusiasm for sports never waned. He participated in football while at boat camp at Parris Island and while training at Camp Pendleton in Southern California.

The island of Iwo Jima was of strategic importance because of three operational airfields. The fighting that took place there was some of the most vicious in the entire Pacific Theater. On March 15, 1945, the Fifth Marine Division encountered hardened Japanese troops. In the combat that took place, Joe fought with valor and determination killing five enemy soldiers.* P.F.C Floyd Vaughn was with Lenzi on that day and responded "I personally owe him my life."* It is believed by his family that Joe was hit with shrapnel from a grenade and that he suffered a fatal wound in his abdomen.

Years after his death, the city dedicated a park across the street from Joe's house in Wooster Square. The plaque there reads:

On this ground where once he tread
A vow was made, here's what he said
"I never shirk nor desert the fight
Till I know my Lord that all is right."

*Interview Michael Persico.August 14, 2011.

Photo Courtesy of Michael Persico

A Sailor's Story-William Rossi

William Rossi was born on December 9, 1912, in New Haven. His parents Dominic and Filomena Maturo Rossi emigrated from the Naples region in 1905. In high school, Bill learned the plumbing trade. In the late 1930's, he joined the National Guard and at the outbreak of the Second World War, Bill became a Seabee.

While in the service, Rossi was stationed in the south Pacific on Saipan and Tinian Islands. He accidently discovered an active volcano on Tinian that is still called "Rossi's Crater." Later, Bill helped to assemble the first atomic bomb abroad the cruiser USS Indianapolis. After leaving Tinian Island, this vessel was torpedoed by a Japanese submarine on July 30, 1945. Roughly, three hundred sailors died in the attack. The remaining nine hundred men were left in shark infested waters for days. Hundreds of young men were picked off by the apex predators or died of dehydration. Finally, a routine patrol spotted the men in the Pacific Ocean. Three hundred sailors survived the horrific event. Luckily for Rossi, he was ordered to stay on the island before the ship departed.

In 1949, Rossi married the former Christine Giaquinto of New Haven and in 1952 their only child Marc was born. Today, Marc is a professor at Berkley School of Music in Boston. The couple divorced and Bill married his second wife Melatina who passed away in 1991.

In his professional life, Bill taught at Platt Tech High School and he and his brother Anthony owned "Rossi Brothers Plumbing and Heating." Many years later, he worked as a building inspector, until he retired at the age of eighty-six.

In the twilight of his life, Bill spoke to high school students about his experiences during the war. He always focused on peace with war only occurring as a last result. Mr. Rossi was especially well received by the students at Branford High School who found him to be affable and funny.

Bill and his close friend Dorothy Catinello (originally from Brooklyn) enjoyed the parks in Wooster Square. They fed the squirrels as Bill played the guitar. Dorothy passed away in November of 2009. A few months later (April, 19, 2010), he followed her after a brief illness.

Bill Rossi and Branford High School student Daniele Vitello in front of Tony and Lucille's in April 2007. Bill was taking apart in the "Anthony Bescher Veterans Appreciation Day" later that day at Branford High School. Daniele lived on Wooster Street but went to school in Branford.

Portland class cruiser-USS Indianapolis

(Photo Courtesy of Bill Rossi)

A Soldier's Story-Gennaro Santore Sr.

Gennaro Santore was born as one of eight children to Vittorio and Angelina Smiraglio Santoro on May 18, 1920. Vittorio emigrated from Atrani to New Haven in 1910. His wife originated from Amalfi and she arrived to America in 1902. The couple married at St. Michael Church in 1913. To earn a living Vittorio worked at Sperry and Barnes.

Gennaro was delivered by a mid-wife at 76 Wooster Street. His godfather Frank Chermoli owned the building which consisted of two flats and a grocery store. The family lived on the first floor in a four room apartment. The four brothers and four sisters slept in separate bedrooms, four to a bed. Eventually, the family moved across Wooster Street and then to 136 East Street.

The Santore's lives drastically changed when Angelina died of a blood clot while only in her forties. Jerry and his sister Antoinette told their father that they would financially provide for the family if he ran the household. They did not want their father to remarry. As a result, Gennaro left school at sixteen and worked for 10 cents an hour at Parex Shirt Shop.*

In 1942, Dr. Mongillo at St. Raphael Hospital performed a hernia repair operation on Gennaro. He was recovering for two weeks in the hospital when he was drafted into the Army. He completed basic training in Tennessee and was then sent to England. While in England, by chance, Gennaro came across members of his brother Louis unit who were serving under General Patton. Surprisingly, the two brothers, thousands of miles from home, met at a movie theater. After his training was completed in England, Gennaro was sent to Scotland where he again saw Louis.

The Santore Brothers in World War II.

Top- Phillip (Pacific Theater). Bottom left Louis and the bottom right Gennaro.

(Photo Courtesy of Jerry Santore Jr.)

In 1944 and 1945, Gennaro was in Germany. At the same time his brother Phillip was stationed in the Pacific. On May 8th, Germany surrendered to the Allies. Gennaro was scheduled to leave the European Theater and join the fighting in the Pacific. Luckily, while on leave, the Japanese surrendered and Santore returned to the Elm City.

In 1948, he married the former Maria Luciola at Blessed Sacrament Church in Hamden. The couple moved to Hamden in 1961 and raised their three children Anthony, Jerry Jr., and Angela. For over forty years, Gennaro worked at Geometric Tools and he served as president of the union.

A cordial and heartfelt man, Gennaro and his wife have remained active in senior groups well into their nineties.

*Interview Gennaro Santore Sr. July 29, 2014.

World War II

Their Reflections

"During the war, I was stationed in Australia. While there, I met up with of my buddies from New Haven. They were Chris Reynolds and Frank Savino. Savino lived with me on St. John Street. I was also a childhood friend of Joe Lenzi. It was terrible what happened to him."

Gabe Cognato

"It was a Sunday afternoon and I was at Loew's Poli Theater with friends. Around 5:00 P.M. the movie just stopped. The manager got on stage and told us we were going to hear from President Roosevelt. The president told us we were at war. The Japanese had attacked Pearl Harbor. The manager made us all stand and recite the Pledge of Allegiance. We also had to sing the national anthem. I was terrified. I could not wait to get home. That was over seventy-five years ago."

Rita Silvestro.

"I do remember in school having air raid drills. The boys from the area got drafted. My brother Andrew joined the Navy after Pearl Harbor. He was stationed on the USS Soley, a destroyer. I would often hear my dad crying at our fish store on Wooster Street. He was worried about Andrew."

Marie Cangiano

"On Wooster Street, we found out about the attack on Pearl Harbor during the day time. The people were crying in the street. My father owned 77 Wooster Street which was a twelve family tenement building and 75 Wooster Street which had five families. In our buddings alone, nine boys served in the war."

Vincent Donarumo

Their Stories in Wooster Square

Al Lauro

Carmella Avalone Simonelli

Antoinette Bottino

Al Lauro-Al was born as one of two children to Michael and Pauline Lauro. Michael worked at Sargent for forty-four years while his wife worked in the garment industry. Al married the former Antoinette D'Agostino of Collis Street in 1955. The couple had two sons. For twenty-five years, Al owned a catering business with a partner in East Haven. Al and his wife (Antoinette passed away in November of 2011) lived at 190 Wooster Street.

Carmella Avalone Simonelli-Carmella was born on Ferry Street to Italian American parents. Her husband Nick grew up on Dixwell Avenue. In 1947, the couple married at St. Michael Church and moved to 175 Chestnut Street. Nick worked as a police officer and the couple had two children.

Antoinette Bottino-Antoinette was born and raised on Wooster Street. As a young adult, she went to Atrani to visit her father. While there, she met and fell in love with her future husband Mario. Today, the couple resides in a home overlooking scenic Atrani.

Images From Little Italy

Columbus Park-1950

<u>Back Row</u>-Jerry Silvestri, Alex DePino, and Anthony Fronte.

<u>Second Row</u>-Tommy Scalzo, Michelina D'Agostino, Annette Ventura, Ralph Anastasio, Mike Balzano, Matilda Lucibello, and Ed Candela.

<u>Front Row</u>-Frank Marino

(Photo Courtesy of Mike Balzano)

Joe Savo (L) and his brother in law Ronnie Rosarbo.

Wooster Street residents Summer of 2011.

Faith, Family, Friends

St. Michael Church

Mission Statement

Our parish is open to all people who seek to give glory to God through the centrality of Jesus Christ in the Eucharist and in sharing the gifts and traditions of the Roman Catholic faith. Enlivened by the Holy Spirit, we strive to create a vibrant, welcoming faith community for worship, education and outreach to our neighbors, community, and the southern Italian Societies through the Lordship of our Savior Jesus Christ.

Children of Mary

St. Michael Church-1924

(Teresa Falcigno Collection)

Pastors of St. Michael Church

Rev. Vincent Astorri	**1889-1890**
Rev. Oreste Alussi	**1890-1894**
Rev. Francis Beccherini	**1894-1895**
Rev. Francis Zaboglio	**1895-1896**
Rev. Vincent Sciolla	**1896-1897**
Rev. Louis Lango	**1897-1900**
Rev. Bartolomeo Marenchino	**1900-1904**
Rev. Francis Moretti	**1904-1905**
Rev. Oreste Alussi	**1905-1916**
Rev. Leonardo Quaglia	**1916-1949**
Rev. Raphael Larcher	**1949-1951**
Rev. Ugo Cavicchi	**1951-1954**
Rev. Francis Minchiatti	**1954-1964**
Rev. Guido Caverzan	**1964-1967**
Rev. Joseph Bizzotto	**1967-1975**
Rev. Thomas Carlesimo	**1976-1978**
Rev. Tarciso J. Bagatin	**1978-1989**
Rev. Francis Minchiatti	**1989-1996**
Rev. Michael Tarro	**1996-1999**
Rev. Andrew Brizzolara	**1999-2004**
Rev. Michael Tarro	**2004-2008**
Rev. Ralph Colicchio	**2008-2015**
Msgr. Gerard Schmitz	**2015-**

St. Michael Church

1889-1989 Facts and Statistics

(Source-100th Anniversary Souvenir Book)

Researcher: Teresa Falcigno

Opening Day-September 1, 1889

Opening Day Baptisms:

1. Enrico Conte (The future Dr. Conte)
Godparents-Philip Castellano and Marianna Sangesse

2. Rocco Cristiano
Godparents-Louis Guardile and Carmella Guardile

3. James Papacado
Godparents-Joseph Capo and Alphonsina Sansone

First Wedding:

Vincent Spinelli and Angelina Melone
Witnesses-Salvatore and Maria Esposito

Baptisms 1889-1998	**33,820**
Peak Year-1914	**1,175**
Marriages 1889-1998	**6,291**
Peak Year-1913	**190**

Church of Saint Michael

Early Years

With the influx of Italian immigrants to Wooster Square, the need for a place to celebrate their Catholic faith heightened. During the 1880's, the Italians attended mass at St. Patrick's Church. St. Patrick's was established in 1851 and was the second Catholic church in the city. The parishioners were mostly Irish and they were not cordial to the newly arrived southern Europeans. Father John Russell earnestly tried to make all of his parishioners feel comfortable.

St. Patrick's Church

(Photo Courtesy of John Ragozzino)

In 1884, Paul Russo, a prominent scholar and businessman, led a small Italian delegation to Hartford to meet with Bishop Lawrence McMahon. McMahon was appointed the fifth Bishop of Hartford on May 16, 1879. A visionary, he oversaw the opening of forty-eight parishes during has fourteen year tenure as Bishop. McMahon gave the Elm City residents permission to raise funds for a new church.

In autumn of 1885, Father Riviaccio celebrated mass in a hall on Wallace Street and Grand Avenue. The building was the property of St. Patrick's Church. A young William Verdi assisted Father Riviaccio as an altar boy. Verdi was born in Italy. In 1894, he graduated from

Yale with a degree in medicine. Years later, he was one of the founders of St. Raphael's Hospital. With the funds that they raised, the Italians were able to establish a chapel on Union Avenue and later in a flat on the seventh floor of a building on Chapel and State Street.

On September 1, 1889, Father Vincent Astorri, a Scalabrinian, conducted the first mass at St. Michael the Archangel. The church was named in honor of the Patron Saint of Gioia Sannitica, Caserta. Astorri, who had previously served on Atwells Avenue in Providence, raised the funds to purchase a Lutheran Cathedral on the corner of Wooster and Brewery Street. Paul Russo and Dominic Bergonzi were the trustees.

The second Pastor of St. Michael was Father Oreste Alussi who served from 1890 to 1894. Father Alussi had over four thousand parishioners in the rapidly expanding Italian enclave. The church also housed the St. Michael Society, the Rosary Society, the St. Louis Society, and the Madonna del Carmine Society.

Father Francis Beccherini was appointed the third Pastor on August 16, 1894. During his tenure, the church was enlarged. The next two Pastors were Father Francis Zaboglio (1895-1896) and Father Vincent Sciolla (1896-1897). As the Italian community continued to inflate, a more spacious building was needed.

New Church

Father Louis Lango petitioned Rev. Michael Tierney in Hartford to purchase a Protestant church in Wooster Square. This structure overlooked picturesque Wooster Park. A series of fires damaged the building and the Protestants were happy to sell the church to the Italians for $25,000. On April 23, 1899, Archbishop Sebastiano Martinelli dedicated the one thousand seat house of worship.

In early winter of 1904, a devastating fire again struck the church. Around 10:00 A.M. Rev. Bartolomeo Marenchino (1900-1904) discovered the blaze and rang the bell. The firemen had difficulty reaching the building due to snow. Sparks from the inferno reached homes on Chestnut Street. Lt. Fleming of Engine Company Four and Fireman Fitzpatrick of Company Seven were injured. Over thirty thousand dollars of damage took place.*

On December 21, 1904, the church was rededicated. For this special event, Dr. Verdi donated a pipe organ.

In 1903, Bishop Tierney established St. Anthony Church in the Hill section to fulfill the needs of New Haven's other Italian enclave. Father Bartolomeo Marenchino became the first Pastor of St. Anthony.

*Source-The Day January 4, 1904.

New Haven Catholic Parishes 1913

(Source-*City* by Douglas W. Rae pp. 150)

Church	Founded	Neighborhood	Parishioners
St. John's	1834	Hill	3,429
St. Mary's	1851	East Rock	3,314
St. Patrick's	1853	Wooster Square	3,300
St. Francis	1867	Fair Haven	4,219
St. Boniface (German)	1868	Downtown	1,000
St. Aedan	1872	Westville	
Sacred Heart	1874	Hill	4,870
St. Louis (French)	1889	Wooster Square	1,200
St. Michael (Italian)	1899	Wooster Square	24,470
St. Joseph's	1900	East Rock	2,828
St. Peter's	1902	Hill	1,941
St. Stanislaus	1902	State Street	3,000
St. Anthony (Italian)	1903	Hill	1,700
St. Rose	1907	Fair Haven	3,100
St. Casimir (Lithuanian)		Wooster Square	1,500
St. Brendan	1913	Dixwell	2,000

Father Leonardo Quaglia

The most significant and longest serving Pastor of St. Michael was Father Leonardo Quaglia. Father Quaglia served from September 1916 to May 1949, leading his parishioners through both World Wars. In 1923, Father Quaglia oversaw the building of St. Michael Hall which was paid for by the selling of the old church on Wooster Street. The hall was the site of plays, productions, wedding receptions, and meetings.

In 1936, Father Quaglia founded the parochial school. The students who attend the school were in grades 1-4. In September of 1940, the new school was opened and for decades offered a challenging curriculum to the children of the neighborhood. After his services at St. Michael, Father Quaglia returned to Italy.

St. Michael Hall-2010

In May of 1949, Father Raphael Larcher replaced Father Quaglia. After only a few years at the parish, he was assigned to a new position in Rome. Father Ugo Cavicchi arrived to New Haven in November of 1953. An energetic man, he oversaw improvements to the interior of the church before he was given a new appointment in England in April of 1954.

St. Michael School
Building

2009

Father Francis Minchiatti was promoted from an assistant under Father Cavicchi to Pastor in 1954. During his tenure, which lasted a decade, he oversaw the renovation of the existing properties. Father Minchiatti also had to contend with Mayor Lee's Redevelopment program and its dire effects on the St. Michael community. Many dedicated parishioners were forced to flee the city and settled in East Shore and the suburbs.

Father Francis Minchiatti 1954-1964

(Teresa Falcigno Collection)

Father Guido Caverzan was ordained in 1950. He had previously served at St. Peter's Italian Church in Syracuse and St. Mary of Mt. Carmel in Utica before arriving at St. Michael in September of 1964. As Pastor, he tried to rebuild the parish hurt by Urban Renewal. Father Caverzan oversaw the 75th Anniversary Celebration of the church. In January of 1967, he was sent to Our Lady of Pompeii in Manhattan.

75th Anniversary Altar Boys

(Teresa Falcigno Collection)

The Symbol of Wooster Square turns 75 years old.

(Teresa Falcigno Collection)

Father Thomas Carlesimo in 1977

(Teresa Falcigno Collection)

Father Joseph Bizzotto

(Teresa Falcigno Collection)

Post Urban Renewal

In January of 1967, Father Bizzotto became the Pastor of a church in transition. Father Bizzotto united the Italian community by airing weekly radio programs and by publishing a monthly journal called "*Eco Italiana*." A kind man, he worked well with all segments of the parish before leaving in November of 1975. From 1977 to 1985, Father Bizzotto was at St. Anthony Church in the Hill section.

In January of 1976, Father Thomas Carlesimo became the inaugural Italian American Pastor of St. Michael. Father Carlesimo was born in Utica, New York in 1924. He was a humorous and encouraging man. While at the parish, he had the confessionals replaced following the liturgical rules.

In November of 1978, Father Tarcisio Bagatin began his long and productive tenure at St. Michael. Father Terry was born on April 5, 1928, in Vicenza. He had previously served in Canada. Father Terry's tenure was challenging. He was committed to having the school provide a quality education and he was a strong proponent of the Italian societies. Father Bagatin joined prominent Italian American leaders to create the Italian American Historical Society of New Haven.

In preparation for the 90th Anniversary, he had the church painted and he oversaw many renovations during his eleven year stay. After guiding the parish through its centenary anniversary (1989), Father Terry left to serve at Our Lady of Pompeii in Greenwich Village.

Father Terry in 1979 along with Teresa Falcigno and Theresa Argento.

(Teresa Falcigno Collection)

Father Minchiatti returned as Pastor from 1989 to 1996. The parish had a fraction of the parishioners when Father Minchiatti had previously served. In 1993, St. Michael School sadly closed its doors unable to compete with the expenditures of running a parochial school. Father Minchiatti left St. Michael in 1996. He passed away in March of 2008.

Father Michael Tarro enjoyed two stints at St. Michael. The first was from 1996 to 1999. He was called back in 2004 to reside over a healing parish community.

Father Andrew Brizzolara arrived at St. Michael in 1999. Previously, he had served at St. Charles Borromeo in New York, St. Tarcisius in Massachusetts, Our Lady of Pompeii in Manhattan, and St. Joseph in New York City. In January of 2004, he resigned in face of sexual abuse allegations from his work at St. Tarcisius in 1983.* His legal problems shocked and angered the parishioners of St. Michael. Bishop Peter A. Rosazza informed the parish during a Saturday evening mass.

*Sources: New Haven Register January 18, 2004
        Boston Herald January 19, 2004

The popular Biagio DiLieto celebrating the St. Andrew Society Procession Mass at St. Michael in 1985.

(Teresa Falcigno Collection)

The Future of St. Michael Church

Father Ralph Colicchio became the Pastor in April of 2008. He was born on July 28, 1940, in Waterbury. Father Colicchio studied for the priesthood at St. Thomas Seminary in Bloomfield and Christ the King Seminary at St. Bonaventure University. He was ordained on May 4, 1967. From 1980 to 1990, he was a Pastor at Mary Magdalen Parish in Oakville, Connecticut. From 1990 to 1998, he served as a chaplain at Hartford Hospital and Yale New Haven Hospital. Father Ralph retired in the summer of 2015.

Father Ralph Colicchio-2012.

Father Ralph-2013

(Photo Courtesy of John Varone)

The future of St. Michael Church is in question. After the school closed, the church rented property for learning academies. The revenue from the rentals greatly augmented the parish savings and paid for operating expenses. The parishioners have remained dedicated but most continue to commute to the church. The fear is that with a declining number of parishioners that the church will not be able to survive. St. Casimir, a former Lithuanian church, located at 339 Greene Street, closed in October of 2003 after existing for ninety years. Sacred Heart, established in 1876 and located at 25 Gold Street in the Hill merged with St. Anthony.

In 2016, St. Michael still had roughly three hundred families listed in the parish community. This architectural marvel, and the heart of the Italian American community, continues to have an emotional and spiritual influence on the parishioners. For generations, the church has persevered despite deadly fires, Redevelopment, and financial struggles. Nonetheless, there is optimism that St. Michael will rebound and thrive as it has done countless times during the past century.

Deacon Richard Santello in July of 2012. He was ordained in October of 1976 by Rev. John Whealon, the Archbishop of Hartford. Deacon Santello and his wife Angela have four children and have been married for over fifty years.

Father Minchiatti circa 1960.

(Photo Courtesy of Marie Cangiano)

The former St. Casimir Church-2008.

*Source-<u>100th Anniversary Church of Saint Michael</u>

St. Michael School during the 1960 Columbus Day Parade.

(Theresa Argento Collection)

First Holy Communion Parade-Wooster Place Circa 1960.

(Photo Courtesy of Marie Cangiano)

The Four Seasons of Worship

Saint Michael Church

Winter

Spring

Summer

Fall

Societies of Wooster Square affiliated with St. Michael Church

During his tenure at St. Michael (1890-1894), Father Oreste Alussi oversaw four societies. They were the Madonna del Carmel Society, Rosary Society, St. Louis Society, and St. Michael Society. For well over a century, Italian American societies have housed their statues within the church. This list includes:

St. Andrea Society founded November 1, 1900

St. Andrea Ladies Society founded 1923

St. Ann Society

St. Catello Society founded 1901

St. Maria Maddalena Society founded May 1, 1898

St. Maria Maddalena Female Society founded 1925

St. Michael Alter Society founded 1949

St. Trofimena Society founded 1908

Santa Maria delle Vergini Society founded 1906

The Falcigno's (left) and the Argento's-June 1985.

(Teresa Falcigno Collection)

Santa Maria delle Vergini Statue-St. Michael Church.

(Photo Courtesy of Ruby Proto)

1953 St. Michael First Holy Communion.

(Photo Courtesy of Marie Cangiano)

Italian Parishes of New Haven

St. Anthony

Washington Ave.

St. Donato

Lombard Street

St. Michael

Wooster Place

Church of St. Michael

125th Anniversary Celebration

Raymond Saracco Jr. (Left) and John Serra.

Over a century ago, Italian immigrants gathered at St. Michael Church to celebrate their Catholic faith in an environment that was familiar and comfortable. Since the inception of the parish, St. Michael has served as the spiritual center of the Italian American community in Wooster Square. Today, the majority of the parishioners at St. Michael are the grand children and great grandchildren of the immigrants.

On September 28, 2014, the church celebrated its 125th Anniversary. Father Ralph Colicchio elegantly performed mass to the proud and dedicated parishioners.

Father Colicchio-2014

The festivities included honoring a police officer and a firefighter that has contributed to their community. Connecticut State Trooper John Serra and New Haven Firefighter Raymond Saracco Jr. were the recipients of the Service Award.

John Serra was born in Stratford as one of four children to Anthony and Mary Serra. He graduated from Milford Academy and attended Memphis State University. John enlisted in the Air Force and he served in the Security Forces. Before being honorably discharged, he obtained the rank of Sergeant.

Officer Serra enjoyed a long and distinguished career with the Connecticut State Police serving in numerous capacities. He retired in August of 2014. Today, he is the propitiator of a company that trains pet dogs.

Raymond Saracco Jr. was born and raised in New Haven. His parents Raymond Sr. and Linda DiPaola Saracco had four children. He graduated from St. Michael School in 1984 and matriculated to Notre Dame High School where he completed his diploma in 1988.

In 1997, Raymond became a New Haven Fireman and he was assigned to the Dixwelll Avenue station. During his career, he has served in various capacities within the department.

Saracco Jr. was one of the original founders of the East Rock Festival. Currently, he is involved in politics in his home town of North Haven.

Following mass, a festive banquet was held at Anthony's Ocean View in Morris Cove. St. Andrew Society President Frank Gargano served as master of ceremonies and local band, The Jassmen, performed to the delight of the three hundred people in attendance.

Toastmaster-Frank Gargano

Past Honorees

Capt. Andrew Consiglio
Sgt. Joseph Buonome
Det. Peter Brennan
Asst. Chief Stephanie Redding
Officer Anthony Santatcangelo
Officer Michael Novella Jr.
Officer Peter Krause
Sgt. Rose Turney
Firefighter Salvatore Camera

Sgt. Achilles Generoso
Lt. Harry DeBenedet
Det. Peter Carusone
Officer Lisa Scaramella
Det. Andrew Faggio
Officer Frank Lombardi
Det. Martin Buonfiglio
Firefighter Andrew Bonito
Firefighter Michael Ciaburro

Det. Julius DelGuidice
Capt. James LaBanca
Officer Ralph Consiglio
Officer Tim Fanning
Det. Sgt. Muro
Officer Marianne Petrillo
Sgt. Louis Cavaliere
Sgt. Vin Anastasio
Officer Dennis Mastriano

Wooster Street residents and St. Michael parishioners.

Joe Colello and his family.

St. Michael Church Event Circa 1975.

<u>Front Row</u>-Teresa Falcigno, Nettie Balsamo, Hilda Riggio, Professor Franesco Riggio, Francesca Lodge, and Rosemary Prete.

<u>Back Row</u>-Yolanda Coda, Father Tarcisio Bagatin, Mary Mauro, Congressman Robert Giamo, Gov. John Lodge, Father Joseph Cogo, Carla Lukas, and Father Mario Bordignon.

(Teresa Falcigno Collection)

The Wedding of Alphonse Lauro and

Nettie D'Agostino at St. Michael Church

September 10, 1955.

(Photo Courtesy of Al Lauro)

The Passing of Reverend Michael A. Tarro

(Source-*St. Catello Society Newsletter*. Issue 44 August 2015)

The Reverend Michael A. Tarro, C.S., 87, a Scalabrinian Missionary Priest, passed away July 15, 2015, at the Scalabrini Villa Health Care Center in North Kingstown, Rhode Island. Born in Providence on August 13, 1927, he was a son of the late Anthony and Rose Lozito Tarro. After serving briefly in the Army, Fr. Michael entered Congregation of the Missionaries of St. Charles Scalabrinians in 1951. He completed his theological studies at the Pontifical Gregorian University in Rome, and he was ordained a priest on July 6, 1958, while in Rome.

Upon his return to the United States, Father Michael, served as Pastor in the Scalabrinian missions and parishes in the Boston area, Connecticut, New York, and Toronto. While in New Haven, assigned to Saint Michael Church, he served as Chaplain to the Saint Catello Society and the Southern Italy Religious Societies.

Andrew Consiglio (L), Monsignor Gerard Schmitz and Frank Gargano (R)

Saint Maria Maddalena Society Procession-July 2015.

Monsignor Gerard Schmitz

In July of 2015, Father Ralph Colicchio retired. Sadden by his retirement, the parishioners anxiously awaited news of their new spiritual leader and the future of the church. Immediately upon his arrival, Monsignor Schmitz made an impression and developed a rapport with his parishioners.

Monsignor Schmitz was born as one of three sons to a German Irish father and an Irish mother. His father earned a living as a salesman and his mother was a part time clerical worker. The family resided in Fair Haven and the boys enjoyed a happy childhood. Gerard attended St. Francis School and then graduated from Notre Dame High School in 1959. He enrolled and graduated from St. Thomas Seminary.

Monsignor Schmitz-Columbus Weekend Wreath Ceremony Procession-2015.

On May 23, 1968, Gerard was ordained to the delight of his proud parents. During his esteemed career, he has served at St. Augustine in North Branford, St. Margaret in Madison, St. Rita in Hamden, and St. Bernard in Tariffville. In 2001, Monsignor Schmitz began his twelve year tenure as President Rector of St. Thomas Seminary. Legendary Pope John Paul II. appointed him Monsignor.

Adored by his parishioners, Monsignor Schmitz is also a board member at Notre Dame High School and at St. Raphael Hospital. He also serves as the Chaplain of the Connecticut Senate, the St. Catello Society, and for the Southern Italian Religious Societies.

In a reflective mood, the Monsignor commented "I have enjoyed a very rewarding career. I have developed lifelong friendships and have met people at critical points in their lives. The nice thing about St. Michael is the connection between the people and the neighborhood."*

*Interview. Monsignor Schmitz. November 12, 2015.

Their Stories in Wooster Square

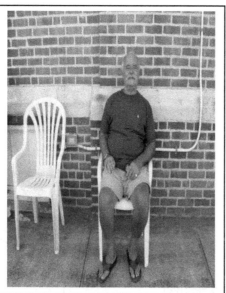

Ann Norman   Angelo Ciaburro   Theresa "Dolly" Dogolo

Ann Derrico Norman-was delivered by Dr. Amatruda at 191 Wooster Street. Her parents, Angelo and Anne, had two children. Angelo worked twelve hour days at the railroad while his wife worked at J&R Shirt Factory. Ann's uncle owned Carlucci's Market. Ann and her husband Ron Norman had three boys and they lived in North Haven. In this photo, Ann is with Sister DeMatsiana at St. Michael School.

Angelo Ciaburro-Angelo was born as one of two children to Fred "Bang Up" and Olga Ciaburro. The Ciaburro's lived in Capri, Italy until moving to New Haven in 1946. Fred worked as a Teamster while his wife worked in the garment industry. The family lived on Warren and Water Street until Angelo was twelve. As a result of Redevelopment, the family moved to 193 Wooster Street. For over thirty years, Angelo and his wife Therese lived in the Columbus Mall at 190 Wooster Street. The couple had four children named Anthony, Louis, Michael, and Kellie.

Dolly Dogolo-Dolly was born as one of two children to Philip and Mildred Pacileo at 116 Wooster Street. Dolly married John Dogolo who originated from Warren Street. Both John and Dolly worked at Sargent. They had two children named Roseann and Christopher.

Images From Little Italy

Ralph Buccetti (C) 1995 Festival.

(Santa Maria Maddalena Society Archives)

Theresa Argento (holding the flowers) and Mrs. Susan Amendola (her right) and the St. Andrews Ladies Society in 1996.

Members of the Galardi family on Wooster Street mid-1940's.

(Galardi Family Collection)

1950 Religious Procession-St. Michael Church.

(Galardi Family Collection)

Chapter Five *Le Strade de Wooster Square*

(The streets of Wooster Square)

The boundaries of Wooster Square have been debated for years. Old timers considered the boundaries to be centered around Wooster Street and St. Michael Church. Another predominately Italian American neighborhood located around the Wallace Street area existed with most of those residents attending St. Patrick Church. The inhabitants of Wallace Street did not consider themselves to be Wooster Square residents. Despite their objections, the city does recognize that area as a section of Wooster Square.

Today, streets such as Collis Street no longer exist, a victim of urban renewal. Hundreds of families were displaced making the ward a fraction of what it once was. Nevertheless, the stories of achievement and assimilation need to be understood and honored whether they unfolded on Wooster Street, Chapel Street, or Wallace Street. It is tribute to the courageous men and women who left Italy to settle in New Haven and allowed their families to prosper in the Elm City.

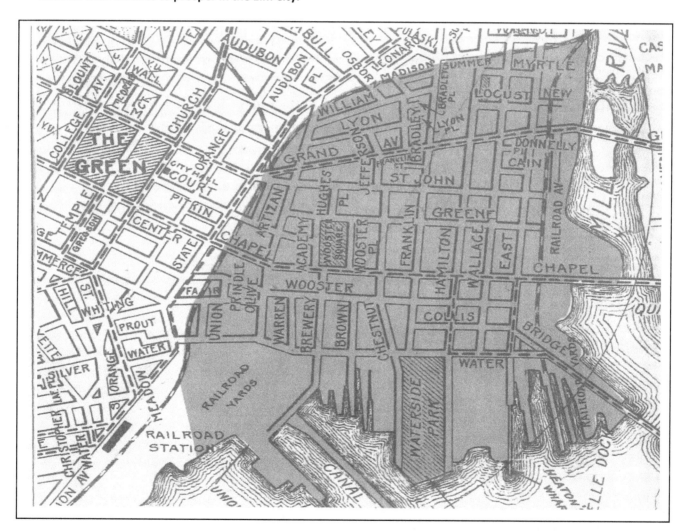

Map of Wooster Square

(Source-New Haven Museum)

Academy Street

Academy Street was named after a private school that was built is 1809. The institution, the "New Township Academy," was a boarding and day school. Today, Academy Street is lined with exceptional homes facing the picturesque Columbus Green.

The Edward Rowland House, built in 1857, is located at 42 Academy Street. The original owner, built and restored homes. After making a profit, Rowland moved on to other restoration projects.

Giuliano Family

Michael Giuliano was born in 1878 in a small village outside of Palermo, Sicily. In 1906, he arrived to America. Michael and his spouse (she was also from a village outside of Palermo) raised their two sons and four daughters at their home located at 26 Academy Street. To support his family, Giuliano operated a banana importing business on Grand Avenue. Michael's cousin Joe Guglielmino was also in that trade.

Giuliano's son Jake married the former Philomena Panza at St. Michael Church in 1941. The following year, at the age of twenty-two, Jake established West Haven Plumbing and Heating. The couple had eight children and lived in Orange.

In 1992, the Giuliano family sold their property on Academy Street.

10 Academy Street.

26 Academy Street

Bradley Street

In 2014, the New Haven Museum, created a display entitled "Wooster Square Beyond the New Township." Included, was a city directory explaining the origins of the streets. According to this document, Bradley Street was named after Abraham Bradley who opened the road in the 1830's. Henry Bradley, a wealthy carriage maker also lived in the vicinity.

Michael LaBonia, lived at 6 Lyon Street. His apartment was located just yards away from Bradley Street. As a child, in the 1940's, he played on John Palo's fish truck with his buddy Tommy Holland. In July of 2015, LaBonia spoke about his early years. He stated "I had many friends on Bradley Street. The Verderame, Rescigno and Greco families lived there. Later in life, I became a mailman and fellow postal workers Pat and John D'Albis came from there. Gabe Capuccio owned a market at 42 Bradley Street and there was Adinolfi Ice House on the corner of William and Bradley. Kids from Bradley Street went to Eaton School and the people went to St. Patrick or St. Michael Churches." *

*Interview. Mike LaBonia. July 26, 2015.

Legendary Wilbur Cross basketball coach Red Verderame (with the rose) at a dinner with former players. Red was born at 17 Bradley Street.

(Photo Courtesy of Ann Verderame)

Lawrence Frank Pisani

Antonio Pisani met his future wife Dora in 1900 in Italy. Two years later, they arrived to New Haven and settled on Bradley Street. An exemplary writer, Antonio established a newspaper called *L'Indipendente* in 1904. In 1913, along with Giorgio Mazzacane, he created *Le Forche Caudine*, a weekly publication which ran for a quarter of a century. Pisani was also a correspondent for *Il Corriere d'America* which was a popular Italian newspaper in New Haven.

Antonio's son Larry graduated from Hillhouse High School and later Yale. He continued his education by earning a decorate degree from the Ivy League institution. In 1934, Larry joined the Boys Scout Troop based out of St. Michael Church. He was involved with that organization for over eighty years.

Professionally, Pisani taught Sociology at Southern Connecticut for over five decades. Well-liked and respected, Larry was a founding member of the Italian American Historical Society of New Haven. Many years ago, in 1957, he authored an outstanding book on Italian Americans entitled "*The Italian in America*."

Dr. Pisani on October 8, 2011-Columbus Park.

Rescigno's

Julius and Nellie Rescigno lived on Bradley Street in the 1930's through the early 1940's. Early in their marriage they both worked at the New Haven Clock Shop. Eventually, Julius was hired as a maintenance man at Yale. The happy couple had five children named Julius, Roseanne, Joseph, Gloria, and Tony. Tony was born on February 26, 1945, at 191 Franklin Street, in the projects. In 1955, the family moved to 37 Pearl Street.

Tony was a very popular First Selectman in North Haven from 1989 to 2000. In 2000, he accepted the position as President of the Greater New Haven Chamber of Commerce. Rescigno firmly believes that his childhood experiences helped to prepare him for his professional career in public service. As a child, he attended Hamilton and Skinner Schools. He graduated from Wilbur Cross in 1962 and earned a B.S. degree in Business Administration from the University of New Haven. On July 29, 2015, Tony looked back on growing up in Wooster Square. He claimed, "living in that neighborhood got me started in business at the age of eight. I was given a shoe shine box with a number. I was assigned a corner which was on State and Olive. Tony's Apizza was next to my corner. Ironically, years later, I went to work for the owner Tony Porto. Back then it was safe. My parents did not have to worry about me. From that job I got a sense of business and street smarts. The neighborhood was a large and close community. It was a big family and I had many, many friends."*

*Interview.Tony Rescigno.July 29, 2015.

Skinner School

(Photo Courtesy of John Ragozzino)

Brewery Street

During Colonial times, Brewery Street ran from Wooster Square to the harbor. At that time, located in the vicinity were many industries including breweries.

Al Lauro, a major contributor to this book, lived on Brewery Street as a child in the mid 1930's. According to Al, there was one residential home on the street. Mr. Fiore owned the Fiore Building located at 185 Brewery Street. He was the Registrar of Voters for the Tenth Ward.

Today, there are no residential homes on Brewery Street. The most notable building in the area is the United States Post Office.

Pepe's-1995

Sal Montagna holding Cam Gravina. Cam's aunt Laura Rinaldi is enjoying the moment.

(Photo Courtesy of Gary and Denise Gravina)

Salvatore Montagna was a tall and distinguished looking man. Sal possessed a calm demeanor which made him extremely popular with the customers at Pepe's. While only in his teens, he began to work for Frank Pepe. For over sixty years, he was a loyal and dependable employee.

Montagna was born as one of five sons and two daughters to Giuseppe and Marie Cretella Montagna. The family resided on Wooster and Brewery.

Brown Street

Brown Street was named after prominent members of the Brown family that lived in the area in the late 1700's. Jabez Brown was the wealthy owner of a dock on Water Street. He married the former Rebecca Smith on November 18, 1773, at the North Congregational Church. Other members of the family included George H. Brown a carver, Robert Brown a candle maker, and Andrew and Daniel Brown who were builders.

Today, the street is well kept and quite. Located at the midpoint of Wooster Street, Brown Street has thirteen homes including 20 Brown Street which was built in 1846. Currently, there are no commercial businesses on the road and the residents are Italian American or young couples. Rightfully so, Brown Street is considered prime real estate in the city.

Brown Street-Fall of 2013

Al Lauro can vividly recall the residents of Brown Street going back to the World War II era. Families such as the Accurso's, Langello's, Gambardella's, Scaramella's, Barletta's, Diana's, Vanacore's, Gargano's, Ricciutti's, Cinque's, Vitagliano's, Casanova's, Esposito's, and Consiglio's formed a tight knit community. The road was primarily residential with DiBenedetto Dry Goods located on the corner of Wooster and Brown. Alphonse Bonito owned a small fish market on the street near the Accurso home. Sal and Sebastian Siena had a gas station at the corner of Brown and Water.

Vitolo's

Aniello Vitolo and Nicoletta Perrilli Vitolo lived at 527 Chapel Street in the Esposito Building. The couple married on July 19, 1925, at St. Michael Church. Aniello's father Antonio, who grew up at 22 Brown Street, and his mother Rafaella who came from Atrani, Italy to celebrate their wedding. Rafaella did not enjoy America and immediately returned to Italy. Antonio made the voyage a few times. In fact, he brought the original statue of Atrani to St. Michael Church.

Aniello and his wife Nicoletta had a son and two daughters. To support his family, he worked as a Longshoreman (hatch boss) at the New Haven Terminal and Cilco Terminal in Poughkeepsie for forty-four years. Nicoletta worked at Sargent for thirty-five years.

22 Brown Street

Rafaella and Antonio Vitolo

(Photo courtesy of Tony Vitolo)

Anthony "Flash" Consiglio was born at 13 Brown Street. His father Gennaro and his mother Marie Annette Basso originated from Amalfi. When Anthony was in his teens the family moved to the Hill section.

During World War II, "Flash" was in the Military Police. He was a driver and bodyguard for General Clark in the 5th Army. Anthony spent a great deal of time during the war in Italy. After the war, he worked at the Post Office.

Anthony Consiglio relaxing in Italy.

(Photo Courtesy of Teresa Consiglio)

"Flash" met his future wife Teresa Leonzo at a picnic. Teresa asked him for a ride home to Campbell Avenue in West Haven. The couple married on May 29, 1943, at St. Anthony Church. After their honeymoon, they resided at 107 Columbus Avenue in the Hill. Eventually, the couple moved to North Branford to raise their daughter Marie.

Celia DeMayo Agnellino was born at 21 Brown Street. Her parents Nicholas DeMayo and Rafaella Consiglio had two children. Nicholas worked at Connecticut Steel in West Haven as a welder. Rafaella worked at C. Cowles.

Giuseppe Agnellino

St. Andrew Procession-2013.

At the age of five, Celia's family moved to 22 Franklin Street. The family enjoyed the larger living space which included four rooms and their own bathroom. Nicholas paid a hefty twenty-four dollars a month for rent.

In 1962, Celia met her future husband Giuseppe Agnellino at the Feast of St. Michael on Wooster Street. Giuseppe had recently arrived to New Haven from Cusano, Italy. Two years later, the couple married. To earn a living he worked as a tailor at Chips on Eld Street. The Agnellino's moved to Morris Cove to raise their family.

Brown Street during Redevelopment.

(Photo Courtesy of Harry DeBenedet)

Salvatore Consiglio

Salvatore Consiglio was born as one of three children to Thomas "The Lord" and Josephine Nastri Consiglio. Originally from Spring Street, Sal grew up at 19 Brown Street. In 1951, his grandmother Annunziata purchased the three story home. Occupying the first flat was his Aunt Anna Consiglio. Sal and his family lived on the second floor and his grandparents resided on the third floor.

As a ten year old kid, Sal earned a few dollars by sweeping the floor at "The Big Apple," his family's restaurant. A few years later, Consiglio waited tables and washed dishes on Sundays. His maternal grandfather was a shoe maker with his storefront located on the corner of Wooster and Chestnut.

Growing up on Brown Street was similar to the other streets in Little Italy. The families were close and dozens of children played in the street. The residents especially enjoyed the legendary July 3rd firework celebrations that would last for hours. Consiglio claimed, "it was unbelievable until Chief Ahern tried to stop them. One year the police tried to arrest people and a riot broke out."*

After graduating from Notre Dame High School in 1960, Sal went to work as an electrician and in the auto body business. At the age of twenty-six, he purchased the home at 17 Brown Street. At one time, Consiglio owned four homes on the street.

Consiglio concluded, "it was a great place to grow up. Behind Brown Street was Dante School. Hundreds of guys would play dice in the school yard. Behind my house were garages that were occupied by Blue Jay Cleaners. My dad passed away at eighty-six. He bartended for fifty-six years and he was a great joke teller always laughing himself before the punch line."*

*Interview Salvatore Consiglio. June 30, 2014.

17 Brown Street

Spring of 2015

Chapel Street

Chapel Street was named after the Yale College chapel. The edifice was located on the corner of Chapel and College Streets.

<u>Theresa Argento</u>

Proud, dedicated, and dignified are just a few words that can describe Theresa Argento and her three quarters of a century of contributions to the New Haven Italian American community.

Theresa's parents Matteo and Antonetta Carrano were born in Amalfi. Matteo came to America at the age of four and his future wife at sixteen years old. They became part of the thriving Amalfitani community in New Haven. Matteo worked hard at his fruit market called "Carrano's" located at 460 Chapel Street to support his seven children.

Matteo in front of his market.

(Theresa Argento Archives)

While at Commercial High School, Theresa studied business. The skills that she obtained would help her immensely in the years to come to organize and budget many different programs.

In 1983, Mayor DiLieto appointed Theresa as the chairwoman of the Amalfi-New Haven Sister City Program. This program had included academic scholarships, sponsoring exchange students, and the hosting of the honorable mayor of Amalfi. Argento stated, "the Sister City Program was wonderful for the Americans as well as the Italians. Both groups had the opportunity to understand one another's shared heritage and culture."*

Theresa (Right) and Rosa DeLauro on Wooster Street.

July of 2011

Argento's fervor and enthusiasm are impressive especially for a women in her mid-nineties. She has been the President of the St. Andrews Ladies Society and a member of the St. Andrews Festival Committee for decades. Theresa is also the chairwoman of the Columbus Day Parade and the Wreath Laying Ceremony in Columbus Green.

A pious individual, Argento has tirelessly raised money for the Cathedral of St. Andrew in Amalfi. Furthermore, she is involved in many activities for the Church of St. Michael including the church's cookbook, and annual banquet. "My mother raised money for the Cathedral of St. Andrew for fifty years. She passed her love of Amalfi on to her children. My late husband Pasquale never held me back from being involved. He was great. I met him when he owned a dry cleaning business out of my father's building. He would say to me "good job" after a function."*

In her private life, Theresa was married to her husband Pasquale for fifty-six years before he passed away in 2003. They had two daughters. Sadly, her daughter Francis, succumbed to cancer at a young age.

Theresa's newest endeavor is an effort to get younger people, including her granddaughter Jessica Muoio involved. Argento concluded, "in the last year, twenty young women have joined our society. It is important to get the young people involved for the future. For me it has been a labor of love."*

Few if any, have done more in New Haven to bring the Italian American family together.

*Interview. Theresa Argento. November 10, 2015.

Frank Carrano

For thirty-seven years, Frank Carrano was employed by the City of New Haven Board of Education. Throughout his long and distinguished career, Frank made an impact in the classroom and as the president of the teacher's union. In 1975, the teachers went on strike demanding an increase in their salary. A judge ruled that the educators must return to their classrooms. In the vanguard, negotiating for better wages, Frank refused the court order and spent eight days in jail.

As a child, Frank's parents encouraged him to focus and excel in school. He attended Dante School until enrolling at St. Michael School in the 4th grade. Carrano graduated from

Notre Dame in 1955. He continued his studies at Southern Connecticut Teachers College, graduating in 1961.

Frank's maiden assignment was as a Special Education instructor at Sheridan Junior High School. Concurrent with his duties as a teacher, he served as President of Local 933 of the union. Dr. Carrano retired in 1999. Retirement was a misnomer for Frank as he remained extremely active. He became an adjunct professor at Southern Connecticut State University and he worked in Washington D.C. for the American Federation of Teachers. Carrano has also served on numerous educational committees including the Connecticut Commission for Education Excellence, the President of Connecticut Coalition for Justice in Educational Foundation and the Chairman of the Branford Board of Education.

Frank and his wife Angela have two sons. Matthew is the Curator of Dinosaurian at the Smithsonian Museum of Natural History. Frank Jr. is a doctor in Massachusetts.

Theresa organizing the 2012 St. Andrew Procession.

Matteo Naclerio Jr.

Foxon Park Soda, Pepe's Apizza, and Louie's Lunch are Elm City establishments that are recognized on the local and national levels. Over the course of time, these businesses have increased in their popularity. Rightfully so, patrons can enjoy "a slice " from Pepe's and satisfy their taste palate with one of eighteen different Foxon Park flavors.

Matteo Naclerio Sr. arrived to New Haven from Agerola, Italy at the age of twenty-seven. Matteo and his wife Louise Papagoda Naclerio had eight children and they resided at 458 Chapel Street.

To provide for his family, Matteo started to bottle water and he sold the product for two cents. When the Great Depression struck, twenty-five percent of Americans were jobless. Few people had the means to spend money on water. In a clever effort to re-invent himself, Matteo purchased property on Foxon Boulevard. In 1922, he established Foxon Park Soda. In the 1940's, his sons Joseph, Edward, and Anthony inherited the company.

Another son, Matteo Jr. attended Wooster Street and Columbus Schools. A capable student, he graduated from Hillhouse High School in 1946 and he went on to major in biology at Providence College. After completing his course work, Matteo worked in the jewelry and cable fields. Many years later, in 1970, he created Tri-State Tire in Wallingford.

Matteo married the former Marie Esposito of 235 Wooster Street. They had four children.

Today, the Naclerio family still owns and operates Foxon Park Soda and Tri-State Tire. Both companies are thriving.

Matteo and Marie Naclerio

(Photo courtesy of Marie Naclerio)

Gennaro Ruocco

At the age of nineteen, Gennaro Ruocco emigrated from Naples. In the early 1920's, he established a shoe repair business. His shop was located at 478 Chapel Street. Gennaro specialized in making and repairing shoes for Polio victims who were crippled or disabled.

Gennaro and his wife Jennie had four boys. The family lived above his store.

Chestnut Street

Chestnut Street received its name from the Chestnut Tree. Today, the street is a far cry of what it was before Redevelopment and only contains a few homes. Mayor Lee's program devastated the street replacing factories and homes with Conte School and campus.

Rita Silvestro exudes vitality for a lady her age. An octogenarian, her face contains no wrinkles and her mind is sharp. Her secret to longevity and health is simple. Rita stated, "I stay very active, involved with St. Bernadette Church and other organizations."*

Rita's story began on November 6, 1929. She was delivered by Dr. Conte at 23 Chestnut Street. The legendary doctor was assisted by Louise LaFemina, a mid-wife and the sister of Dr. LaFemina. Michael Proto, a cousin of Rita's family owned the six family property at 23 Chestnut Street which was located across the street from C. Cowles. The Cavaliere family (including Emiddio and Silvio the future owners of the market on Wooster Street) were also tenants.

Andrea Della Spina, fought in two conflicts while serving in the Navy in Italy. A citizen of Amalfi, he saw action against Yugoslavia and later in World War I. Prior to being deployed in the Great War, he told Anna Langella, "God willing, if I return we will get married." In 1919, the couple married at St. Andrew Cathedral in Amalfi.

Andrea left his young bride in Italy and immigrated to Rutland, Massachusetts. His brother-in-law was able to secure him a job. Two years later, Anna joined her husband in Rutland. Andrea's cousin Carmen lived in New Haven and was worked in the fishing industry. In time, Andrea moved to the Elm City and Carmen got him a job at Sargent. Anna stayed at home and raised their children Nicoletta, Ciro, Carmella, and Rita.

Rita was a happy and well adjusted child who performed well in school. At Dante and Columbus Schools, she was a model student. At Commercial High School, her favorite teacher was Dr. Floyd Blackman who taught accounting. The skills that she mastered served her for decades in her professional career.

At the age of sixteen, Rita went to work for Mr. DiBenedetto at Ideal Shirt Factory. The owner liked and trusted her. Aside from his factory, Mr. DiBenedetto had real estate properties including an apartment building at 258 Cedar Street in the Hill section. Each month, she collected over two thousand dollars in rents for her boss.

After a few years, Rita left Ideal and found a job at A.C. Gilbert. She worked in the accounting and payroll department for twenty years. On June 4th, 1997, she retired from Yale after thirty-five years of service.

In 1958, Angela Santoro, a friend of Rita's, had a child. Rita traveled by bus to Hamden to Angela's home. On that fateful day, she met John Silvestro. John's grandfather, a Sicilian, owned Catania Bakery of Blatchley Avenue. The two married on April 25, 1959, at St. Vincent De Paul Church. In 1963, the couple purchased a home on Ley Street in Morris Cove. John was a welder by trade. He passed away on May 25, 1997. Today, Rita lives with her nephew Andrew Donarumo.

Pleasant and proud, Rita concluded, "during the Depression my father made my brother a shoe shine box. His station was on Elm Street with the Yale students. On prom night, Ciro shinned the shoes of a future president and congressmen. My former boss, Mr. Gilbert, gave Ciro his first pair of roller skates."*

*Interview. Rita Silvestro. July 12, 2015.

Rita Silvestro in July of 2015.

Andrea and his wife Anna with their daughter Nicoletta and son Ciro (baby). The photo was taken in Amalfi in 1920.

(Photo Courtesy of Andrew Donarumo)

Collis Street

From its origins in the 1840's, Collis Street was a densely populated area until Redevelopment. The building of the highway erased the road from the landscape of New Haven.

In the early 1920's, there were eight family owned markets on Collis Street. The Afragola's operated a grocery at 29 Collis Street and the Acampora's rented the storefront from John Orso for their grocery at 36 Collis Street.

John Frank Orso came to America from Amalfi in 1919. A commercial fisherman, Orso boarded his boat "The Onward" at 4:00 A.M. and fished until 5:00 P.M. Tirelessly, he kept this daily schedule from the age of seventeen to seventy-two. John and his spouse Adeline had three children and they resided at 36-38 Collis Street. The family owned the tenement building which included seven apartments, the Acampora Market and Harbor Grille.

John Jr. followed his dad's footsteps and became a fisherman. During his company's peak years, Orso had two lobster and two clam boats operating daily. He stated, "the people on Collis Street were very tight. The majority were Italian and there were many stores in the neighborhood. Cousins lived with cousins."*

*Interview. John Orso. March 16, 2015.

Alphonse Paolillo lived at 15 Collis Street. He married the former Maggy Luciano and they moved to 16 Taylor Avenue in East Haven. This photo was taken on Collis street in the 1930's.

(Teresa Falcigno Collection)

Court Street

The row houses on Court Street were constructed prior to the Civil War. By the early 1920's, they were occupied mostly by wealthy single families. The residents were small business owners. Within a few decades, the buildings were dilapidated and occupied by transient workers.

Steven Esposito Marker

Court Street

Perhaps, more than any other road in Wooster Square, Court Street benefited from urban renewal. The row house were skillfully renovated making the area a hot spot for young artists, college students, and professionals.

DePalma Court

   In September of 1989, the city dedicated DePalma Court in honor of Michael DePalma. In 1903, DePalma was born on Collis Street. He served the Elm City for a half century as an Alderman, and on boards, and committees. Today, DePalma Court is the home of Russo Park and the site of a weekly farmers market.

East Street

During Colonial times, East Street was a major avenue of trade and travel along the Mill River.

Michael Lavelle was born on November 13, 1896, in Faicchio, Benevento, Italy. As a young boy, his family moved to New Haven and settled on Brown Street.

In 1914, Europe erupted in conflict. President Wilson was determined to keep the United States out of the war. Finally, on April 6, 1917, America declared war on Germany. Millions of young Americans were drafted or enlisted to serve in the military. According to the website warmemorial.us, eleven hundred men from the state of Connecticut were killed or wounded in action. From the Elm City, Privates Matthew Amarante and Valentine Asprelli died as a result of disease. Private John Amato perished in a combat zone accident.

Lavelle served with the 301st Field Artillery Battery C. While fighting in France, Lavelle's unit was gassed by the Germans and he was critically wounded. Michael returned to New Haven and lived on East Street. However, his health continued to deteriorate and he died on January 11, 1922, at the Veteran's Hospital. Michael was laid to rest at St. Lawrence Cemetery on Derby Avenue.

Fair Street, the Banana Capital of New England

Fair Street, just north of Wooster Street, was at one time the banana importing capital of New England. The street, a combination of residential structures and commercial businesses, had a rich history before being drastically reduced during Redevelopment.

In 1904, the Bridgeport Herald (July 24) reported that the Feast of St. Maria Maddalena began on Fair Street and concluded at the end of Wooster Street. The "Festa" was a gallant multi-day event that attracted thousands of recently arrived immigrants.

In the city directory of 1928, over ninety percent of the inhabitants of Fair Street were Italian. Two of the families that lived on the street at that time were the Mercurio's and the D'Amico's. Matteo Mercurio immigrated to the Elm City from Sicily. He married the former Josephine Murano and they had seven children. The family lived at 29 Fair Street.

Raffaele D'Amico was a part of the massive wave of Italian immigration from Atrani to New Haven. He and his wife Nancy Apicella D'Amico lived in a cold water flat at 16 Fair Street with their nine children. A son named Alphonse, joined the Civilian Conservation Corps (CCC) during the Great Depression. In time, Alphonse and his wife moved their son and daughter to Fair Haven. To support his family, he worked as a machinist at A.C. Gilbert and Winchester.

Following the pattern of assimilation, Alphonse's son Ron was able to leave Fair Haven and to purchase a home in the suburbs. For over fifty years, he has owned "Ron's Barber Shop" located at 4 Linsley Street in North Haven.

1936-Fair Street Area.

John Riccio (Left), Nancy D'Amico, and Alphonse D'Amico

(Photo courtesy of Ron D'Amico)

In the late 1920's, a variety of businesses thrived on Fair Street. Mario Picardo, Maria Vece, Rosario Setaro, and Mrs. Fiengo ran small grocery stores. Klein Sausage (8 Fair Street-Rear), Atlantic Bottling Company (30 Fair), Perrigo Plumbing (45 Fair), and Maiorino Real Estate (50 Fair) were also located in the neighborhood.

However, it was the Sicilian owned banana companies that marked Fair Street on the New Haven landscape. They were: Dattilo (7 Fair), Corso (36 Fair), Guglielmino (31 Fair), Mascari (8 Fair) and Cedro.

Dattilo Banana Company

(Photo Courtesy of Billy Mascari)

Mascari Bananna Company

At a youthful age, Antonio Mascari boarded a transatlantic steamer and sailed to America. He made the voyage with his cousins. His parents remained in Termini, Sicily and never joined him in the United States. Life was a grind for Antonio, as he barely earned a living, as a push cart vendor in the neighborhood.

Antonio married Caterina Guglielmino and they had three children; Salvatore, Joseph, and Josephine. Antonio, a hard working and frugal man, was able to purchase property at 8 Fair Street which included the rear building.

In 1936, Salvatore established Mascari Banana Company at 8 Fair Street. The first floor of the building was occupied by Antonio and his wife and the storefront where the business was situated. In the basement, the bananas were kept on hooks. The fruit was imported by sea from Central America. Once in New York, the product was transported by rail to New Haven. The second floor flat was inhabited by Josephine and her husband Frank Farace.

Originally, Joseph had attended school to become a cabinet maker. He joined forces with his brother after being strongly encouraged to do so by his mother. The brothers quickly established a reputation for their honesty and for the quality of their bananas. As their business expanded, both men had to serve their country during World War II. Salvatore fought in the Philippines and Joseph in France.

Throughout the Great Depression, the banana dealers were friendly competitors. These hard working men converged at Sil's Tavern on Fair Street and enjoyed a drink after a long day at work. Silvio Antonelli was the proprietor of the bar.

In 1960, Mayor Lee's Redevelopment program forced the Mascari's from Fair Street to 179 Main Street in Branford. Previously, the Martone family owned a chicken farm at that location. The Mascari's remained there until 2003.

During the 1980's, the Spanish population rapidly grew in sections of the city, especially Fair Haven. To meet the need of the Spanish residents, the Mascari's expanded from selling bananas to other fruits such as mangos, and avocados. At this time, Antonio's grandson Joseph and his two sons Billy and Joe were directing the company. They bought out Phil and Vito Cedro and renamed the corporation "Cedro Banana and Mascari Enterprises."

Billy and his brother took the company to the next level. Today, they are a direct importer and service the local dealers. Furthermore, they are the largest importer in the state of Connecticut.

The industry has changed a great deal in the past century. Today, the product is shipped unripe on pallets from Central America. Climate control technology is utilized to prepare the fruit for sale.

Billy and Joe claimed to have the industry ingrained in them. As babies, they sat in crates with blankets at their dad's shop. In high school, Billy would load up a pickup truck with fruit and peddle it within the Spanish community in Fair Haven. This provided him with spending money and a valuable education for the future. Billy concluded, "we work seven days a week. I am married to the business. This is all I know how to do. It is in my blood."*

*Interview Billy Mascari. July 7, 2013.

Alphonse D'Amico (Left) and his brother-in-law Julias Viscio on Fair Street. This photo was taken on October 3, 1936. The D'Amico family lived at 16 Fair Street.

(Photo Courtesy of Ron D'Amico)

Fair Street Residents-1913

(Source-*Carriages&Clocks* by Preston Maynard and Marjorie Noyes. pp. 82-83)

In 1913, ninety-five percent of the residents living on Fair Street were Italian. The recently arrived immigrants were not highly educated. Therefore, forty-one percent were laborers helping to build the infrastructure of the city. Another twelve percent of the population were employed in the banana or importing industry.

Address	Resident	Occupation
1 Fair Street	Raffaele Freccia	Owner of Freccia Company 634 Chapel Street
6 Fair Street	Dominico Prete	mason
7 Fair Street	Guiseppe Carrano	laborer
7 Fair Street	Mrs. Jennifer Nanton	widower
8 Fair Street	Gaetano Dattolo	fruit vendor
8 Fair Street	Michele Dattolo	
8 Fair Street	Tommaso Cretella	laborer
9 Fair Street	Sabato Del Franco	
12 Fair Street	Antonio Carrano	Sargent Company
12 Fair Street	Andrea Costantinopoli	
12 Fair Street	Anotoni Cretella	laborer
12 Fair Street	Bonaventure Savino	laborer
12 Fair Street	Luigi Laudano	Sargent Company
13 Fair Street	Giovanni Sica	laborer
13 Fair Street	Mrs. Giovanni Colavolpe	
15 Fair Street	Antonio Cicalese	laborer
15 Fair Street	Cosimo Gargano	laborer
15 Fair Street	F. Roveta	
15 Fair Street	Giacomo Perretti	laborer
15 Fair Street	Pasquale Testa	Sargent Company
16 Fair Street	Aniello Amatruda	barber-224 Wooster Street
16 Fair Street	Antonio Proto	laborer

16 Fair Street	Filippo Corso	laborer
16 Fair Street	Francesco Scappace	laborer
16 Fair Street	Giovanni Durso	laborer
16 Fair Street	Maria D'Amico	widow-Alfonso
16 Fair Street	Raffaele D'Amico	laborer
16.50 Fair Street	Rosalio Variety Store	resided at 12 Warren Street
20 Fair Street	G. Ferrailo	horse dealer
20 Fair Street	Giuseppe Scappace	laborer
20 Fair Street	Vincenzo Scappace	laborer
22 Fair Street	Pasquale Surrentino	laborer
25 Fair Street	Fair Street School	
26 Fair Street	Antonio Consiglio	Sargent Company
26 Fair Street	Antonio Dattolo	fruit dealer
26 Fair Street	Cosmo Williams	fruit dealer
26 Fair Street	Ernesto Barbato	salesman W.H Galvin produce-253 Water St.
26 Fair Street	Gioacchino Cretella	laborer
26 Fair Street	Guiseppe Cavallaro	peddler
26 Fair Street	J. Cavallaro	wholesale fruit dealer
26 Fair Street	Pasquale Volpe	barber
26 Fair Street	Vincenzo Paulillo	laborer
29 Fair Street	Gennearo Consiglio	Candee Company
29 Fair Street	Massimo Del Pizzo	laborer
30 Fair Street	Joe Williams	fruit dealer
31 Fair Street	Angelo Langella	peddler
31 Fair Street	Guiseppe Nisto	shoemaker 77 Lamberton Street
32 Fair Street	Cosmo Williams Fruits	
32 Fair Street	Pasquale Mangini	Sargent Company
32 Fair Street	Vincenzo Lettieri	laborer
34 Fair Street	Tripoli Athletic Club	
35 Fair Street	Luigi Amatruda	laborer
35 Fair Street	Michele Amatruda	shoemaker
35 Fair Street	William Olson	
36 Fair Street	Iragi Rosario	

36 Fair Street	Pasquale Corso Fruit Dealer	
36 Fair Street	Vincenzo Pauso	laborer
37 Fair Street	Domenico Raiano	Sargent Company
37 Fair Street	Ferdinando Roveta	confectioner
37 Fair Street	Filippo Mangier	painter
37 Fair Street	Francesco Pacilio	driver
37 Fair Street	Geraldo Cappiello	laborer
37 Fair Street	Mrs. Raffaela Perrelli	
37 Fair Street	Tomasso Corso Fruit Dealer	
39 Fair Street	Gargano Firovante Grocery	
40 Fair Street	Rosario Setaro Grocery	
40 Fair Street	Francesco Di Mello	laborer
42 Fair Street	Filippe Gambuto	laborer
42 Fair Street	Philip Sansone Fruits	
43 Fair Street	C. Costello	
45 Fair Street	Israel Hershman	paper stock dealer
46 Fair Street	Guiseppe Della Sala	Sargent Company
48 Fair Street	Antonio Guglielmino Fruit Dealer	
50 Fair Street	Leopoldo Colavolpe	laborer
50 Fair Street	Salvatore DiPalma Meat Market	
50 Fair Street	Antonio Apuzzo	laborer
52 Fair Street	Alfonso DeMaio Saloon	
52 Fair Street	Maiorino Brothers Saloon	

Franklin Street

Franklin Street was named after James Franklin. In the 1830's, Franklin and Joseph Jenkins bought and developed land in the New Township area.

In the decades preceding central heating, many families in Wooster Square heated their tenements with kerosene oil. In the basements of the buildings were storage tanks. Most flats had a stove in the kitchen and a smaller heating source in the parlor. Five gallon drums were used to carry the fuel from the cellar to the apartment.

Marie Cangiano grew up at 151 Wooster Street. She vividly recalled the smell of the kerosene and her parents using a stone and vinegar to clean the stove. She stated "the stove provided a little heat but it was still cold in the bedrooms. We would go to sleep with our coats on in bed."*

Caspar Amodio married Jennie Perelli. Both were born in New Haven. In 1929, during the Great Depression, he created Blue Flame Oil. At that time, Caspar and his driver Tony Scaramella of Brown Street, delivered the kerosene in five gallon drums. Eventually, a hose was added to his truck which facilitated the deliveries.

Driver Tony Scaramella with Jennie Amodio.

(Photo Courtesy of Rae Somma)

*Interview. Marie Cangiano. August 8, 2012.

Amodio also ran a candy store out of his building at 24 Franklin Street. Jennie raised their three children and she served as the bookkeeper. The Amodio's owned and lived at 96 Wooster Street. Casper and his family occupied two apartments on the first floor and rented out the other flats.

During the summer months, Casper daily drove one hundred miles to Providence to pick up fresh seafood. He then delivered the product to markets in New York City.

Today, Casper's grandson Pat is the president. Despite being the owner, Pat still enjoys the grunt work of the industry such as installing a new heating system. Blue Flame Oil serves twenty-seven towns and cities in the greater New Haven area.

483 Chapel Street

The corner of Chapel and Franklin.

40 Franklin Street

Winter of 2010.

Grand Avenue

"Being on Grand Avenue was the best spot in the city. I would go to DiLungo's stand with a crew of guys like Cosmo Amendola, Ally Gambardella, Sally Filipelli, and Dickie Annunziato. On some nights, Midge Renault would stop by and buy the entire wagon of clams for the guys."

Egisto Filipelli

During the mid-1800's, Jewish immigrants settled on Grand Street which was renamed in 1871 to East Grand Street. Sixteen years later, the street became known as Grand Avenue. A second wave of Jewish settlers arrived in the late 1800's.

By the 1890's, the southern Italians began to arrive to the bustling area. At the time, Giuseppe Gagliardi resided at 586 Grand Avenue and he walked to work at the New Haven Clock Shop.

From 1900 to Redevelopment, Grand Avenue was the hub of Italian and Jewish commercial businesses in the Elm City. Residents from Fair Haven and Wooster Square fondly remember their childhood and adult shopping excursions on Grand Avenue.

"To me, Grand Avenue was the place. In five minutes, you could walk down Grand Avenue and take care of all of your shopping. We had drug stores, barber shops, food stores, clothing stores, furniture stores, and bakeries. It was all right there on the avenue."

Ronnie D'Amico

Jewish businesses in the area included Rosner's Grocery, Feinberg's Fine Clothing, Greenberg's Furniture, and Smolen's Furniture. Establishments such as Perlmutter's, and Mac Millers were popular clothing stores. For entertainment, locals frequented The Dreamland and Apollo Theaters.

Italian merchants such as Tony's, Cusano, and Baldo's bakeries, Sabby's, and Jimmy's Luncheonettes, Musco Jewelry, Battista's Shoes, Martone's Florist, Malafronte's Market, and Teresa's Furniture were neighborhood hot spots.

Cosmo Perrelli

Cosmo Perrelli in his store.

(St. Maria Maddalena Society Collection)

Cosmo Perrelli was born in Ravello, Italy. Later, his family moved to Atrani. After completing the transatlantic voyage in the 1890's, Perrelli lived on Greene Street. Cosmo married his first wife in his native country. Sadly, she passed away young and he remarried in the Elm City. Between both matrimonies, Cosmo had eight children.

An astute businessman, he owned properties on Chestnut and Wooster Streets. Cosmo also operated a liquor store at 369 Grand Avenue and a grocery store at 852 Orange Street.

A leader in the Italian American community, Perrelli served as the third President of the Santa Maria Maddalena Society.

The spiritual needs of the thousands of Catholics in the area were met by St. Patrick and St. Michael Churches. For a decade (1949-1959), Father Joseph Graziani guided the parishioners at St. Patrick's. The outgoing priest had a deep passion for sports and he took great pride in the youth teams of the parish. Father Joe often transported the basketball team in his 1954 Chevy station wagon. Vincent DiBerardino, a nephew of Father Joe, describe his uncle as being "a priest of the young." A few years after Father Joe was transferred to St. Mary's in Derby, St. Patrick's was torn down.

Father Joe died on May 3, 2009, at the age of eighty-eight.

Father Joe at Payne Whitney Gym

Cross vs. Hillhouse-1959.

(Photo Courtesy of John Ragozzino)

Father Joe Speaking at a Banquet.

(Photo Courtesy of John Ragozzino)

Today, there are a few Italian merchants on Grand Avenue. Lucibello's at 935 Grand Avenue, Ferraro's located at 664 Grand Avenue, and Vinnie's Importing at 799 Grand Avenue continue to thrive. The majority of the Grand Avenue merchants are Spanish, representing the most recent immigrant group to arrive to the Elm City.

Pasquale DiLungo

"The Clam Man of Grand Avenue"

Pasquale DiLungo

(Photo Courtesy of Anthony DiLungo)

Pasquale DiLungo was born on May 21, 1895. Six years later, he arrived to the Italian colony in New Haven residing at 143 Wooster Street. Years later, he relocated to 685 Grand Avenue and finally to 171 Chestnut Street.

During the daytime, Pasquale worked at the New Haven Clock Shop. However, it was his second job that made him a local legend. From his residency on Chestnut Street, he pushed a cart loaded with clams to the corner of Grand and Hamilton. Into the early hours of the morning, with a knife, he skillfully shucked and served clams on the half shell. Locals, as well as men returning from area watering holes, frequented his stand.

At St. Michael Church, Pasquale joined hands with his wife Anna in matrimony. They had five children named Mary, Frank, Catherine, Nicholas, and Pasquale Jr. The "Clam Man of Grand Avenue" passed away in 1978.

Pasquale Jr. married the former Josephine Vitello. An electrician, he established D.F.G. Electric (DiLungo, Fusco, and Gentilesco). The couple had three sons, Pasquale, Anthony, and Mark. All three boys were elite hockey players at East Haven High School. Pasquale Jr. passed away on May 6, 1999.

Anthony DiLungo on the corner where his grandfather had his stand in June of 2015.

Greene Street

The Neptune was a state of the art vessel built at the Olive Street shipyard. The ship was equipped with twenty guns and a crew of thirty-six. Captain Daniel Greene commanded the ship on a three year voyage (1796-1799) to the Far East. The boat returned to New Haven with valuable silk, porcelain , tea, and other expensive items valued at $280,000.* Greene Street was named in honor of Daniel.

*New Haven Museum. *Beyond the New Township Wooster Square*.

Vincent Aitro

Vincent Aitro was born on April 13, 1912. He was brought into this world by a mid-wife at 205 Greene Street. Vincent's parents, Joseph and Assunta Ferrera Aitro originated from a small village in the vicinity of Naples. The couple had seven sons and two daughters.

Life was arduous for the Aitro family. Their flat located on Greene Street had five rooms for eleven people. Furthermore, there was no heat. A coal stove in the kitchen was used to heat the apartment.

In 1958, as a result of Redevelopment, Vincent moved to 46 Hellstrom Road in East Haven. His wife, Florence Camarra Aitro was an Italian American from Cambridge, Massachusetts. Florence and her husband were married for seventy-three years until she passed away in 2011. They had two sons named Richard and Vincent Jr.

To support his loving family, Aitro worked as a welder for A.B. Hendryx making bird cages. Later, he owned an amusement company (pinball and other gaming machines) which was located on Olive and Grand.

A lifelong Yankee fan, Vincent and his twin brother Carmen yearly went to Fort Lauderdale to watch spring training games. At the time, Joe DiMaggio was a hitting instructor. The Aitro's became friendly with the "Yankee Clipper" often enjoying breakfast with the legend.

Mr. Aitro was involved with dozens of sporting committees and functions. In 1945, the "Aitro Twins" coached the Connecticut Yankees female basketball team to the state championship. Vincent volunteered to coach many area teams including the St. Michael

Church basketball squad as well as Police Athletic League (P.A.L.) softball teams. He served as baseball commissioner for the Richard Lee Pony League.

An altruistic individual, Vincent was on the board of directors for the Walter Camp Football Foundation, New Haven Tap Off Club, the New Haven Football Foundation, and the Special Olympics. The twins also financially sponsored baseball teams for over fifty years.

Vincent was a longtime member of the St. Catello Society and a proud parishioner at St. Michael Church.

In April of 2012, Vincent celebrated his one hundredth birthday. The Centurion had retained a sharp mind and a passion for life. He passed away on May 10, 2015, at the age of one hundred and three.

Vincent holding a picture of himself and his twin brother with Joe DiMaggio.

(Photo Courtesy of Vincent Aitro)

Beverly Carbonella

Beverly Carbonella was an exceptional woman with a myriad of talents and abilities. A beautiful woman, Beverly had a sense of style and fashion. She was also energetic and had great determination. For a half of a century, she was a leader in the Wooster Square area. For example, Beverly was a co-founder of the Cherry Blossom Festival, and a founding member and past president of the Historic Wooster Square Association.

Beverly was born as one of two children to James and Mildred Bradshaw in Naugatuck. Her father was a talented baseball player who played catcher in the minor leagues. Beverly graduated from the Gilbert School in Winsted. She then attended the Pratt Institute of Arts and Design in Clinton Hills, Brooklyn. Her experiences in the city left a lasting impression.

As a young lady, Beverly met John Cassidento of Hamden at the Owenego Club in Branford. In January of 1964, the couple married at St. Michael Church. At that time, the Wooster Square area was in turmoil as a result of Redevelopment. Longtime residents were forced to leave or left on their own volition. Beverly immediately felt a connection to Court Street. The brownstones reminded her of her collegiate years in Brooklyn.

The newlyweds moved into a unit on Greene Street and then to 15 Court Street with their children John Jr. and Christina. In 1970, John and his wife purchased the Italian Consulate home at 20 Academy Street. The structure, built in 1890, needed costly repairs. They invested $36,000 to renovate their home. Professionally, John was working in the legal system. He had attended the University of Illinois and graduated from Uconn Law School.

In 1973, Cassidento successfully defended Alfred Baldwin III., the grandson of former Connecticut Governor Raymond Baldwin, in the Watergate Trials. In early 1974, Governor Richard Meskill appointed John as a Superior Court Judge. He passed away of a heart attack on June 10, 1974.

A strong woman, Beverly focused her energies on raising her two children who attended St. Michael School. The close knit Wooster Square community helped the grieving family. John Jr. reflected, "it was a terrific place to live. The park was right there. I attended St. Michael School for nine years and I knew all the kids from the neighborhood, including those who lived on Wooster Street. I have so many memories. In September, there was a block party. Right on Court Street, I played football, Wiffle ball and Frisbee. It really was a great neighborhood."*

Beverly remarried to Joseph Carbonella in 1981. He founded the New Haven Food Terminal and the couple moved to 295 Greene Street. Joseph passed away in 1996. Well into her retirement years, she remained an active force in the neighborhood. "My mother saw the potential of the area. The classical architecture reminded her of her school years in Brooklyn. She always wanted to improve the area" stated her son John.* On May 18, 2015, Beverly passed away at the age of eighty-eight. Her legacy in Wooster Square will carry on for decades to come.

*Interview. John Cassidento. August 11, 2015.

The Resume of Beverly Cassidento Carbonella

Co-Founder of Historic Wooster Square Association

Co-Founder of Court Street Association

Member of New Haven Historical District Commission for a decade.

Board Member of New Haven Preservation Trust

Board Member New Haven Colony Historical Society

Appointed by Mayor Guida to City Historical District Commission in 1970

Beverly and her daughter Christina in Columbus Park in 1967.

(Photo Courtesy of Christina Greene)

The Cassidento family participating in a procession in Wooster Square in the late 1960's.

(Photo Courtesy of Christina Greene)

Hamilton Street

Hamilton Street was named in honor of the great American patriot Alexander Hamilton (1755-1804). During his esteemed career, Hamilton served as chief staff aide to General Washington and he founded America's financial system.

Norma Zito Bailey

Norma Bailey, an active and energetic woman, often can be seen walking from her apartment on Wooster Street to downtown. Norma also regularly walks down Hamilton Street to Grand Avenue to Ferraro's Market. Amazingly, she has walked these same roads for eighty years.

Joe Zito and his wife Virginia Repoley Zito raised their family on Chestnut Street. During the Great Depression, he worked for the W.P.A. Joe came from a family tradition in music as he, his dad, and his uncle were professional musicians. Zito played the saxophone at local night clubs.

Academically, Norma excelled at Hamilton School and later Commercial High School. At Commercial, she studied business.

Shortly before World War II, the Zito's relocated to the Farnam Court Projects. The housing units were a drastic improvement from Chestnut Street. Norma commented "the projects were just built. They were great. There was even baseboard heating. On Chestnut Street we had to share a bathroom in the hallway."*

Norma on Wooster Street September of 2015.

In the late 1940's, Norma met Kessler Bailey who hailed from West Virginia. He had served in World War II as a Chief Petty Officer in the Navy. In 1950, the couple married at Center Church in New Haven. The newlyweds took up residence in a flat at 71 Hamilton Street. The couple had a son Kessler Jr. and a daughter Norma Jean.

Today, Norma enjoys spending time with her family and friends. She stated "I have lived on Wooster Street since 1964. It is nice but not the same. In the old days, the feast went from Olive Street down Wooster to Water Street. It was great. As a young girl, I played "kick the can" in the street. We did not have much. I attended St. Patrick's Church. It was beautiful. At that time, the parishioners were Irish, Italian, and some Polish. It was really special."*

*Interview. Norma Bailey. April 21, 2015.

St. Patrick's Church
(Photo Courtesy of John Ragozzino)

Filomena Carbone Gambardella

Filomena Carbone was born on April 8, 1913, as one of eight children to Joseph and Jenny Carbone. The family resided in a six apartment tenement building at 19 Hamilton Street. Mike's Butcher Shop was located on the street level of the building.

As a young women, Filomena met a guy from the neighborhood named Tommy Gambardella. He was a popular boxer in the featherweight division who fought under the name of Tommy Gam's. Gambardella participated on boxing cards at the New Haven Arena and at Savin Rock.

Tommy married Filomena at St. Michael Church. Their marriage produced a son and two daughters. For twenty-five years, he worked at Sargent and Filomena at Mode Dress Shop on Hamilton Street.

Surrounded by her loving family, Filomena celebrated her one hundred and second birthday in April of 2015. He daughter Rose Pane commented, "as a child, my mother took us to Waterside Park to play on the swings. Each summer the circus came to the park and that was a big deal."*

*Interview. Rose Pane. April 23, 2015.

Filomena (Center) and her family in April of 2015.

(Photo Courtesy of Rose Pane)

Hughes Place

During the early 1800's, Samuel Hughes lived in the vicinity. His property was decorated with glorious gardens and contain a stable for horses. A prominent business man, Hughes was a partner of Titus Street. Samuel passed away in 1864.

Today, in the spring time, the Yoshino Japanese Cherry Trees form a breathtaking canopy over the short road.

Hughes Place

Spring of 2015

Jefferson Street

Thomas Jefferson was an early American hero. The principal author of the Declaration of Independence, Jefferson also served his country as the third president. Jefferson Street was named in his honor.

In 1915, the Boys Club of New Haven moved to Jefferson Street. At that time, the Italian population in Wooster Square was rapidly growing. Many of the neighborhood boys were members of the club and were allowed to use the swimming pool. Down the street, at the corner of Grand Avenue and Jefferson Street, was a prosperous chicken market.

Tony and Caterina Valentino arrived to New Haven from a small village outside of Naples in 1951. Originally, the couple lived at 171 Chestnut Street. Tony supported his wife and three children by working for the Water Company. Caterina raised the children and worked at a nearby garment factory. In 1971, the couple purchased a home at 6 Jefferson Street. Today, Tony and Caterina are active parishioners of St. Michael Church. They enjoy spending time with their family and tending to their flower and vegetable gardens.

On a warm summer day in June of 2014, Caterina reflected on her journey to America. She stated, "I lived twenty minutes outside of Naples. A village called Santa Maria a Vico. There was no work in Italy. At the age of twenty-six, I came to America and got a job in a dress factory. I worked twelve hour days. Back in Italy, my father had a farm with ten workers. In America, at first I cried every day. On the trip over it took two weeks. I was sick as a dog."*

*Interview. Caterina Valentino. June 24, 2014.

The Valentino's in their gardens in the Summer of 2012.

Lyon Street

Lyon Street was created in the 1830's by Sidney Stone. Stone, a gifted architect, was born in May of 1803. His sphere of influence was felt throughout the Elm City. In the early 1830's, Stone designed New Haven's St. John's Episcopal Church. He also designed the Solomon Collis House at 75 Wooster Street and the Thomas Trowbridge Home situated at 45 Elm Street.

In the late 1840's, Stone drafted the design for his home located on the corner of Olive and Lyon Streets. In fact, his work was so prevalent that the area was known as "Stoneville." The Stone family moved to Elm Street in 1855.

Ferraro Family

Michael Ferraro was born as one of ten children to Michele and Dolly Fico Ferraro. Michele was born in Naples where he apprenticed as a baker. In America, he worked at Danese Bakery and later at Narcisco's. Dolly's father at one time owned a market on Wooster Street.

Baker Michele Ferraro

(Photo Courtesy of Mike Ferraro)

In 1940, Michele purchased a three family home at 21 Lyon Street from the Germanese family. The Ferraro's lived on the first floor and slept three boys to a bed. An uncle, Joseph Casanova and his wife Blanche occupied the third floor.

Down the road from the Ferraro's, Ed DeMaio operated Littlemore Beverages. DeMaio lived on Orange Street and he worked full time at Winchester. His soda company was popular during the 1940's and his product was delivered to residential and commercial customers. His biggest customer was Pepe's. Michael and Pasquale Ferraro worked for DeMaio.

The former site of the Littlemore Beverage Company in September of 2013.

Fred Frese, an industrial arts teacher at Old Saybrook High School, grew up at 69 Lyon Street. As a child in the 1950's, he recalled the Buffa's, DeRosa's, Gambardella's, Taddei's, and Falcigno's who all were neighbors. Fred's grandfather, Joe Cuomo owned a plumbing company from the 1930's to the 1960's at 69 Lyon Street. In the 1960's, Joe's son took over the small business. Fred's uncle, Jim Nuzzo, from St. John Street ran Willie Mack's Restaurant on East Street. Nuzzo previously was a boxer who fought under the alias of Willie Mack.

Mike and Pasquale Ferraro (r) in front of their former home at 21 Lyon Street.

69 Lyon Street 2013

The Fallen Hero's of Lyon Street

Two young men from Lyon Street perished while fighting for their country. Joe Figaro lived on the first floor of the tenement building at 6 Lyon Street. As a kid, he attended Eaton and Columbus Schools. He was a quick and gifted athlete. On April 18, 1953, Corporal Figaro was mortally wounded in North Korea. He had been serving in the 7th Division.

Bernard Zambrano resided at 69 Lyon Street. Bernard arrived in Vietnam in January of 1969. Two months later, on March 17th, he died in combat.

> 6 Lyon Street
>
> John Palo returned in the spring of 2015 to his apartment for the first time in fifty years.

Richard Damiani

Richard Damiani, future Superior Court Judge was born on Lyon Street on January 25, 1946. His parents Fred and Julia Adinolfi Damiani had three sons. Fred was a city of New Haven Court Judge and a State Senator.

Richard, an exemplary student, graduated from Notre Dame High School in 1963 and Providence College in 1967. He went on to earn his law degree from UCONN in 1970. In January of 1971, Damiani was appointed as an assistant prosecutor for the 6th Circuit Court. He worked in that capacity for five years. The amiable Damiani became a partner in the law firm of Greenberg, Costa, and Damiani in 1977.

On November 5, 1985, Governor O'Neill appointed Richard as a Superior Court Judge. Throughout his career, he was greatly respected in his profession for his fairness. In his personal life, Richard married the former Anna Marie Bonito. The couple had a daughter named Stephanie. She followed her father's footsteps and went into law. She is currently an Assistant State Attorney. Sadly, Richard suddenly passed away at the age of sixty-six in 2012.

Bernard Anthony Zambrano

Olive Street

According to the New Haven Museum, Olive Street received its name from the Olive Branch, a sloop, which was docked in New Haven on September 30, 1784.

Before Redevelopment, there were hundreds of people living on Olive Street of which the majority were Italian. Eddie Angiollo, grew up at 173 Olive Street. As a teenager, he worked for Ralph Amendola who owned a hair supply company named Aimee's Cosmetics. The business, located on the corner of Olive and Lyon Streets, sold products to local barbers. In the 1950's, the Masselli's, Aloi's, Squila's, and Riano's resided on the street.

A-1 Auto Service

29 Olive Street

Corner of Olive and St. John

(Photo Courtesy of Tony Galardi)

Dominic Galardi was a kind hearted and cheerful man who thrived being around people. At a young age, the value of money and the essence of hard work were instilled in him by his loving parents. Despite professional success, Dominic remained a down to earth man who passionately cared for his family and friends.

Galardi was born the fifth and final child of Antonio and Anna Lucibello Galardo on March 4, 1931. Antonio originated from Amalfi and his wife from Atrani. The couple had already been married in Italy when they arrived to America in 1912 aboard the S.S. Saint Anna.

For forty-five years, Antonio grinded out a career at Sargent. Unlike most recently arrived immigrants, the Galardi's owned property in Wooster Square including a tenement building at 82 Wooster Street where they resided. On the second floor, Anthony and Rose Florenzano lived along with their ten children. Anna raised her five children and looked after the Galardi's real estate interests.

As a child, Dominic helped to collect the rents and he worked at his dad's store. This hands on experience benefited him years later as a prominent business leader. Dominic attended St. Michael School and St. Mary's Academy. He was enrolled at UCONN for two years before taking a job at Winchester. During the Korean War, he honorably served his country in the Army.

In 1955, Dominic and his father-in-law Tony Buglione established A-1 Auto Service at 29 Olive Street. The business was multipurpose with a gas station and small dealership. In 1959, they opened a larger business in East Haven.

Altar Boys at St. Michael Church

Dom Galardi (Left),

Ed Naclerio (Center)

and Andy Criscuolo (Right).

(Photo Courtesy of Tony Galardi)

In 1963, the partners took an unprecedented risk by opening a Toyota franchise. At the time, America was still engaged in the Cold War with the communist super powers. Tensions were escalating in Asia and the Red Scare was on the minds of Americans. A Toyota car was not viewed as desirable because they were not American made. Dominic and Tony took the risk of selling Japanese cars and the rest is history. For over forty-five years, A-1 Toyota has been in operation enduring periods of economic hardships.

Dominic married his wife the former Virginia "Gigi" Buglione at the age of twenty-one. They had two children named AnnaLynn and Tony. Both of his children joined him at the dealership.

For over fifty years, Dominic was a member of the St. Andrew and Santa Maria Maddalena Societies. Also, he was a founding member of the Italian American Historical Society of New Haven in 1979. Galardi was honored by numerous organizations including the Knights of Columbus, and Providence College. Dominic passed away on July 10, 2013. His burial services were performed by Iovanne Funeral Home.

Tony and Antoinette Buglione resided at 124 Wooster Street. They had three children named Virginia, Carol, and Michael. Here Michael is driving down Wooster Street during World War II.

Dom (left) and his wife with members of their family on Wooster Street.

(Photos Courtesy of Tony Galardi.)

ST_magdaline Day - 1946

Carol Buglione-July 22, 1946, on Wooster Street.

(Photo Courtesy of Tony Galardi)

Eddie Angiollo (R), Frank Fronte (C), and Richie Mizger (L) Columbus Day Parade-2013.

St. John Street

St. John Street was named after Samuel St. John. He was a wealthy merchant who owned a considerable amount of land in the area. Upon his death in 1844, St. John left his parcels of land to his nieces.

Gabe Cognato was born on November 4, 1922, in Williamsburg, Brooklyn. His father Peter was the second husband of his mother Nina. Her first spouse died of the Spanish Influenza in 1918. The couple had two children and resided at 284 St. John Street.

Gabe attended Eaton and Orange Street Schools. He graduated from Hillhouse in 1940. Two years later, Gabe was drafted into the Army. As a member of the 155th Artillery Unit, Cognato trained in the Mojave Desert in California. After being deployed, his unit was at sea a month before arriving to Australia. Their final destination was New Guinea.

Stationed on the tropical island, the American G.I.'s faced many perils aside from the hardened Japanese soldiers. The jungle was inhabited by poisonous snakes and spiders. Malaria and other illnesses were common. To combat malaria, every soldier had to take Atabrine daily.

Gabe Cognato-Mojave Desert 1943

(Photo Courtesy of Gabe Cognato)

Gabe stationed in New Guinea

(Photo Courtesy of Gabe Cognato)

After the Japanese surrendered, it took Gabe's unit another two months aboard a ship to arrive back in the states. In time, Gabe got a job at Pratt and Whitney in North Haven and Southington. He retired after working for over thirty years for the post office.

In 1950, he married the former Grace Porello at St. Donato Church. Her brother was a priest in Hamden. The couple raised their family in New Haven and later Hamden. Gabe passed away on June 6, 2016.

Theresa Amendola McClure was born on September 11, 1918, as one of nine children to Giuseppe and Carolina Amendola. Theresa was delivered by a mid-wife on Franklin Street. In time, Giuseppe moved his family to 116 Wooster Street in the Pacilio Building. Francesco Pacilio owned the tenement building and lived on the second floor. A few doors down, at 118 Wooster Street, the Pacilio family operated a grocery store. To provide for his clan, Giuseppe worked as a laborer and later at the Sargent plant.

In the 1930's, during the Great Depression, Giuseppe purchased the home at 227 St. John Street. As a young girl, Theresa was enrolled at Wooster Street School as well as Dante and Columbus Schools. She was enthusiastic about her studies and was deeply sadden when she had to drop out at the age of fourteen. Theresa needed to earn money for her family and she found employment at a dress shop on Chestnut Street. At the age of sixteen, she went to work at Lucibello's Pastry Shop. Her mother was a cousin of Frank Lucibello.

On a fateful day in 1937, a young man named Art McClure bought goods at the bustling shop. A French Canadian from Massachusetts, Art took an immediate liking to Theresa. The couple married on June 10, 1939, at St. Michael Church.

During the first year of their union, the McClure's resided at 527 Chapel Street. They later moved into the family home at 227 St. John Street to save money. In 1941, Theresa gave birth to their first child Art Jr. Two years later, at the advice of her father-in-law, the young couple purchased a home in Orange. A second child, a daughter named Beverly was born in 1944. Both of the McClure children graduated from Amity High School. Art Jr. became an engineer and Beverly worked for Travelers Insurance Company.

In 1986, while working as the supervisor of the cafeteria in the Orange School System, Theresa moved back to St. John Street. Her home, was erected in 1849 in the Italianate style for Matthew Elliott. The first permanent occupant of the house was Parnell Booth. Booth was a prominent painter and real estate speculator.

Well into her late nineties, Theresa was still vibrant, and living at the family home with Beverly. Sharp and witty she stated, "in the old days, the boys were lucky to go to the bathhouse on St. John Street. Us girls had to take a sponge bath at home. "*

Until her death on May 20, 2016, Theresa was close to her longtime friends Rae Somma and Caterina Valentino.

*Interview. Theresa McClure. June 24, 2015.

Rae Somma (L), Theresa McClure (C) and Caterina Valentino (R)

June 24, 2015   227 St. John Street

Wallace Street

Wallace Street was named in honor of Captain William E. Wallace, a wealthy landowner. While in Cuba, in 1828, Wallace died. His wife returned to New Haven and took up residency on Wooster Street. By the mid 1800's, the Wallace School was a part of the New Haven Public School System.

Ralph DeFrancesco

Ralph DeFrancesco was one of three children to parents who originated from Sorrento. His dad worked at Quinnipiac Coal located on East Street. A common trend during the Great Depression was for families to "apartment hop" for a cheaper rent. As a result, Ralph's family moved from 400 East Street to 219 Wallace Street and finally to 242 Wallace Street. Living in the tenement buildings was a struggle.

Despite a difficult life during the Great Depression, the children of the area had the ability to have fun. Ralph elaborated, "we played with Polish, Irish, and Italian kids. There was always a ball game in Jocelyn Square. In the summertime, adult counselors supervised the games. They would organize games between different neighborhoods."*

Interview. Ralph DeFrancesco. August 26, 2013.

Harry Trotta

Francesco Trotta was born in Aversa, Italy. In 1908, at St. Anthony Church, he joined hands in matrimony with Maria Cappella. Her family lived in the Hill section. The loving couple had five sons and five daughters.

Financially raising and supporting such a large family was an impossible, but common task, in the Wooster Square area. In 1936, Francesco opened a store selling candy, tobacco, and novelties. Seven days a week, he worked from six in the morning until nine in the evening. Occasionally, a son would relieve him for a well deserved break. Trotta purchased his goods from New Haven Tobacco Company and State Street Candy.

The Trotta's lived in a six family tenement at 149 Wallace Street. The building was owned by Louis Litowf. Francesco paid fifteen dollars a month to rent a seven room flat on the second floor. Strangely enough, his family occupied rooms on both sides of the hallway.

During the Second World War, four Trotta boys served in the military. One day, Francesco was in his store listening to an Italian channel on the radio. A customer, thinking he was a spy, reported him to the federal authorities. Father McDonald from St. Patrick's Church ran over to inform the agents that Francesco was not an Italian sympathizer and that he had sons in war zones.

The oldest son, Harry graduated from Hillhouse High School in 1946. He found employment at a shirt store at 189 Church Street before serving his country in the Korean War. In 1954, Francesco died of a heart attack. His wife survived him by twenty-five years.

Harry stated, "we did not have much. I did not know anything else. The neighborhood was friendly and with good people. We were very, very, family oriented and happy."*

*Interview. Harry Trotta.April 8, 2015.

Harry Trotta-St. Andrew Society.

July of 2015

Warren Street

Warren Street was named in honor of General Joseph Warren. Joseph was born on June 11, 1741, in Roxbury, Massachusetts. At the age of eighteen, he graduated from Harvard. He became a doctor until the Revolutionary War broke out.

Early in the conflict, Warren saw action at Lexington and Concord. Later, he was responsible for recruiting Paul Revere and William Dawes to warn the colonist that the British were coming. On June 14, 1775, Warren was appointed the rank of major general. Just three days later, he was killed while fighting on Bunker Hill.

Rose Cimmino

Rose Cimmino was born on May 7, 1926, as one of eight children. Her father Giuseppe originated from Salerno. As a young man, he married the former Fortuna Volino. In the 1920's and 1930's, he peddled vegetables throughout the Hill section and Wooster Square. Later, he established a grocery store at 52-54 Warren Street.

For many years, Rose worked at Fair Manufacturing. To her close friends she was known as "Rose of Wooster Square." She was an active member of the St. Ann and St. Andrew Societies and a devout parishioner at St. Michael Church. The kind Rose Cimmino passed away on February 23, 2014. At the time of her death, she was still residing at 54 Warren Street.

52-54 Warren Street

Summer of 2009

Candeloro Buccetti

Candeloro Buccetti was born on February 22, 1896, in Atrani. A quiet man, he arrived to America at sixteen. His wife Trofamina was born on December 2, 1902, in Atrani and she made the transatlantic voyage at the age of eleven. The couple married at St. Michael Church and lived on Wooster Street. Eventually, Candeloro was able to save enough money working at Sargent to purchase a home at 50 Warren Street.

At this location, the seven Buccetti children; Joseph, Francis, Ralph, Anthony, Caroline, Susie, and Alphonse grew up. Susie, at the age of eighty-seven recalled, "I can still remember the 1940's and 1950's and all the wonderful people who lived on Warren Street. Families such as the Scarpellino's, Esposito's, DiTulio's, Gatto's, Giamo's, Cimmino's, DePalma's, Labonia's, Malerba's, and the Casanova's. There were also the Carrano's, Amendola's, and Amodio's. We were all close neighbors and we cared about one another. The kids always played in the streets. There was even Solomine's Bar which became an athletic club. Warren Street was beautiful."*

*Interview Susie Buccetti Montaneri. June 20, 2015.

Buccetti Building-50 Warren Street in the Winter of 2012.

Cimmino, Giamo, and Buccetti building on Warren Street around the time of Redevelopment.

(Photo Courtesy of the New Haven Museum)

Water Street

Water Street received its name for its proximity to the New Haven Harbor. During the 1800's, wealthy merchants and sea captains lived in the area. Today, Water Street is comprised of commercial businesses.

Biagio "Benny" Amendola

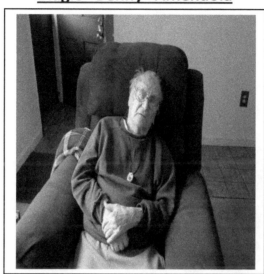

Benny at the age of ninety-three in June of 2015.

Benny Amendola was delivered by Dr. Conte on August 18, 1922. His parents, Benventuro and Rose had four children and lived in a flat at 87 Water Street.

Benventuro was the proprietor of a small grocery below his flat. The tenement building was owned by the Mentone family. At the same time, also on Water Street, the Piccolo, DiLieto, and Branchini families ran markets.

Benny graduated from Dante and Columbus Schools. During his high school years, he attended a school for students who were visually impaired.

Amendola, an energetic nonagenarian, gleamed with pride when reminiscing about his childhood. He stated, "we came from nothing but we were happy. Everyone came from a good family. Kids today would never survive. As a teenager, we spent a great deal of time at

Waterside Park. We went to Waterside Park to play in the summer. Those were good times. There was a lot of gambling. Even the cops played craps at Waterside Park."*

To earn a living, Benny worked for the city in the Department of Sanitation. His wife Nancy originated from Woodbridge and the couple had two sons named Nicholas and David.

Biagio passed away on January 2, 2016.

*Interview. Benny Amendola. May 3, 2015.

Large crowd at Waterside Park.

(Photo-SSMM Archives)

William Street

William Street is located on the outer edge of the Wooster Square neighborhood. The street was named after William Leffingwell who was born in 1762. He was a director of the first hospital in Connecticut which was located in the Elm City. Leffingwell passed away in 1831 and was buried at the Grove Street Cemetery.

Maria Luciola

Maria Luciola was born at 178 Franklin Street on March 28, 1923. She spent the majority of her youth and teenage years living at 14 William Street. Her father daily commuted to Ansonia to work in a factory, while her mom remained at home to raise the four children.

Maria attended Hamilton School (K-8), Fair Haven Junior High (9th), and graduated from Commercial High School in 1941. Luciola was a dedicated student who excelled in the classroom. After high school, she went to work for Philip L. Buxbum Insurance Company as a secretary for $7.00 a week. After six months, Maria went to work at New Haven Chamber of Commerce for $12.40 a week. At the outset of World War II, she secured a better paying job at Knights of Columbus for $60.00 a month.

Luciola described her childhood as, "difficult, but good." During the 1930's, William Street would be considered a ghetto occupied by poor working class Italian, Polish, Irish, and Jewish families. Despite their diversity, the neighbors got along and helped one another. She commented, "William Street was safe and clean. It was the cleanest ghetto ever. We would scrub the staircases of our building and wash the sidewalks. We never had to lock our doors and we walked everywhere in the city. Our flat was on the second floor. We had a sink and a toilet but no bathtub. It was bitter cold in the winter. To bathe, we would go to the bath house on St. John Street once a week. For five cents, we got a towel, and a bar of soap. Those were good times. In 1944, I left William Street and moved to Hamden."*

*Interview with Maria Luciola July 29, 2014.

Pat Vissicchio

Pat Vissicchio is a popular member of the St. Michael Church and St. Andrew Society communities. Since his early childhood on William Street, Pat has valued friendship and he has great pride in his Italian heritage. "Growing up on William Street was nice. The neighbors were friendly and ninety percent of the people were Italian. The Graziano's, Fucci's, Criscuolo's, and Andrews were all neighbors. As a child, we had pear and fig trees in the backyard, as well as, grapes " stated Vissicchio.*

Joseph Vissicchio and his wife Gilda raised their son Pat and daughters Marie and Dolores at 42 William Street. The house was occupied by relatives. Carmel Pisano (Pat's aunt) lived on the first floor. She was a cook at Rossetti's Restaurant on Wooster Street. During the Depression, her husband died leaving Carmel to raise their seven children. She never re-married and she out lived her husband by seven decades.

The second floor was inhabited by Joseph and his family. He earned a living at American Steel and Wire on Fairmont Avenue. On the third floor, Joseph Bencievenga (Pat's uncle) resided.

Pat attended Hamilton School for Kindergarten. He transferred to St. Michael School for grades 1-8. In 1964, he graduated from Wilbur Cross High School. Vissicchio retired from Stop & Shop. Pat has a son that resides in New Orleans. Pat and his wife Kathy live in East Haven.

*Interview. Pat Vissicchio. August 21, 2015.

42 William Street-2015

Wooster Place

Rheta Lenzi DeBenedet

Rheta Lenzi DeBenedet was elected the President of the Santa Maria Maddalena Lady Society in 1986. For decades, she has been a leader in the Wooster Square community. Her passion for the preservation of the Italian American culture is reflected by her involvement in numerous committees and organizations. "Becoming a member of the St. Maria Maddalena Society and then being elected president was a way to keep me connected to the neighborhood and the Italian traditions that I grew up with," stated DeBenedet.*

Eugene and Henrietta Civitello Lenzi had six children. Rheta was born on Wallace Street. In her youth, her family moved to 186 Hamilton Street and then to 11 Wooster Place. Eugene served his country in the Navy during World War II. After the war, he earned a living by working in construction. Henrietta raised her family and worked as a waitress at Joe's Luncheonette on Grand Avenue. The Lenzi family attended mass at St. Patrick and St. Michael Churches.

Rheta attended Hamilton School, and Fair Haven Junior High before graduating from Wilbur Cross High School. In 1966, she married Harry DeBenedet at St. Michael Church. Harry was a police officer in New Haven and a member of the bomb squad.

Professionally, Rheta has earned a living in a number of capacities in New Haven. She was employed as a saleswoman for Morrison Clothing Store on Chapel Street and she briefly worked at the gas company. Rheta also worked at Alberts Hosiery for her aunt Louise DeNegre who was the manager. Furthermore, she worked at the law offices of Greenberg and Hurwitz. She was an assistant at the Connecticut Credit Bureau in the Equity and Loan Department. In 2011, DeBenedet retired after working fourteen years as an Assistant Administrator for Century 21 Access America in Branford.

The DeBenedet's have two sons named Michael and Joseph and four grandchildren. They enjoy spending time with their family and being active parishioners in the events of St. Michael Church. Aside from her presidency, Rheta is a member of the St. Ann Society. Harry is on the board of directors for the St. Maria Maddalena Society and he is an energetic member of the St. Andrew Society and the Campania Club. He is also an accomplished writer having articles published in national Italian American publications.

Rheta articulated, "my family has had a strong affiliation to the Wooster Square area due to my grandparents living there all of their lives. The park on St. John and Jefferson Streets was named in honor of my uncle, a war hero, Joe Lenzi. He lost his life on Iwo Jima at a young age. My grandmother Lenzi lived on St. John Street until the late 1980's and my grandfather Diamond Lenzi was a detective who patrolled the neighborhood."*

Harry and Rheta DeBenedet-St. Maria Maddalena Society Procession 1995.

Rheta at the Columbus Day Parade in the early 2000's.

*Interview. Rheta DeBenedet. October 28, 2013.

Dr. Ralph Marcarelli

Ralph Marcarelli was born on October 3, 1935, in the Westville section of New Haven. His parents worked hard and were proud of their Italian heritage and culture. As a child, Ralph spent a great deal of time in the Wooster Square area visiting members of his extended family.

Dr. Marcarelli's educational accomplishments are impressive and extensive. He graduated from Hillhouse High School and went on to study at Fairfield University where he earned an A.B in English Literature and Philosophy in 1959. Three years later, Ralph completed his Masters Degree in Italian Language and Literature at Middlebury College. From 1962 to 1963, he studied at the University of Naples. While at that institution, he taught English and American Literature. A lifelong learner, he wrote his dissertation entitled "In

Principio Erat Verbum" to procure a PhD from Yale University. Many years later, Marcarelli obtained a law degree from the University of Bridgeport.

Professionally, Ralph has been employed in a number of positions. He was the English Department Chairman at North Branford High School for two years in the mid 1960's. He has taught at the University of New Haven, Albertus Magnus, Southern Connecticut State College, Yale University, and the University of Rhode Island. Also, he was the Headmaster at Milford Academy for five years. A man of many talents, Marcarelli completed his career in the public sector by serving as the Worker's Compensation Commissioner for the State of Connecticut from 1998-2007.

Over the decades, Ralph has earned dozens of accolades. In 1972, he was named "Man of the Year" by the West Haven Italian American Civic Association. He also has received the Distinguished Community Service Award by the Santa Maria Maddalena Society, the Distinguished Service Award from the Italian American Historical Society of Connecticut, and the Humanitarian Award from the American Committee on Italian Migration. A linguist, he is fluent in many dialects of the Italian language and he has performed concerts in Neapolitan music for decades in both the United States and Europe.

Proudly, Dr. Marcarelli has been a member of St. Michael Church for over fifty years and he has spoken on many occasions at church functions. In 1970, Ralph purchased his home at 37 Wooster Place which was constructed in 1832. At one time, the Santella family occupied the home. They had a pit dug into the basement floor so that a printer could be used to produce a newspaper called "*Corriere di Connecticut.*"

Dr. Marcarelli in front of his home-July of 2011.

Dr. Marcarelli-St. Maria Maddalena
Distinguished Service Award-1996.

Wooster Street and the Connecticut Little Italy's

The Hartford Courant (February 22, 2011), published an article *"That's Italian, Connecticut Gives other State the Boot, Claims to be Most Italian State."* The piece cited the fact that Connecticut has surpassed Rhode Island as having the largest percentage of Italian Americans. Furthermore, the article stated that according to the 2010 Census, twenty percent of Connecticut residents are Italian American.

The Italian immigrants were drawn to the small but growing cities in Connecticut in the late 1800's. Municipalities such as Bridgeport, Hartford, New Haven, Stamford, and Waterbury had tens of thousands of jobs available in construction, garment industry and manufacturing. As a result, vibrant Italian colonies sprang up throughout the state. One hundred and twenty-five years later, descendants of the original settlers visit the neighborhoods, churches, and cultural centers that their relatives helped to build. Often, the neighborhoods have changed, with the next wave of immigrants replacing the Italians.

Today, Connecticut has hundreds of Italian organizations and societies. A handful of school districts such as North Haven have Italian courses available at the middle and high school levels. Proud Italian Americans, such as Joe LaPorte of Southington, work tirelessly organizing annual festivals. For a young American of Italian lineage, there are plenty of opportunities to learn about the struggles and achievements of their ancestors.

Southington Italian Festa-2014

Southington-Holy Rosary Society

Bridgeport-North End

The Italian immigrants in the Park City originally settled on the East Side. For the immigrants there were jobs available at companies such as Bridgeport Brass, Columbia Records, and Singer Sewing. After World War II, Italians began to leave the East Side for a plot of land in the North End. The residents of the North End took pride in home ownership and kept their lawns and gardens meticulously manicured. Madison Avenue became the heartbeat of the Italian community. Restaurants such as Conte's, La Scogliera, Marisa's, and Testo's were neighborhood landmarks.

Today, Madison Avenue is a hotbed of activity. There are many eateries serving a wide range of cuisine including Asian, Spanish, Brazilian, and Portuguese. Although no longer Little Italy, there are a few holdovers such as Testo's, Micalizzi Ice, and Tuscany (formerly Marissa's).

Micalizzi Ice

Testo's Restaurant

Tuscany Restaurant

Hartford-Franklin Avenue

Around 1900, Italian immigrants, the majority from Sicily, began to arrive in Hartford and settled on Front Street. The East Side quickly became a strong and dynamic community. The immigrants found jobs in the dress shops, construction, and in manufacturing. By 1910, fourteen per cent of Hartford's population was Italian and sixty percent of the residents living on Front Street were Italian.*

In 1891, Carminuccio Battaglia and his wife Emilia resided on Front Street. Their son Crescenzcenzo dropped out of Brown School in the 5th grade to work in a tobacco factory. Later, he took up boxing and fought under the name of Bat Battalino. As an amateur, Bat was the Connecticut State Champion from 1925-1927 and the National AAU Featherweight Champion in 1927. As a professional, he was the Connecticut Featherweight Champion in 1929 and the World Champion from 1929-1932. The legendary Hartford native has been inducted into the National Italian American Sports Hall of Fame, the International Boxing Hall of Fame, and the Connecticut Boxing Hall of Fame.

*History of Italians in Connecticut. Trinity College EDU

The redevelopment of Hartford began in the late 1950's and the building of the Constitutional Plaza pushed the Italians from Front Street to the South End. Franklin Avenue, a two mile strip, became the epicenter of the Italian American Community. Dozens of Italian American restaurants and bakeries, as well as, social clubs thrived. In 1980, forty-five percent of the residents in the South End were Italian.** However, the younger generation desired a home in the suburbs. Furthermore, Eastern Europeans, and Hispanics began to move into the area.

**Italians Flourish on Street. Joseph Rodriquez. Hartford Courant. July 2, 1985.

By the early 2000's, Franklin Avenue had become a diversified neighborhood. The Italian pastry shops, deli's, macaroni stores, social clubs, and restaurants continued to exist. Today, residents are of a variety of ethnic backgrounds including Greeks, Puerto Ricans, and Bosnians. These groups have established popular businesses on Franklin Avenue.

Waterbury-Town Plot

Situated atop of a hill, overlooking the Brass City, is the magnificent Our Lady of Mt. Carmel Church. Every July, for four days, the Italian American parishioners celebrates an "old world" festival.

The climax of the festival is the procession which follows mass celebrated in Italian. A coalition of Italian societies and religious organizations take part in the two mile parade over the challenging terrain. Remarkably, hundreds of elderly citizens along with their children and grandchildren participate in the parade which finishes on the church grounds.

In the 1600's, the first section of Waterbury to be settled was Town Plot. Three hundred years later, Italians from Pontelandolfo and other regions of the south began to arrive to the city. By the early 1920's, the growing Italian community attended mass in the basement of St. Patrick's Church. In June of 1923, Bishop John Nilan appointed Father Lynch as the first pastor of what would later become Our Lady of Mt. Carmel.

On December 8, 1940, the current brick structure with elegant windows and doors was dedicated. In 1957, the school and convent were added to the parish. At this time, the majority of the homes in the area were owned by Italian Americans.

In August of 1955, rains from Hurricanes Connie and Diane created massive flooding in Waterbury. Over five hundred people from the city and in Naugatuck had to be air lifted to safety. Tragically, twenty-four people were killed and hundreds were injured. The fear of another flood drove Italian Americans out of the Brooklyn section of Waterbury to Town Plot reinforcing the Italian community.

Today, Highland Avenue is the main fairway of the Italian section. There are great eateries, deli's, and bakeries. Although the area is more diversified than when President Eisenhower was in office, the atmosphere remains Italian American. The parish is thriving, and the Italian American community is determined to continue their traditions for many decades to come.

Wooster Street

Wooster Social Club-Before Redevelopment.

(Photo Courtesy of Al Lauro)

In the spring of 2015, WTNH produced a weeklong series on Italian American contributions to the Nutmeg State. Segments were filmed in Middletown, Hartford, Waterbury, and New Haven. There was a great emphasis on Wooster Street including a live broadcast from Columbus Park.

For decades, Wooster Street has been written about in books and newspapers and filmed for documentaries. Today, the neighborhood is more gentrified, but it continues to be the symbol of Italian Americans in New Haven.

Billy "O" Oronzo

John Oronzo was born on Wooster Street in 1908. While in his teens, Oronzo peddled fruits and vegetables from a cart in the neighborhood. In his early twenties, John met and fell in love with a local girl named Marie DeFilio. The young couple married in 1929 at St. Michael Church.

Around the time of his matrimony, Teamster Local 443 was established and John was a charter member. The Oronzo's had two sons, William and Pasquale. "Jerusalem," (John's nickname given to him by his buddies) was a loyal family man and friend until he passed away in 1984.

John Oronzo

Best Man at Luigi DePalma's Wedding in 1928.

(Photo Courtesy of John Oronzo)

William Oronzo was born on March 9, 1930. In his youth, his family resided on Chestnut Street. While in his teens, the Oronzo's moved to Main Street in West Haven.

Young and adventurous, "Billy O" joined the Navy at seventeen to see the world. Furthermore, his love of World War II propaganda films, inspired him to serve his country. From 1947 to 1951, Oronzo was stationed aboard the USS Moale, a destroyer.

After being discharged, Billy returned to West Haven. In 1954, he went to work for Akers Motor Lines in West Haven and he was a valuable employee until 1981. One day, he arrived for work only to see a padlock on the door. The company inexplicably shut down. By nature, a kind, quiet and hard working man, Billy quickly got a job at Steven Fiore Travel on Campbell Avenue. Simultaneously, Oronzo also tended bar at Captain's Gallery. The epitome of a family man, Billy worked a third job as a custodian for the West Haven Board of Education to put his children through college.

Billy Oronzo in 1952.

(Photo Courtesy of John Oronzo)

In 1983, Billy served as the President of the Italian American Club in West Haven. A few years later, he purchased a home in Coconut Creek, Florida. Billy and his wife, the former Marie DePino, had four children. Billy passed away on March 10, 2015. Fittingly, he joined his beloved wife in Heaven exactly one year to the day of her death.

Billy (bottom left) playing cards with longtime friend Mike LaBonia (bottom right) at the Italian American Club in Branford in August of 2013.

The Neighborhood-Their Reflections

"I was born at 22 Warren Street almost ninety years ago. Warren Street was like an Italian village. We were all family over there. On Sunday morning, every family was cooking the same meal. It was different then. Women did not work until World War II. It was great. We had our own bakeries and shops."

Frances Malerba Erba

"Growing up in Wooster Square was very nice. We all hung around together. At night, they would let us play basketball at Dante School. I use to pal around with Benny D'Agostino, Frank Amici, Abe DePalma, and Mike DePalma. We lived on Collis Street. In the winter, my brother use to hang a box outside our third floor window. This would be our refrigerator. In the summer, it was very hot. We had an ice box. At night the people would sit outside on their stoops and talk about the old days. Also, on Collis Street, we would shut down the road and put up lights. We had a block dance. Abe DePalma was a good dancer."

Salvatore "Provolone" Consiglio

"Wooster Street means the world to me. What we did there as kids could never be done again. The people were forced to leave and it was terrible. I would go back to those times in a heartbeat."

Vincent Donarumo

"Growing up on Chestnut Street, we were poor but we did not know it. We had food on the table every night and clothes. We had family and the holidays. We were happy kids."

Josephine Esposito

"I was born at 19 Brown Street. As a kid, I remember playing a baseball card game against a four story building on Wooster Street. I played with my cousins Al Lauro and Hank Cappella. I attended Dante and Columbus Schools before my family moved to the Hill. Later, I moved into the Rocco Candela building at 44 Olive Street. One night, I was at Sally's, and Frank Sinatra stopped in to see his friend Sal Consiglio. I got to meet Sinatra."

Vin Pantera

Their Stories in Wooster Square

John and Louise Ricciuti

Joseph and Gilda Vissicchio

Andrew and Rosalind Proto

John Ricciuti-grew up at 16 Brown Street. On April 21, 1950, he joined hands in matrimony with Louise Esposito at St. Michael Church. Louise was born on Collis Street but she was raised on Wooster Street. To earn a living, John was a plumber by trade. He retired as a plumber from St. Raphael Hospital. Louise worked at a dress shop on Hamilton Street and then at W.T. Grant Department Store. The couple had children named Anthony and Mary Ann.

Joseph Vissicchio-married the former Gilda Bencivenga on June 4, 1934, at St. Michael Church. The couple had a son and two daughters and they resided on William Street. To earn a living, Joseph worked at American Steel and Wire. He retired after thirty-one years of service. In August of 1984, the Vissicchio's celebrated their 50th Anniversary at the Annex Club.

Andrew "Butch" Proto- grew up at 10 Hamilton Street. Butch worked for twenty-two years at Alba Dress in the old New Haven Clock Shop. In 1986, he was hired by Yale University and he worked there until he retired in 2008.

On July 12, 1969, Butch married his wife Rosalind at St. Michael Church. Rosalind grew up on Wooster Street. Her father ran a chicken market and later a grocery store. Rosalind taught for a year in the Branford Public School System and for many years in the North Branford System before retiring in 2004. Both Butch and Rosalind are active in the St. Michael community and with various Italian American organizations. They reside at 109 Wooster Street.

Image From Little Italy

The Wedding of William Regan and Louise Maiorino at the Marchegian Club in 1950.

The Maiorino family owned and lived in the building located at 48-52 Fair Street. William and Louise had children named Gail and William Jr. William was employed as an engineer at Winchester.

(Photo Courtesy of Al Maiorino)

St. Andrew Society Procession-2014.

The People of Wooster Square

St. Maria Maddalena Procession 1996.

Bob and Ruby Proto-1996.

Amarone Family

Mr. and Mrs. Amarone walking down Wooster Street.

(Photo Courtesy of Judy Amarone)

The Amarone family was one of the largest in the history of New Haven. The patriarch, Andrea was born on November 3, 1888, in Atrani. His wife Giuseppina Nazzario Amarone was born on February 28, 1889, in Minori. She arrived to the Elm City in 1911. Andrea and Giuseppina met on Wooster Street in the heart of the expanding Italian community.

The couple's first child, Giovanni was born on January 3, 1913. In total, the Amarones had seventeen children with another two passing away before birth. Amazingly, Andrea supported his family while working as a polisher at Sargent. He was employed at the company for forty-nine years. Later, he worked at Marlin Firearms on Willow Street for six years. To augment his income, Andrea changed grates on wooden stoves in the neighborhood.

As the family expanded, Andrea moved to different locations in the neighborhood. At one time or another, the family resided at 138 Chestnut Street, 143 Wooster Street, and 159 Wooster Street before purchasing a home at 180 Wooster Street.

Rose Panzo, was a mid-wife who lived on Wooster Street. She delivered fifteen of the seventeen Amarone children. The other two children were born in the hospital.

The Amarone Children:

1. Giovanni-born January 3, 1913, and passed away on February 1, 1994.

2. Antoinette-born April 9, 1914, and passed away on March 4, 2001.

3. Carolina-born March 21, 1916, and passed away on May 11, 1953.

4. Carmelina-born January 9, 1918, and passed away on November 7, 1928. She died of Chronic Rheumatic Fever and Bacterial Endocarditis.

5. Pasquale-born on October 24, 1919, and passed away on June 8, 1920, of Pyemia.

6. Lucy-born on March 23, 1921.

7. Stella-born on January 25, 1923, and passed away in 2012.

8. Biagio-born on June 11, 1924, and passed away on March 2, 1945.

9. Madeline-born on June 15, 1926, and passed away in 2011.

10. Raffaela-born September 15, 1927.

11. Pasquale-born on November 1, 1928. He died on July 28, 2013.

Amarone Brothers

(L to R) Andrew, Nick, John, Joseph, and Pasquale.

(Photo Courtesy of Judy Amarone)

12. Trofimina-born November 1, 1928.

13. Carmelina-born November 2, 1929.

14. Andrew-born January 31, 1931, and passed away on December 29, 2004.

15. Joseph-born August 12, 1932, and passed away on February 26, 2010.

16. Nicholas-born January 31, 1935, and passed away on August 26, 2008.

17. Pamela-born 1934.

Joseph Amarone

President of Santa Maria Maddalena Society- 2003.

(Photo Courtesy of Judy Amarone)

Michael P. Balzano

The life story of Michael Balzano is both an inspiration and an example that, with perseverance, one can overcome any obstacle. Michael was born on November 6, 1935, at 63 Warren Street. Legendary, Dr. Harry Conte brought him into the world. His father, Michael Sr. was born in Salerno and worked at the Winchester plant. The matriarch of the family, Jennie, an Italian American, was born in New Haven and for fifty-four years, worked at Sargent.

Michael attended Dante, Columbus, and St. Michael schools before dropping out of Wilbur Cross High School at the age of sixteen. Incorrectly, considered unmotivated by his educators, Michael was not diagnosed as being dyslexic. This learning disability prevented him from achieving good grades at that juncture of his academic career.

In the early 1950's, Balzano was employed as a garbage collector for the Department of Sanitation. While working, he injured his back which incapacitated him and left him unable to earn a living. Occasionally, as a side job, he played guitar in a band with a neighborhood friend named Ray Boffa. Michael's brother Anthony "Tappy," a harmonica virtuoso, also played with them from time to time. Later, Boffa got Michael a job with an optical company in Stamford. In 1957, Michael returned to Hillhouse High School at night and earned his degree while working full time.

On Wooster Street-March 4, 2012.

Left to Right-Pete Gatto, Michael Balzano, Anthony Giordano and Mike Novella.

Now a licensed optician, he decided to take a course at the University of Bridgeport. Michael received an "A" in that class and then embarked upon a sensational career in the academic and political realms. In 1966, Balzano graduated from the University of Bridgeport. At the commencement ceremony, he was the recipient of the Top Scholar Award. Five years later, he obtained a PhD in Political Philosophy from the prestigious Georgetown University.

Balzano, an accomplished scholar and gifted orator, drew the attention of the Nixon Administration. The thirty-seventh President of the United States liked and trusted Michael. President Nixon felt that Michael's real life experiences enabled him to communicate with the people. For two years, he served as a special assistant to Nixon in the field of labor unions and ethnic groups.

In all, he has worked for six presidents and many members of Congress. When Ronald Reagan was campaigning for the 1980 election, he visited Wooster Street. Michael planned Reagan's itinerary, which included stops at Pepe's, and Libby's before Reagan delivered a speech on the steps of the Saint Maria Maddalena Society building.

In the mid 1980's, Michael established Balzano Associates which is a nationwide firm specializing in communications in the workplace. In his spare time, Michael enjoys reading the classics including Plato and Socrates and he has an affinity for public speaking. Balzano has lectured at a number of universities including Columbia, Georgetown, and San Diego St. Michael has also published numerous works including: *Reorganizing the Federal Bureaucracy: The Rhetoric and Reality, The Peace Corps: Myths and Prospects and Federalizing Meals on Wheels.*

Michael and his wife Denise married in 1972. They have two sons and three grandchildren.

Mike Balzano in front of Harvey and Lewis where he worked as an optician.

(Photo Courtesy of Mike Balzano)

Bobby Esposito

For over forty years, Bobby Esposito has been the proprietor of Branford Book and Card Shoppe in the center of Branford. The values and lessons that he acquired growing up on Wooster Street have helped him as a leader in the Branford community. Esposito commented, "the sense of family and the devotion to family and friends has enabled me to relate to my customers."*

Salvatore Esposito arrived to Wooster Square from Amalfi in the late 1920's. A reserved man, Salvatore married Adeline Gambardella at St. Michael Church. Adeline was born in the neighborhood and as a teenager, she worked in a grocery store that her family owned on Olive Street.

The Esposito's had five sons and three daughters. At first, the family rented the property at 267 Wooster Street. In time, Salvatore was able to purchase the single family home. To support his family, he worked at Sargent and then for many years at Sperry and Barnes. In his free time, he liked to play bocce and to tend to his garden. Salvatore was a dapper dresser. He passed away in 1949 at the age of fifty-seven. Adeline survived her husband by many years. She was a warmhearted person, an affectionate mother, and a terrific cook.

Adeline Esposito at Branford Book and Card Shoppe in 1989.

(Photo Courtesy of Bobby Esposito)

Bobby attended St. Michael School in Kindergarten before transferring to Dante School. He also attended Columbus School. While in the 6th grade, he worked six days a week assisting an older gentleman on a paper route. Two years later, he took the corner at George and Church Streets selling newspapers. Each morning, from five to seven, he greeted his customers who generously tipped him. At that time, in the mid 1950's, he was making fifty dollars a week. With a sense of style, Bobby spent a great deal of his earnings on clothes. "Growing up on Wooster Street was a lot of fun. I hung around with guys like Gabe Solomini, Joe "Duck" Scarpellino, Johnny "Boy" Coppola, and Frankie Esposito. We were always playing sports and we were involved with the P.A.L. and C.Y.O. programs. I played in the Eddie Sheehan Little League under coach Ed Torello. Frankie Esposito and I took the bus to Blake Field to participate in the games. The summers were great because of the Italian festivals," stated Esposito.*

In high school, Bobby attended Fair Haven Junior High School and then Wilbur Cross. As a Governor, Bobby played under the legendary Red Verderame. Red's historical teams won two state championships, a New England title, and were victorious in forty-seven consecutive games. Esposito graduated in 1959.

Shortly afterwards, he married his wife Maria who grew up in Fair Haven. He went to work for C.P.I (Community Progress Inc.). His job description included educating residents on federal programs, food stamps, Adult Education, and employment opportunities. After a few years, he went to work for a similar agency, Skill Center Job Corps, directed by Larry Amendola on Cedar Street in the Hill.

In February of 1974, Bobby and Maria established Branford Book and Card Shoppe located across the town green. The Esposito's have three children named Salvatore, Roberta, and Tami. They are the proud and adoring grandparents of Angelo, Salvatore, Maria and Amy, and great grandparents of Adeline and Salvatore.

On September 18, 2008, Bobby was honored as "Man of the Year" by the Historical Wooster Square Neighborhood Reunion. Bobby has remained a devoted parishioner of St. Michael Church. He concluded, "St. Michael Church has always stayed with me. I attended the church, I played on the basketball team, and I coached the basketball team. The church is in my heart."*

*Interview. Bobby Esposito. April 10, 2016.

Bobby Esposito in his store in May of 2016.

Teresa Falcigno

Teresa Falcigno was a determined, energetic and talented individual. Admired by those who were fortunate to have interacted with her, Teresa will be remembered for her devotion to her family. Furthermore, her passion for St. Michael Church, St. Andrew Society, and the Italian American community was legendary.

Teresa was born on January 7, 1902, on Collis Street to Salvatore and Louisa Del Preto. Salvatore arrived from Amalfi in 1894 and Louisa made the transatlantic voyage in November of 1900.

In his native land, Salvatore worked in a macaroni factory. Modern machinery took his job and then his brother encouraged him to head to America. Salvatore worked at a lumber yard on Water Street to support his wife and their five children.

The Del Preto Family Portrait-1909.

Louisa and Salvatore with their children Andrew, Mary, Teresa, Michael, and Fred. Salvatore was one of the founding members of the St. Andrew Society.
(Teresa Falcigno Collection)

In a time, when "apartment hopping "was common, the family moved to 31 Collis Street. Located on the first floor of the "Apicella Building" was a candy and tobacco store that Louisa operated for twelve years. The second floor was a four room flat where the family resided. Teresa attended Wooster Street School and then Greene Street School (which became Columbus School). An accomplished student with aspirations of becoming a teacher, she had to leave school at the age of fourteen to go to work. However, at the age of seventy-nine, she returned to formal schooling and obtained a G.E.D.

Initially, Teresa found employment at a garment shop on Collis Street. She next took a job that she did not enjoy at Sargent packing locks for seven dollars a week. Desiring a better occupation, she attended night school at Hillhouse studying business English, shorthand and typing. At the age of seventeen, she earned a certificate and briefly worked at First National Bank.

While she worked at the bank, P.J. Kelly, the owner of a nearby furniture store, would come in to relax. He immediately took a liking to Teresa and offered her a job at his store. On August 9, 1919, she began working for Mr. Kelly. Teresa was fond of P.J. whom she trusted and respected for his kind temperament and old fashioned Irish manners.

Kelly Furniture store in the 1930's. The business was located at 817-823 Grand Avenue. The founder, P.J. passed away in 1921. His son took over the business.

(Teresa Falcigno Collection)

Pasquale Vincent Falcigno grew up on Wallace Street. He met Teresa through his older brother. For two years, Pat courted Teresa taking her to the movies and plays. The couple became engaged in December of 1924, and on June 28, 1925, they married at St. Michael Church. A cousin of Pat owned a farm on Evergreen Avenue in Hamden where the reception attended by sixty people took place. The newlyweds honeymooned in upstate New York.

After returning from their honeymoon, Pat and Teresa lived with her parents on Brown Street. At the time, Pat was employed as a lock assembler at Sargent. He passed the examination and became a custodian for the New Haven Board of Education. Pat took a pay cut with his new job, but he acquired job security for his young family. He continued his career with the Board of Education until his retirement, thirty-six years later.

On April 22, 1926, the couple's first child Agnes was delivered by Dr. Conte. The sons of P.J. Kelly wanted Teresa to continue to work part time. Her mother agreed to watch Agnes so that Pat and his wife could both work. On November 21, 1930, their second child Paul was born at 199 Wooster Street. In 1933, the Falcigno's were able to purchase a spacious home at 31 Lyon Street.

Teresa in front of her home at 31 Lyon Street in the early 1950's.

(Teresa Falcigno Collection)

In 1937, the Kelly family sold their business to Cain Furniture. A son of P.J. broke off and started a store on Grand Avenue and Teresa joined him as a partner. Later, she bought him out and established Teresa Furniture at 879 Grand Avenue. Amazingly, she was a labor force of one acting as owner, salesperson, and bookkeeper. Pat would assist her after his shift at school. Teresa's store had four floors and sold complete living room, dining room, and bedroom sets. She also sold appliances and had a high end gift shop. In 1963, Teresa sold the business and went into semi-retirement working as a bookkeeper for Zimmerman Construction Company for twenty years.

In retirement, Teresa was very active. In 1964, Pat and her sold their home on Lyon Street and moved to Townsend Avenue in Morris Cove. Along with her good friend Theresa Argento, she was a mainstay at the St. Andrew Society diligently serving on many committees. She volunteered two days a week at St. Raphael Hospital, and one day a week at St. Michael Church and at the Shubert Theatre. In her free time, Teresa enjoyed spending time with her children and twelve grandchildren. The lovable and proud Teresa Falcigno passed away in 1994.

Pat and Teresa celebrating their 50th wedding anniversary in front of St. Michael Church.

(Teresa Falcigno Collection)

Paul Falcigno was highly educated and he embarked upon a remarkable career. Paul attended Eaton School (K-6) and Columbus (7-8) before graduating from Hillhouse High School in 1948. After high school, Paul studied at Quinnipiac College where he served as the president of the student government. Before graduating in 1954, he also helped to create KDM (now TEKE) a fraternity, and he directed the first blood drive on campus.

From 1954 to 1956, Paul served in the Army. After the military, he attended the prestigious Wharton School of Finance (University of Pennsylvania) on the G.I. Bill of Rights. In September of 1958, he returned to Lyon Street and was hired as a marketing instructor at his alma mater.

Paul served his country at Fort Dix in New Jersey.

(Teresa Falcigno Collection)

Coinciding with his teaching career, Paul had a profitable consulting firm (1960-1980) named Paul A. Falcigno and Associates. His business consulted dozens of companies including Plasticrete Corporation owned by Philip Paolella in Hamden and the New Haven Register. Paul was proud of his numerous accomplishments at Quinnipiac College. He founded the Quinnipiac Polling Institute in 1987. Today, this is recognized as a creditable polling service nationwide.

Paul also was very active in civic affairs. He joined the Boy Scouts at St. Michael Church, under the direction of Larry Pisani, became an Eagle Scout and a Scoutmaster. He was active in Scouting until 2011. Paul served three terms as Alderman in New Haven and he chaired the Urban Development Committee under Mayor Richard C. Lee.

Intrigued by different cultures, Paul traveled to over two dozen different countries. He had been to Japan nineteen times, and Italy and China five times, as well as Africa, Australia, South America, and most of the United States. Paul lived in Hamden with his wife Judy and their dog Frankie. He passed away on September 1, 2013.

Paul and his sister Agnes touring the Grand Canyon in 1997.

(Teresa Falcigno Collection)

31 Lyon Street in the Winter of 2013.

Agnes Falcigno attended Eaton and Orange Street Schools. She graduated from Hillhouse in 1944. After high school, she attended Larson College and earned a degree in secretarial studies. Agnes married Salvatore Zichichi, a Sicilian, and they had twelve children.

In 1947, they moved from Lyon Street and bought a home in Northford where they raised their family. Agnes died in 2006 and Sal in 2007. All twelve children and their families still live in the New Haven area.

1975-St. Andrew Procession

Teresa is on the far right dressed in green.

(Teresa Falcigno Collection)

Biagio Fronte

121 Wooster Street

For over a century, the Fronte family has been a presence on Wooster Street. At one time, Biagio and Alessandra Fronte as well as their eleven children resided at 121 Wooster Street in the Santa Maria Maddalena Society Building. At that time, the locals commonly referred to the structure as the "Fronte Building."

Biagio Fronte was born in 1900 in Atrani. In 1907, he made the laborious transatlantic voyage to the Elm City settling on Collis Street. Alessandra Ianuzzi, who was also born in 1900, immigrated in 1913. Biagio and Alessandra met on Wooster Street and in 1916, the young couple married at St. Michael Church.

Biagio and Alessandra Fronte

(Fronte Family Archives)

Alessandra was a kindhearted woman as well as a terrific cook. During her child bearing years, she had thirteen pregnancies. In total, the couple had six sons named Andrew, Biagio Jr., Dominic, Frank, Louis, and Tony as well as daughters named Ann Marie, Ida, Josephine, Mary, and Patricia. To provide for his family, Biagio worked two jobs. He was a polisher and a buffer for a company located on Wooster Street. At night, he worked on the docks unloading the liner "Richard Peck." After the completion of his arduous day, Biagio ate alone. Earlier in the evening, Alessandra feed the children in shifts and tucked them into bed. The children slept three or four to a bed in their third floor apartment.

Biagio was a popular man in the Italian American community. Throughout his life, he was devoted to Atrani and the Santa Maria Maddalena Society. He served as a longtime president of the organization and he influenced his sons to become active members. For enjoyment, Biagio played cards at the clubhouse. An exceptional player, he played his paesani for chocolate that after he won he gave to his beloved children.

In July, for four days, the feast of Santa Maria Maddalena was the signature family event of the year. Biagio and his sons set up tables in their backyard. After the festival, dozens of family members and friends would gather until four in the morning conversing and drinking wine.

Biagio Fronte (center right) receiving an award at a local banquet.

(Fronte Family Archives)

Biagio Jr. declared, "the festival was about the family. We had a very big and close family. My aunts, uncles, and cousins were close. The festival and holidays were unbelievable. All year long, we had nothing. But every Christmas, my parents made sure we had a tree and gifts."*

Redevelopment forever altered the fabric and landscape of Little Italy. Mayor Lee wanted to demolish the Santa Maria Maddalena Building. Biagio, who had ties in city hall, convinced the mayor to spare the property. In return, the society had to invest in costly renovations of the building.

Fronte family gathering at 121 Wooster Street.

(Fronte Family Archives)

In 2016, Frank Fronte, the youngest child, resides on Wooster Street along with his daughter and granddaughter. Frank has been a dutiful member of the society for sixty years. His brothers Biagio Jr. lives in North Haven tending to his gardens. Biagio Jr. concluded, "living on Wooster Street was a wonderful experience. The people were great and there was camaraderie. We looked out for one another. Next to us were the Gargano's, Perrilli's, and Staino's. In the summer, it was hot in our flat. We would all sit on our stoop. Everyone in the neighborhood was on their stoop. We would talk all night long about the children, sports and everyday happenings."*

*Interview. Biagio Fronte Jr. April 26, 2016.

Anthony "Dickie" Gambardella

Anthony "Dickie" Gambardella

Anthony Gambardella was born as one of five children on August 2, 1933, to William and Philomena Gambardella. The family was a mainstay on Warren Street for decades.

Dickie graduated from Wilbur Cross High School in 1951. As a Governor, he was the captain of the baseball team. After graduating, he served in the Navy during the Korean War.

Following his tour of duty, Gambardella began his distinguished career in the New Haven Fire Department. He was appointed to the department on May 20, 1956. In 1978, Dickie became a Lieutenant and in 1997 a Battalion Chief. In total, he served thirty-two years on the force. In retirement, Dickie worked as a Judicial Marshall for the State of Connecticut well into his seventies.

The lifelong Wooster Square resident married the former Barbara Conte Gambardella. They had five children named Phyllis, Laurie, Theresa, Jackie, and William. Dickie was a member of the St. Andrew Society, the St. Maria Maddalena Society and the New Haven Firefighters Italian American Society. The jovial Gambardella loved to hang out on Wooster Street especially at Tony and Lucille's Restaurant.

On May 28, 2009, Dickie passed away. Two years later, in May of 2011, the city dedicated the corner of Wooster and Warren Streets in his honor.

Paolo Russo

Paolo Russo was an extraordinary man of many talents. In the early history of the Italian colony in Wooster Square, he was the most influential civic leader. Russo had strong ties in local and state governments, as well as, the Catholic church.

Russo was born on April 19, 1859, in Basilicata, Italy. His parents Michael Angelo and Annie had children named Josephine, Joseph, and Ralph. In 1869, the family immigrated to New York City. Three years later, they arrived in the Elm City.

As a nine year old boy, Paul earned money as a street violinist. In the evening, he read books and studied many subjects that would help him in the years to come.

Paolo Russo building located at 533 Chapel Street.

In 1879, Russo opened an Italian grocery store on the corner of Congress Avenue and Oak Street in the Hill section. At the age of twenty-three, the 6'2 tall and distinguished looking Russo, served as an interpreter in the city courts aiding Italian immigrants. Remarkably, he also found time to teach night school at the Whiting School helping immigrants learn their citizenship rights.

In 1884, Paul led a delegation from Wooster Square to summit with Rev. Lawrence McMahon in Hartford. The Elm City residents wanted to convince Rev. McMahon that the flourishing Italian community needed their own cathedral. On April 23, 1899, after a series of temporary sites, Archbishop Sebastiano Martinelli dedicated St. Michael Church. Shortly thereafter, a raging fire devastated the building. The church was rebuilt and rededicated on December 21, 1904. Russo and Dominic Bergonzi were the first trustees of St. Michael Church.

The Paolo Russo Bank.

(Photo from the collection of Theresa Argento)

Russo's contributions to his countrymen were far from complete. In 1884, the tireless pioneer along with Lorenzo Mattei, Frank Mona, Antonio DiMatti, Sal Maresca, and Pasquale LoGruidice founded a benevolent society called "La Fratellanza." Members had to be Italian males, and a parishioner of the church. The organization sponsored religious festivals, dances, banquets, and provided sickness benefits for the members.

In 1885, he ventured into the banking business along with Angelo Proto, Frank DeLucia, and Antonio Pepe. Italian immigrants who were skeptical of banks entrusted Russo with their savings. The Paul Russo Banchiere was located on Chapel Street.

A diversified man, with multiple projects occurring simultaneously, Russo ran the first Italian newspaper in Connecticut. *La Stella D'Italia*, was a popular weekly publication from 1892 to 1912. Also, in 1892, Paul was a leading promoter of the drive to erect the Columbus Statue in Wooster Square Park.

Paul, still intrigued by the court system, attended Yale Law School. In 1893, he became the first Italian to receive a diploma from that institution. For two decades, he was a prestigious criminal lawyer in New Haven, as well as, New Jersey, and Massachusetts. He left the profession in 1911 to concentrate on his banking and real estate interests.

In 1911, Russo purchased 3,500 lots in a wooded section of Foxon. He sold the lots to families that paid him a small sum weekly. Furthermore, Paul was instrumental in helping Italians get jobs at the Malleable Iron Fitting Company (M.I.F.) in Branford. These immigrants represented the first Italians in that shoreline community. M.I.F. had a workforce of roughly 1,200 employees from Italy, Scotland, Ireland, and Finland. The company was a mainstay in Branford for over a century.

In his personal life, Paul was blessed with a compassionate wife and three wonderful children. On May 23, 1889, he married the former Lucy Francolini of New York. Lucy originated from an influential family. Her father, Dr. Biagio Francolini was a renown surgeon in New York. Her uncle Joseph Francolini was the President of the Italian Savings Bank of New York.

Lucy gave birth to their daughter Rose in 1890. Rose went on to marry Dr. Genesis Corelli on New Haven. In 1892, Michelangelo was born and in the following year, Biagio followed. Both of his sons graduated from Hopkins and joined Paul in the real estate business. Sadly, Lucy was bedridden for years before passing away in 1927. Russo survived his wife by fifteen years passing away in May of 1942.

Paolo Russo

The Paolo Russo Park in the Winter of 2011.

Paul's devotion to the Italians in New Haven and his kind spirit enabled him to be adored by many. At the age of seventy-three, he was awarded the Cross of Cavilere, by King Vittorio Emmanuel of Italy. This honor was bestowed upon Russo for his work with Italian immigrants.

At the advanced age of seventy-eight, Paul performed Ave Maria at the midnight mass at St. Michael Church on New Year's Eve. Fittingly, he gave of himself to others to the end of his enriching life.

Salzo Family

Josephine Salzo on Olive Street in 1921.

(Photo Courtesy of Doug Guidone)

Simultaneously, the legendary Amarone and Salzo families resided within walking distance of one another. The matriarchs, Giuseppina Nazzario Amarone (her first child was born in 1913), and Josephine Serritillo Salzo (her first child was born in 1914) began motherhood within months of one another.

In 1910, Michael Salzo arrived from Sicily to New Haven. Two years later, he sent for his fiancée Josephine of Amalfi to join him in America and they quickly married. To support his wife in Little Italy, Michael worked as a carpenter. In 1914, the couple's first child Carmelino was born. Sadly, the infant passed away. The following year, Josephine gave birth to a child named Carmel. In 1916, the Salzo's welcomed twins named Philip and Mary.

On May 9, 1921, Michael and his wife made national news. Dr. Conte delivered quadruplets named Angelina, Michael, James, and Salvatore. At the time of their arrival,

Michael was thirty-two years old and Josephine was twenty-seven and they resided at 238 Wooster Street. When news of the Salzo quadruplets reached the White House, President Harding sent a letter to the couple. Tragically, in July of 1922, Angelina, James, and Salvatore died of complications due to pneumonia.

After eleven years of marriage, Josephine had given birth to fifteen children. In total, she had twenty-two children including triplets, and two sets of twins. However, only nine of the children lived into adulthood. In 1939, Josephine died suddenly at the age of forty-four. At the time of her passing, the clan lived at 259 Wooster Street.

After the death of his wife, Michael remarried. In 1964, he married his third wife Maria who was the sister of Josephine. A hard working and humorous man, Michael also was a skilled cook. He passed away in 1983.

Philip A. Scarpellino

Philip A. Scarpellino was raised in a large and close knit family at 197 Wooster Street. As a child, Phil learned to respect people and he developed strong friendships and a sense of neighborhood pride. These unique qualities enabled him to become an outstanding educator and later prosecutor and judge.

Philip "Flippy" Scarpellino on Wooster Street in 1950.

(Photo Courtesy of Theresa Scarpellino)

Phil was born one of two children to Hank and Theresa Scarpellino on November 29, 1947. His parents emphasized the importance of earning an education to Phil and his sister Patricia. In Kindergarten, he attended Dante School. The following eight years, Phil was enrolled at St. Louis Catholic School which was located on Chapel Street. The majority of his friends that he played with for long hours in the park on Wooster Street went to St. Michael School or Columbus School. A dedicated student, Phil excelled for three years at Notre Dame High School in West Haven. He ended up graduating from Wilbur Cross High School in the Class of 1965.

A tradition within the Scarpellino family is the game of baseball. All male members of the family played the national pastime in the neighborhood. Phil "Skippy" and Phil "Do" were outstanding players at Wilbur Cross. Flippy began playing at a young age. He was a member of the Neighborhood Athletic Club team, and later, he also played at Wilbur Cross. At that time, Wooster Square was exclusively "Yankee" territory with Joe DiMaggio and Mickey Mantle serving as idols.

Patricia and Phil on Warren Street in 1953.

(Photo Courtesy of Theresa Scarpellino)

After high school, Phil attended UCONN and he graduated with a degree in political science in 1969. He obtained his Master Degree in Education from the University of Bridgeport in 1971. With a strong desire to work with children, he taught at Betsy Ross School in New Haven for a decade and for four years at High School in the Community.

In 1983, he retired from teaching and embarked upon a career in law. In 1986, Phil earned his Juris Doctor Degree from Nova Southeastern Law Center in Ft. Lauderdale. The following year, he was hired as a prosecutor in Middletown. From 1990 to 2000, he served in the same capacity in New Haven. In 2000, former Governor John Rowland appointed him to the Superior Court as a judge. As a trial judge, Phil has presided on mostly criminal cases.

Phil graduating from law school shown with his sister in 1986.

(Photo Courtesy of Theresa Scarpellino)

After a decade on the bench, Phil is still passionate about his profession. He stated, "growing up on Wooster Street had a great impact on my life and career. It helps me as a judge understand all sides during an argument. My childhood helped to make me a complete person. I always try to help people as long as it is within the law. I remember where I came from. I believe that people can change and learn from their mistakes."*

Phil has been the recipient of many accolades. On September 22, 2005, along with Abe DePalma, he was honored at the 40th Annual Wooster Square Old Timers Reunion. The previous year, he was honored by the Festa di San Giuseppe Organization.

In his personal life, Phil enjoys spending time with his daughter Julia. She was an outstanding softball player earning All Oronoque Division honors while at Branford High School.

The Scarpellino's named Phil (1986 Branford).

(Left to right) Phil (Junie's son), Flippy, Skippy, Phil Do, Junie, and in the front, Phil Do's son.

(Photo Courtesy of Theresa Scarpellino)

*Interview. Philip Scarpellino. October 30, 2012.

Michael Quiello

Michael Quiello in the Marines.

(Photo Courtesy of Theresa Scarpellino)

For decades, Warren Street has enjoyed stability with members of the Scarpellino, Gambardella, Buccetti, Cimino, and Giamo families residing in the area. Political leaders, teachers, athletes, and civil service employees can trace their roots back to this small, but distinctive road. Michael Quiello, a product of Warren Street, has achieved numerous accolades as a pilot in the military and for commercial airlines.

Michael was born at Saint Raphael's Hospital and grew up at 67 Warren Street. His paternal grandparents were Michael Archangel Coviello and Rosa Canali Coviello. At some point, their last named was altered to Quiello. Michael and Rosa were married at St. Michael Church in 1913 and they had seven children.

His maternal grandparents were Felippe "Lefty Burke" Scarpellino and Mary DeGale Scarpellino. "Lefty Burke" and his brother "Sally Burke" were stellar minor league baseball players. The national pastime as well as basketball would become a family tradition with many members playing on the high school and collegiate levels.

John Quiello met his future wife Mary while she was working at the First National Store in West Haven. The couple had three children named Michael, Mary, and Rose. Michael had an enriching childhood. Living on Warren Street allowed him to spend considerable time with his extended family. Their building had twelve apartments of which most, if not all, were occupied by relatives in the Scarpellino, DePalma or Gambardella families. During the summertime, the extended family ate in three seating's in the basement of the building. The young children ate first followed by the teenagers. Lastly, the adults dined as the cousins played baseball in the backyard.

Academically, Michael was a good student. He attended Columbus School in Kindergarten followed by St. Michael School. Quiello continued his parochial school education by enrolling in Notre Dame of West Haven. He graduated in 1970 and matriculate to the University of New Haven. Michael graduated with a degree in Civil Engineering in 1974.

During his teenage years, Michael developed an affinity for aviation. He went to local libraries and read countless articles and books on the subject. Michael expressed his desire in becoming a pilot to his parents and he followed his dream after meeting Don Santacroce at New Haven Airways.

Commercial Pilot-Michael Quiello.

(Photo Courtesy of Theresa Scarpellino)

Mary went to the bank with her son and took out a six hundred dollar loan so that he could take the eight hundred hours of lessons to earn his license. At the age of seventeen, Michael completed the necessary requirements and became a certified private pilot.

The following year, on his eighteenth birthday, he enlisted in the Marine Corps as an officer candidate and attended Marine Corps Officer Candidate School. Upon graduating from college, he was commissioned as a 2nd Lieutenant in the United States Marine Corps and attended U.S. Navy Flight School in Pensacola, Florida. During his time in the military, he served stateside and abroad including Japan. Quiello also did a tour flying EA-6 Intruder aircraft on the aircraft carrier USS Midway. Michael credited the Marines for teaching him discipline and leadership skills.

In 1981, he began to fly commercial jets for Delta Airlines. For the next twenty-eight years, Michael worked for that corporation and he was based in Atlanta, Boston, Cincinnati, and Miami retiring as a Vice President. In 2009, Quiello left Delta and became the Vice President of Corporate Safety, Security, Quality, and Environment for United Airlines. His stellar career in aviation enabled him to be inducted into the Aviation Hall of Fame.

Today, Michael is still employed by United. He also proudly serves as Board Secretary and the Chairman of the Board of Nominations at the National Aviation Hall of Fame in Dayton, Ohio. Annually, the organization inducts four individuals into the hall of fame. The banquet is a gala affair with over one thousand people in attendance. Michael is humbled to have been able to meet many of his aviation idols who inspired him at a very young age. He also serves on the Board of Trustees at the University of New Haven and as a board member of the Flight Safety Foundation in Washington.

In his personal life, Michael is married with three children. Today, he lives in both Chicago and Atlanta with his wife Anne.

Some Scarpellino Kids About 1915

ScarpKids

Members of the Scarpellino family on the steps of 67 Warren Street in 1915.

(Photo Courtesy of Mike Quiello)

The Russell Hotchkiss House-7 Wooster Place

The Hotchkiss family were an early presence in Wooster Square. In 1844, during the Greek Revival Period, the exquisite house was constructed. A few years later, the iron balconies were added and in 1873, the third floor was built.

The second owner of the property was Edward Stephens. Stephens was the manager of the New Haven Clock Company.

Joseph Bromley House

231 Greene Street

The Joseph Bromley House was constructed in 1849. Joseph Bromley was the proprietor of a small store out of his residency. He sold expensive items and garments from Paris. Throughout the decades, the home had been remolded on a number of occasions.

In 2012, Albert A. Annunziata and his cousin Frank Toro III., purchased the home. At that time, the historical landmark was deteriorating. Albert, a prominent young lawyer in the Elm City, had previously restored close to fifty homes. He took great pride overseeing the work on the Bromley House. The New Haven Preservation Trust awarded the project with the Merit Award. Today, the Bromley House is comprised of three condominiums.

Brownstone Row

552 to 562 Chapel Street

The Italianate architectural style of the Brownstones located from 552 to 562 Chapel Street were built in 1871. Prominent Elm City architect David R. Brown designed the structure. Brown worked closely with Henry Austin on many projects in the city. Originally, "Brownstone Row" was comprised of six individual homes that were three stories tall and fitted with elegantly designed windows and palatial facades.

During and after Redevelopment, the units were refurnished. Today, "Brownstone Row" is made up of single homes and condominiums.

558 Chapel Street-2010.

Cherry Blossom Festival

In 1971, picturesque Wooster Square was designated as the first historical district in New Haven. Three years later, the New Haven Historical Commission along with the Parks Department, planted seventy- two Yoshino Japanese, Cherry Blossom trees. The official dedication ceremony took place on April 22, 1974.

For over forty years, in the month of April, the Cherry Blossom Festival has been celebrated in Columbus Park. Over the years, the festival has expanded and increased in popularity. Today, the one day event includes food vendors, photo exhibits, as well as local artists and authors.

2012

Master of Ceremonies

Bill Iovanne Jr.

2014

SSMM Society

2016

St. Catello Society

Cherry Blossom Festival

April 24, 2016

Constable "Sonny" and Jean Quartiano

The Wooster Square area and the Down Neck section of Newark, New Jersey were similar in many ways. During the waves of mass immigration, both neighborhoods were flooded by thousands of southern Italian immigrants. Two Catholic parishes, St. Michael (New Haven) and Our Lady of Mt. Carmel (Newark) serviced the spiritual needs of the recently arrived. The neighborhoods were also parallel with a deep sense of family, dozens of small family operated businesses, and fraternal organizations. Furthermore, the areas were essentially blue collar. The Quartiano family had ties to both Italian American enclaves.

Vincent Quartiano was born in the Naples region and his future wife Caroline Mentone on Water Street in New Haven. The couple had four sons, and three daughters. Two other children died in infancy. All of the Quartiano children were born in Down Neck. To support his family, Vincent worked at the A&P warehouse in Newark. Over the course of time, Caroline wished to be close to her family in New Haven. As a result, Vincent commuted back and forth between the two municipalities.

Sonny was born in 1930. He attended schools in New Jersey, until the age of fourteen. He arrived at Columbus School only weeks before the end of the year and thus he graduated in New Haven. For two years, he attended Hillhouse High School. At the age of sixteen, he went to work at C. Cowles. He fulfilled a variety of tasks for twelve years. Surprisingly, in 1953, he was drafted into the Marines.

Sonny and Billy Abbagnaro (also from Wooster Square) went to Parris Island together. A few weeks before being deployed to Korea, the war ended. Sonny did not enjoy being away from home especially because he had been a newlywed. On May 5, 1951, he married his wife Josephine at St. Michael Church.

Honorably discharged in 1955, Sonny returned to C. Cowles. At the advice of his brother- in- law, Angelo Chieppo, he changed occupations. Angelo was a business agent for Teamsters Local 443 and he helped Sonny secure a job at Yale Transportation. He retired as a driver for Connecticut Container in 1992.

Josephine, a loving wife and mother, was also employed. She worked at Robby Len and then Sero Shirt Company. Sonny and Josephine had three children named Caroline,

Joanne, and Vincent. The couple also has seven grandchildren and a great grandchild. After sixty-four years of marriage, Josephine passed away on December 8, 2015.

Jean attended Ann Street School from K-8 in Newark. While at East Side High School, she was a cheerleader. After graduation, Jean stayed in New Jersey. For many years, she worked in reservations for Eastern Airlines. When the company was purchased, she moved to East Haven and got a job in the I.T. Department for the Teamsters.

Today, Jean has fond memories of living in Down Neck. As a teenager, Jean and her friends went to dances where future icon Connie Francis sang. Nasto's Ice Cream was a neighborhood landmark enjoyed by Jean and her family.

Sonny and Jean are actively involved in the affairs of St. Michael Church. During Lent in 2016, Jean approached Monsignor Schmitz about establishing a program to make Palm Crosses. Jean and a small group of parishioners worked diligently making dozens of crosses that were deeply appreciated by the parish community.

Sonny Quartiano and his sister Jean.

2016 Cherry Blossom Festival

April 24, 2016 at Columbus Park

Anne Potenziani (Left) and Antoinette Salvo (Right).

Anne Potenziani and Antoinette Salvo have been dear friends for decades. Both are Eucharist Ministers and assist mass at St. Michael Church. Furthermore, they are members of the St. Ann Society, and they can trace their roots back to the Wooster Square neighborhood.

Anne Naclerio Potenziani was born as one of eleven children to Tomasso and Teresa Nacelerio at 85 Hamilton Street. Tomasso worked at a lumber yard on Water Street. As a child, Anne attended Wooster and Columbus Schools. She graduated from Commercial High School in 1948.

After graduation, she was employed by the State of Connecticut Department of Transportation as a secretary in the Permits Department. Anne met her husband Harold after the Korean War. Upon his discharge from the Army, Harold was employed by the Department of Transportation as a crew leader. The couple married at St. Michael Church in 1956 and they had three children.

Antoinette Apicella Salvo was born to Fortunato and Trofimena Salvo at 518 Chapel Street. Trofimena suffered from high blood pressure and as a result, lost three previous children. In the seventh month of her pregnancy with Antoinette, Dr. Conte told her to seek the advice of Dr. Mendillo. He assigned Trofimena to bed rest and he was able to successfully deliver Antoinette by Caesarean Section.

Fortunato was a barber and a musician. His shop was situated on Franklin Street around the corner of Trotta's Pharmacy on Chapel Street. In between cuts, Fortunato played the Flamenco guitar. He also skillfully played the trumpet in an orchestra.

Antoinette attended St. Michael Grammar School before graduating from St. Mary High School in 1949. She went on to study medical technology at Larson College. Afterwards, she got a job as a medical technologist at St. Raphael Hospital in the clinical laboratory. In time, Antoinette fell in love and married Michael Salvo, a musician, at St. Michael Church. Michael was the co-owner of Cummings Steel Company. The couple had three children.

Columbus Monument

In 1825, the city established Wooster Square Park (the Italians of the area proudly refer to the parcel of land as Columbus Green) in honor of General David Wooster. The scenic park has been a popular destination for relaxation and play for close to two centuries. Michael P. Russo, the son of the legendary Paolo Russo recalled, "in the early 1900's, a bobby helmeted policeman was always on hand, night and day, strolling through the park. Common sights were nursemaids pushing wicker baby carriages, ladies with long sweeping skirts walking arm and arm with gentleman in derby hats, and children racing after hoops or playing marbles in the paths."*

On Columbus Day in 1892, twenty thousand Italians gathered on Chapel Street to celebrate the unveiling of the Columbus Monument. Civic leader Paolo Russo presided over the ceremony and Mayor J.B. Sargent was in attendance.*

In 1955, the monument was re-casted in bronze at a cost of five thousand dollars. On October 10, 1992, the Columbus Day Committee re-dedicated the monument. Today, people who visit the park continue to be in awe of the structure. Standing eight feet tall and on a six foot triangular pedestal, the Columbus Monument dominates the southern entrance of the park. Each October, Theresa Argento oversees the Wreath Laying Ceremony. Over three dozen local organizations including the Southern Italian Religious Societies, pin wreathes on the iron fence surrounding Columbus.

*Citizens Park Council. _New Haven Outdoors_. New Haven. pp. 34.

Philip Galpin, a local businessman, lived on Greene Street. Galpin served as mayor of the Elm City from 1842 to 1846. Philip designed the iron fence that replaced the wooden fence around Wooster Square Park. The six acre parcel of land once included a water fountain in the center of the park and in the winter a ice skating rink.

1891 Columbus Statue Committee:

Paolo Russo-Chairman

Father Vincenzo Astori

Gaetano Bruno

Pasquale Cafiero

James Caporale

T. Conti

Michele Del Greco

Dr. Vincenzo D'Elia

Rocco DeVita

Ludovico Lombardi

Lorenzo Mattei

Willis Bristol House

584 Chapel Street

The Willis Bristol House was designed by Henry Austin and built in 1845. Austin was born on December 4, 1804, to parents named Daniel and Adah. Originally, Austin was a carpenter before becoming a prominent architect specializing in "Italianate Style" structures. For a half of a century, Henry left his mark in New Haven designing dramatic buildings including the James English Home, Dwight Hall (Yale), and the John Pitkin Norton House on Hillhouse Avenue.

Willis Bristol House-Summer of 2012.

Henry also served on the New Haven City Council and he was a Mason for fifty years. Austin died in 1891 and he was buried at Grove Street Cemetery. Ironically, he designed the entrance gates for the graveyard.

For the past one hundred and fifty years, the Bristol House has served as a home, school, congregation, beauty parlor, and today apartments owned by Neil Rapuano. Lastly, while attending Yale School of Drama (Class of 1975), film icon and Academy Award Recipient, Meryl Streep lived in an apartment at 584 Chapel Street.

Wooster Street

Archway

Dedicated July 16, 2000

The Wooster Street Archway was dedicated on a humid day in July of 2000. To celebrate the occasion hundreds of people, many former residents of Little Italy, lined the streets. Gary Garibaldi, the President of the Wooster Street Business and Professional Association, provided a warm felt welcoming. After the National Anthem, which was sung by Ms. Lisa Pietrosimone, Rev. Brizzolara of St. Michael Church blessed the crowd and the event. On this historical day, music was performed by the Top Hatters, Marc Garafalo, Ralph Marcarelli, Anthony Minutillo, and Nina Pane Sanseverino.

The arch was designed by Gary Waterman. Situated in the middle of Wooster Street, near Russo Park, the structure is a symbol of a century of the Italian community and contributions in the area.

Founding Businesses:

Lupoli Brothers Funeral Home est. 1883

Maresca Funeral Home est. 1888

Longobardi Funeral Home est. 1911

Libby's Italian Pastry Shop est. 1922

Iovanne Funeral Home est. 1928

Cavaliere's Grocery Store est. 1934

Consiglio Restaurant est. 1938

Tony and Lucille Restaurant est. 1953

Frank and Mary's Sub Shop est. 1968

Abate Restaurant est. 1992

Tre Scalini Restaurant est. 1995

Alto Basso Restaurant est. 1997

Sally's Apizza est. 1938

Frank Pepe's Napoletana Pizzeria est. 1925

Wooster Spa

In memory of our deceased members Societa Santa Maria Maddalena est. 1898.

In memory of the men and women of the Societa Sant Andrea Apostolo est. 1900.

Winter of 2016.

Part Two

Neighborhood Guys-Circa 1960's.

(Photo Courtesy of Al Lauro)

Longtime friends Frankie Florenzano (L) and Joe Amarone (R) on Arthur Avenue in the Bronx in the mid-1990's.

(SSMM Archives)

Chapter Six-Franklin Street Fire

The comprehensive history of Wooster Square could not be complete without coverage of the Franklin Street Fire. The event took place on January 24, 1957, in the Hugo Building. The structure was built in 1871 and was not equipped with a sprinkler system. Sadly, the dilapidated building was scheduled to be destroyed that same year as a part of Mayor Richard C. Lee's Redevelopment Program.

At 2:56 P.M., frantic calls were received at New Haven Fire Department Headquarters. A rapidly spreading fire was raging at 62 Franklin Street in a building that housed the S.L. Stanley Company, Andy-Tommy Dress Company, Morris Baer Dress Company, Nylco Manufacturing Company, Thomas Machinery, and Jo-Al Dress Company. In frigid temperatures, workers were trapped on fire escapes as crowds gathered on the street to watch the tragedy unfold.

Caterina DeMartino was a young garment worker at Andy-Tommy Dress Company. In 1955, she immigrated to Wooster Street from Sicily with her husband who was a policeman in the "old country." A diligent worker, Caterina heard women screaming. However, she did not comprehend the chaos around her. In Sicily, there were few fires because the homes and businesses were made of brick or marble. DeMartino made her way to the fire escape which was damaged and not functioning. Fearing for her life, she jumped, violently landing on the hood of a car. Although she sustained injuries to her face and shoulder she was lucky to have survived the "death trap." Caterina reflected, "my English was poor, but I heard the screams. I lost a friend on the third floor who had four young children." *

Fire investigators were not able to determine the exact cause of the most deadly fire in New Haven's history. They believed that the blaze originated on the ground level near the elevator shaft. There was a large pile of fabric scraps that were to be discarded the following day. In total, five people died inside the inferno, four died trapped on the broken fire escape and six others succumbed, later at the hospital, as a result of burns. Lt. John Tiedemann, a twenty-eight year veteran of the fire department stated, "the following day I helped to look through all the rubble for the victims. It was a long time ago, but those images have never left me." **

The death toll could have been even higher if not for the courageous acts of five individuals. Morris Baer, the owner of a small garment company yelled "just get out girls" as he escorted his employees to the fire escape." He then returned inside the building to look for the rest of his workers. Morris and ten of his employees died and another twenty were rushed to the hospital.

*Interview. Caterina DeMartino. July 11, 2011.

**Interview. Lt. Tiedemann. July 11, 2011.

Thomas Dobrowski and three cousins, Stanley, Frank, and Walter Myjak worked for S.L. Stanley Company. The four brave men climbed on the hoods of cars with a ladder to help women who were trapped on the fire escapes.

The tight knit people of Wooster Square were deeply saddened by the tragedy that claimed so many lives.

Hugo Building-Business Owners

Morris Baer	M. Baer Dress Company
Thomas Gagliardi	Thomas Machinery
Anthony LoRicco	Andy-Tommy Dress Company
Stanley Myjack	S.L. Stanley Company
Joseph Nastri	Jo-Al Dress Shop
Richard Stiner	Manager of Nylco Manufactoring

Nearby Eateries

Dominic Mangine	D and J Luncheonette (64 Franklin Street)
Frank Teodosio	Frankie's Restaurant

Those Who Perished

Angelina DeRienzo	18 Years Old
Josephine Marotta	51 Years Old
Jessie Mongillo	43 Years Old
Joseph Nastri	48 Years Old
Grace Pitman	41 Years Old
Thelma Grillo Lynn	49 Years Old

Morris Baer	65 Years Old
Herbert Horowitz	46 Years Old
Alma T. Bradley	47 Years Old
Therese Sullo	43 Years Old
Sophie Christodoulidou	17 Years Old
Winifred A. Freeman	40 Years Old
Angelina Romano	45 Years Old
Anne B. Jones	56 Years Old
Matilda DiRuccio	64 Years Old

Little Known Facts

1. At the time of the fire, approximately one hundred and twenty employees, mostly women, were in the building.

2. The Alderman of the 10th Ward at the time of the blaze was Michael DePalma. Afterwards, he fought for improved safety requirements.

3. A retired fireman named Adam Traub assisted his former buddies in combating the fire.

4. Tom Dobrowski, who worked at S.L. Stanley had two brothers at the scene who were firefighters combating the blaze.

5. Mrs. Mary Iannone was one of the last to survive by jumping off of the fire escape. She had worked for Baer Dress Company for only two weeks before the blaze. Mary and her husband Ralph had two children and they resided at 13 Michael Road in Hamden.

6. Mrs. Alphonse Maselli, a waitress at Frankie's Restaurant, saw the women trapped on the fire escape. It was her first day as a waitress at the restaurant.

7. Carmine E. Prete, a presser at Baer's, slid down the drainpipe two and a half stories to the ground. Before being brought to Grace New Haven Hospital, he helped other workers escape along with Frank Teodosio. Prete suffered severe burns and he shattered his ankle. He endured pain for the rest of his life.

8. Mrs. Nicoletta Esposito worked at a nearby Chestnut Street factory. She rushed over and helped a badly injured woman to rest in a parked car. She then walked home to 66 Warren Street.

9. Ralph Acquarulo, who worked at a fish market in the vicinity, jumped on the hood of a car to try to catch girls leaping from the fire escape. He then assisted Prete who was bleeding profusely.

10. Rev. Vincent LoSavio and Rev. Mario Bordignon of St. Michael Church offered last rites to the victims.

The tragedy on Franklin Street.

(Photo Courtesy of Frank Myjack)

11. Peter Aiello, 38, of 473 Chapel Street ran up to the fire escape and he pulled a woman down. Her clothes came off and she was burned from the waist down. Aiello was sent to Grace New Haven Hospital.

12. Mary Penta, of 138 Greene Street, fell to safety when Stanley Myjack released a pin holding the fire escape.

Interview with Frank Myjack

August 7, 2011

"I never wanted people to pat me on the back. However, I can never forget what happened. Even today, if I see a fire, I immediately go back to the Franklin Street Fire. Some people cannot talk about tragic events or war. I feel that I have to because it is history."

Frank Myjack

Frank Myjack was returning back to Franklin Street after making a delivery for his brother Stanley who owned S.L. Stanley Company. As he was getting closer to the Hugo Building, he saw a huge cloud of black smoke emerging from the structure. Within minutes, Frank, his brothers, Stanley and Walter, and a cousin named Tom Dobrowski, were frantically trying to rescue the workers trapped on the fire escape.

Question-Where did you grow up and were your parents immigrants?

Frank Myjack-"My parents came from Poland in 1921 and they settled in the Polish community centered around State Street. My father, Anthony was a painter and he installed wall paper. My mother, Agnes cleaned offices and raised the children. There was eleven of us."

Q-How would you describe the layout of the Hugo Building before the fire?

FM-"The building had three levels and it was shaped like an "L". Right behind it was St. Louis Church and School. I worked on the bottom floor in my brother's business. We made panel and electric boards. On the day of the fire, I was out on a delivery. On the way back, I could see black smoke from the Franklin Street area. As I pulled up around the back, the building was an inferno."

Q-What happened next?

FM-"When I got back, my brother Stanley was trying to pull a pin out of a latch to lower the fire escape. My cousin Tom was on top of a car. It was never proven, but someone put the pin there to prevent school kids from swinging on the fire escape. Finally, Stanley got the pin out with a hammer and the ladies came tumbling down, saving their lives. I was dragging people to ambulances and hearses that were being used to get people to the hospital. Eventually, the back of the building collapsed."

Q-As you were helping the injured, did you feel the extreme cold?

FM-"I never felt cold. For about forty-five minutes we were dragging people to safety. The victims had their clothing and hair on fire. Sadly, I knew many of these girls. There was a restaurant upstairs and I would get coffee and talk to the girls every day. Mr. Baer was a hero. He tried to save his workers."

Q-When did the magnitude of the fire set in?

FM-"At first, we did not even think about what happened. We went home and my mom saw us with the smudge on us. When we sat down to eat, it sank in that many people died. My cousin was in the hospital."

Q-What happened to your brother's business?

FM-"It was destroyed. He re-opened on State and Stevens Street in Hamden six months later."

Q-What did you do for work after the fire?

FM-"I went on and worked at Marlins on Willow Street. In the late 1950's, I joined the Army. Then, for close to forty years, I was a police officer in Branford."

***Interview. Frank Myjack. August 7, 2011.

City of New Haven
Department of Fire Services
Awards Ceremony for Valor
September 18, 1994
Shubert Theatre

Certificates of Commendation
Thomas Dobrowski
Frank Myjack
Stanley Myjack
Walter Myjack

Onlookers watch as fire crews and a crane sift through the wreckage after the Franklin Street fire in New Haven.

(Photo Courtesy of Frank Myjack)

Frank Myjack, pointing to the section of Conte School where the fire escape was located on the Hugo Building.

(August of 2011)

Franklin Street Fire

Their Reflections

"I was going to St. Michael School. Around 3:00 P.M., I went to Shartenberg's Department Store. My mother worked behind the jewelry counter. I spoke to her and got on a bus which went by Franklin Street. Later, I came back to the scene with my father who worked at Branch Auto Lines on Hamilton Street. We were very worried about our neighbor Mary Santino who lived on Wooster Street. She got badly burned. That night, my parents and I went to the hospital to visit her."

Joseph Colello

"At the time, I was working for the bus company and on my lunch break. I went to Frankie Lee's place on Wooster Street. I heard the noise and went to Franklin Street. The police would not let us get close. Later that night, I returned and I saw them pulling bodies out of the building. I was living on Lyon Street and a friend of my family, from Italy died. It was very sad."

Michael LaBonia

"The day before, I was reading the meters at the building for my job at United Illuminating. The floors were saturated with oil. Joe Nastri was my cousin. He was a hero. He made it out of the inferno and went back in to save his workers."

Al Lauro

"Rosalie Mongillo and I were friends. As kids we both lived on Wooster Street and played together. She was a really nice person. My dad Angelo and I just stood there and watched the fire. It was very tragic. Rosalie's mother Jesse was only in her forties and died in the fire."

Ann Derrico Norman

Their Stories in Wooster Square

Alphonse Cimino

Hank and Theresa Scarpellino

Soapy Carrano

Alphonse Cimino-was born as one of four children to Pasquale and Marie Cimino at 54 Wooster Street. At the age of fourteen, he began his apprenticeship for Jeremiah and Susan Apicella at their bakery on Houston Street in Fair Haven. Many years later, in 1976, he purchased their business. Today, the company is prospering making over five thousand loaves of Italian bread daily plus other Italian goodies. Al married the former Rose Buttone of Chapel Street and they had three children.

Hank and Theresa Scarpellino-Hank, while home on furlough during World War II, married the former Theresa Vitolo in 1943 at the Church of St. Michael. After the war, Hank was employed in a number of occupations. From 1958 to 1968, along with his brother Junie, Hank owned the Mariner Restaurant. He retired as a supervisor for Arden House of Rehabilitation in Hamden. Theresa worked for the New Haven Board of Education as an administrative assistant for fifty-one years. Their children, Patricia and Philip, both graduated from college and had prominent occupations. Patricia was a teacher and her brother a judge.

Nicholas "Soapy" Carrano-was born on February 4, 1932. His parents Francesco and Agnesa had nine children. Soapy served in the Navy as a cook. He married his first wife Carlene who originated from Maine. The couple had two sons and a daughter from Carlene's first marriage. To support his family, Nicholas worked as a fork lift operator for Yellow Freight Systems. He was a proud member of Teamster Local 443.

A boisterous and popular man, he had many friends on Wooster Street. In retirement, he worked for his best friend Frank Florenzano at Frank and Mary's Sub Shop. Soapy passed away on May 27, 2010.

Images From Little Italy

President Reagan and the First Lady at the Saint Maria Maddalena Society-early 1980's.

(SSMM Archives)

Retired police captain (NHPD) Andrew Consiglio (Left) with his son, Officer Ralph Consiglio on Chapel Street in 2011.

Chapter Seven-Redevelopment and Richard C. Lee

Many former residents of New Haven considered Richard C. Lee to be a focused and powerful politician with a vision of the future. To others, he was a self-serving egomaniac who intentionally planned the destruction on the ward that he could not win.

Lee was born on March 12, 1916. He grew up in a cold water flat in Newhallville. His father, Fredrick worked hard at Winchester to support his blue collar family. In school, Lee was an average student. Years later, he was unable to fulfill his military obligation due to ulcers.

In 1953, Lee defeated Republican Mayor William Celentano. Lee served as mayor from 1954 to 1970, and he became nationally known for his Redevelopment program. Lee proclaimed, "our goal is a slum less city, the first in the nation."

Redevelopment

The Federal Housing Acts of 1949 and 1954 established the Federal Urban Renewal Program. This enabled municipal governments to use eminent domain to take ownership of private property. Mayor Lee, who did have powerful connections on all levels of government, was able to obtain hundreds of millions of dollars of state and federal money for the Elm City. Roughly twenty-five thousand residents of New Haven were forced to re-locate. Foolishly, Mayor Lee assumed that the majority of these citizens would purchase new homes in the city. For many, they were traumatized by the process of being evicted and watching the destruction of their homes. Evicted citizens fled the city for the suburbs.

Households Displaced-Redevelopment (Source-*City* by Douglas W. Rae. pp. 339.)

Wooster Square	2710
Dixwell Avenue	1127
Hill Section	1049
Oak Street	866

Church Street	707
Dwight Street	485
Newhallville	363
State Street	270
Fair Haven	107

Redevelopment had a "push" impact on the people of Wooster Square. The construction of I-91 and I-95 destroyed factories and small family businesses. Close knit families were separated and their homes leveled. Never again would Wooster Square be a cohesive neighborhood. The proud Italians of the area were convinced that Lee, an Irishman, selected Wooster Square to be hit the hardest because he could not prevail in the 10th Ward. Even a half of a century later, the Italian American community is resentful.

Interview with Rod McKenzie on Redevelopment-October 22, 1992

Rod McKenzie worked as a Right Away Agent during Redevelopment. His job was to go into the neighborhoods and purchase property for the government. He described Wooster Square as decaying, but well kept by the Italian people. According to him, the citizens whose homes were to be destroyed were notified by the newspaper, and through the mail. Those affected had to leave. Evictees could appeal to the courts, but the judge would never rule in their favor. McKenzie stated, "the small business owners were hit the hardest. They were compensated for their property, but not for the income that their businesses brought in."

Question-Mr. McKenzie, what were your duties as an agent?

Mr. McKenzie-"I bought property for the State of Connecticut. First, an agent would appraise the property and then I would go and purchase it."

Question-What was the condition of the Wooster Square area prior to the building of the highway?

Mr. McKenzie-"The neighborhood physically was in very bad shape. Basically the area was a decaying slum. However, the Italian people did their best to keep the area clean."

Question-Why was the Quinnipiac Bridge built?

Mr. McKenzie-"President Eisenhower was convinced on building a highway system throughout the United States. The purpose of the highway system was for military use and for public transportation. Building the bridge was cheaper than building a tunnel under the harbor. Mayor Lee and the City of New Haven were very happy to get rid of the slum areas."

Question-How were the people of Wooster Square informed that they had to leave their homes?

Mr. McKenzie-"The State of Connecticut held meetings for those people who were influenced by the highway. It was up to those people to attend the meetings. If the people did not attend the meetings then a letter was sent to their house. There were also newspaper articles. They had plenty of warning."

Question-Did the people of Wooster Square have a choice whether or not to stay?

Mr. McKenzie-"The people who were effected had to leave. They had no choice. From the time they were informed, most people had about ninety days to leave. If they did not leave, the case went to the court. The court would rule in favor of the state."

Question-Were the people of Wooster Square fairly compensated for their loss of property?

Mr. McKenzie-"Many of the homes were ready for destruction. So in that sense the people were fairly compensated because they took the money and bought a house in Branford or Hamden. However, there were many people who did not want to leave. There were many sad stories."

Question-Were the small business owners compensated for their losses?

Mr. McKenzie-"I do not remember how many small businesses were involved. I know that there were many. The small business owners were compensated on the value of their property. They were not compensated for the commission that their business brought in. In that sense, many small businesses were greatly hurt."

Question-The people of the Wooster Square area maintain that their forced departure from the neighborhood was a political move by Mayor Lee. Mayor Lee was out to destroy their ward. Was this true?

Mr. McKenzie-"I do not think so. It did not matter to us what the mayor said. The bridge went through that area because it was flat and deteriorating. However, Mayor Lee was a Democrat and very powerful. He had a great deal of power in Hartford. It could have been a political move to breakdown the ethnic neighborhoods. I just do not know. He was in office for a long time. Many Italians in New Haven must have voted for him."

Mr. McKenzie-"May I add that the Quinnipiac Bridge was obsolete from the day it first opened. The engineers who built the bridge did not anticipate the traffic during peak hours. Of course, in the late 1950's, every family had one car. Then Americans fell in love with cars. This only intensified the problem."

Interview with the Ferraro Family-February 1, 1992

Giuseppe and Antoinette Ferraro originated from a small village forty kilometers south of Naples. The Ferraro's lived on a sixteen acre farm which produced vegetables and had livestock. Aided by a small crew of workers, Joe sold his products to Paesani who came to his farm. In the late 1940's, Joe and his brothers traveled to the Bronx hoping to land a job in construction. Two years later, with employment secured, his wife and four sons; Aldo, Lou, Anthony and Gaetano moved to the United States. In 1953, the Ferraro's moved to Wooster Street. Joe was employed at Sperry and Barnes.

Question-Why did your family leave Wooster Street in the late 1950's?

Joe-"The highway forced us out. Wooster Street use to be much longer."

Question-What was the neighborhood like in the 1950's?

Aldo-"Everyone knew and helped one another. The people cared about each other. The area was safe. You did not have to lock your doors at night. Many people spoke Italian on the street. There were many Italian vendors, doctors, small markets, and pizza shops. There were a few real restaurants. The building we lived in was very old. But the people worked together to keep them clean."

Question-What do you miss the most about Wooster Street?

Aldo-"My friends grew up along the street. We were close and did many things together. Today, Wooster Street is different. All the people are not Italian or close. The neighborhood is no longer Little Italy, it is too commercialized."

Question-What were the big events in the neighborhood?

Aldo-"In September, everyone made homemade wine. The festivals were big. Unlike today, there were no real outsiders. The festivals were just for the neighborhood. Of course, funerals were a big deal. People wore black armbands or black dresses for a year."

Question-What are your most enduring memories of Wooster Street?

Antoinette-"A lot of the people belonged to St. Michael Church. I have many memories of the nice old people. There still are friends living there."

In his personal life, Mayor Lee and his wife had three children. He passed away in February of 2007, at the age of eighty-six.

The highway at the end of Wooster Street-Winter of 2011.

Total Business-Displacement

(Source-*City*. Douglas W. Rae. pp. 343.)

Church Street	785
Wooster Square	450
State Street	385
Oak Street	250
Dixwell Avenue	193
Hill	81
Dwight Street	54
Newhallville	10
Fair Haven	8

Redevelopment

Their Reflections

"I grew up in the Brangi Building at 69 Wooster Street. Johnny Brangi and his brothers sold cold cuts and hot dogs. Their store was on the bottom floor. The government put the highway through the neighborhood. At least one hundred families from Wooster Street, Collis Street, and Hamilton and Wallace Streets were broken up. At night, we use to go out and hang out and have a good time. The neighborhood had little grocery stores, clothing shops, and shoe repair shops. We had it all."

Joe Colello

"At first, many people thought that Mayor Lee was okay. My father, Casper Amodio, was a Democratic Alderman. The building of the highway left a bad taste in the neighborhood. The Italians had to move. The societies and festivals have helped to keep the Italian community together."

Rae Somma

"Purely political. The highway went right through the Italian neighborhood. The mayor tried to break up the Italian ward. The highway forced people to move to Morris Cove, East Haven, and North Haven. Sadly, the population of St. Michael Church dwindled."

Beverly McClure

Their Stories in Wooster Square

Joseph Amarone   Eddie Angiollo   Joann and Corky Santacroce

Joseph Amarone-was born in 1932 as one of seventeen children to Andrea Amarone and Josephine Nazzario Amarone. Joe served in the Korean War and later was a truck driver for Teamster Local 443. He was also a custodian in the East Haven School System. Joe married the former Joan Lord and they had five children. Joe passed away on February 26, 2010.

Eddie Angiollo-was born one of ten children to Angelo and Marie Angiollo. Angelo supported his eight sons and two daughters by working at High Standard in Hamden. The family resided at 173 Olive Street. Eddie graduated from Wilbur Cross High School, where he excelled as a sprinter on the track team. Eddie and his wife Rose have two children and they live in Branford.

Francis "Corky" Santacroce-was born on Fulton Street and his family later moved to Laurel Street. Corky attended Woodward School, Fair Haven Junior High School, and Commercial High School.

His wife Dorothy, originated from Chapel and Ferry Streets. The couple had two children. To support his family, Corky drove a truck and was a member of the Teamster Union. He has been a member of the St. Andrew and St. Maria Maddalena Societies for over forty years. Today, in his mid-eighties, Corky works out every day . He enjoys riding his bike, walking, and lifting weights.

Images From Little Italy

DeLucia Funeral home on Chapel Street-1980's.

(SSMM Archives)

Frank Fronte with close friend Rosa DeLauro on Wooster Street in 2010.

Chapter Eight-Doctors and Politicians

"He was a God in the neighborhood. He was the angel of New Haven. If you could not pay, he would say don't worry about it. When you go fishing save a nice fish for me. He was very charitable. He would sit and talk with his patients."

Teresa McClure on Dr. Harry Conte

"Dr. Conte was a wonderful man. After making a home visit, he would sit down with the parents and have a glass of wine."

Ruby Proto on Dr. Harry Conte

The Italian immigrants in Wooster Square endured many struggles and hardships. Unfamiliar with the customs in America and with a limited command of the language, seeking medical attention was often a frightful experience. In this environment, doctors became prominent members of the Italian colony. Alberto Cupelli, in his book, *Italians of Old New Haven 1847-1900,* listed the following doctors in the 1890's:

Dr. Macaluso	202 Wooster Street
Dr. DeSantis	141 Olive Street
Dr. Francolini	541 Chapel Street
Dr. Simone	758 Grand Avenue
Dr. Elia	866 Grand Avenue

The most beloved doctor, Dr. Harry Conte began his practice years later. Other physicians who practiced in the neighborhood included Dr. DeVita, who married Paul Russo's sister, Dr. Castiglione, a dermatologist, Dr. Saverino, of 231 St. John Street (he had his office in his home), Dr. Ranelli, a dentist, Dr. Erba, on Academy Street, Dr. Frank Amatruda, on Chapel and Olive, Dr. Golia, on St. John Street, Dr. Marrini, on Greene Street and Dr. Montano. Furthermore, Dr. Verdi, a founding member of the Hospital of St. Raphael, was a product of the area. Dr. Verdi was born in Italy and he was a 1894 graduate of Yale. As a boy, he was the first altar boy at St. Michael Church.

Dr. Charles Bove

Charles Bove was delivered by a mid-wife on June 7, 1913. In 1906, his parents, Andrea and Maria came to the United States from the Naples region. Andrea and his first wife had two children named Rocco and Therese. Sadly, she passed away at an early age. Andrea and Maria had eight children and they also adopted three orphans.

Columbus School basketball team.

(Photo Courtesy of Charles Bove)

Maria was a strong and dynamic woman as well as a talented entrepreneur. During the Great Depression, she owned rental property on Wooster Street and a gas station on Chapel Street. Additionally, Maria imported olive oil from Italy. Andrea, was a barber by trade.

As parents, Andrea and Maria were determined to have their children succeed. They insisted that all of them earn college degrees. As a result, their sons Joseph and Tony became attorneys. Joseph's clientele were from the Wooster Square area and Tony worked in the Lee Administration. For many years, Tony was the Marshal of the Columbus Day Parade.

Maria and her son Charles celebrating his graduation from Fordham.

(Photo Courtesy of Charles Bove)

Charles was an accomplished student. He completed his undergraduate work at Fordham University in the Bronx in 1936. He continued his studies at the University of Pennsylvania where he obtained a degree in dental surgery in 1942.

During the Second World War, Charles was a Lt. Col. in the 100th Century Division. In December of 1944, the German Army made a last, desperate attempt to push back the Allies. For his valor in setting up medical clinics during the Battle of the Bulge, Bove received a Bronze Star.

After the war, Charles enjoyed a long and prosperous life. He practiced medicine full time until 1985. He continued to work part time until the age of ninety. In the medical community, he was very close to Dr. George Montano and Dr. Castiglione who were both from the Wooster Square area.

Charles and his wife of sixty-five years Grace had two sons named Charles and Andrew. Dr. Bove passed away on April 14, 2009, at the age of ninety-five in Fort Myers, Florida.

Lt. Col. Bove in his military uniform.

(Photo Courtesy of Charles Bove)

Dr. Harry Albert Conte

Arguably, the most revered individual to ever reside in Wooster Square was Dr. Conte. Harry was born the tenth of twelve children to Luigi and Marie Pietropuolo Conte on August 3, 1889. Luigi had arrived in America from Naples on May 22, 1885. To sustain his large family, he worked as a laborer for the Redfield Corporation.

Dr. Harry A. Conte

(Photo Courtesy of Brian Conte)

A gifted scholar, Harry graduated from high school in 1907. He attended and graduated from Yale in just three years. In 1912, Conte earned his degree from Long Island Hospital Medical College in Brooklyn. Specializing in childhood diseases, Dr. Conte interned at St. Barnabas Hospital in Newark.

During his career, Harry had offices on Wooster Place, 5 Elm Street, and 312 St. John Street. It is estimated that he delivered approximately nine thousand babies. On May 9, 1921, he delivered the "Salzo Quadruplets." Michael and Josephine Salzo had twenty-two children. The only female of the quadruplets was named Angelina. She died a victim of pneumonia in June of 1922.

A kind hearted man, Dr. Conte often charged his patients what they could afford. Theresa Argento claimed "Dr. Conte would deliver a baby sometimes for a chicken or a bottle of wine." Harry married the former Mary McLaughlin, who was a nurse. The couple had two sons Bernard and Harry Jr.

Mr. and Mrs. Conte

(Photos Courtesy of Brian Conte)

Dr. Conte earnestly wanted his sons to become doctors. Bernard was five years older than Harry Jr. The brothers were very close. They both graduated from Yale and became physicians. Harry Jr. married Kate Clancy and they had four children. Bernard and his wife had a son named Harry who became a doctor in the Greater Hartford area.

Dr. Conte Sr. passed away in April of 1961, as a result of a heart alignment. Mayor Lee recognized his enormous contributions to the Italian American community by naming a school in his honor. The school is located at 511 Chapel Street.

The entrance of the Harry A. Conte School.

2010

Dr. Gabriel Cusanelli

Nicholas and Erminia Varrone Cusanelli had two children named Gabriel and Gilda. Nicholas worked at the New Haven Trolley Company.

Gabriel was born on December 6, 1921, on Cedar Hill Avenue. The family later moved to Fair Haven and then to Orange Street. As a child, Gabe was an outstanding student and in his free time, he enjoyed playing baseball. Upon graduation from Hillhouse in 1939, Cusanelli enrolled at Yale graduating in 1943.

Erminia was a positive and passionate presence in the lives of her children. She strongly encouraged Gabe to attend medical school. In 1946, he graduated from the State University of New York Downstate Medical Center in Brooklyn. Dr. Cusanelli then served his country in the Army. He was stationed in Japan and Korea. Gabe was discharged in 1949 and returned to the New Haven to establish a medical practice.

As a physician, Dr. Cusanelli worked tirelessly in a number of capacities. For thirty-five years, he was the plant doctor at the Sargent Company. Many of the workers he treated were Italian from the Wooster Square and Fair Haven neighborhoods. By late morning, he went to his office at 235 Bishop Street to treat his patients for his private practice.

Dr. Cusanelli in 1946.

(Photo Courtesy of Mrs. Cusanelli)

In addition to his office hours, Dr. Cusanelli also made house calls throughout the greater New Haven area and he delivered babies into the late 1970's. Gabe was very proud to be a doctor and he enjoyed the interaction with his patients. His sister Gilda Lavorgna worked in his office.

In 1959, through friends, Gabe met Emilia DeVita. After a brief courtship, the couple married. The Cusanelli's had two children named Gabriel Henry and Elizabeth Clare. Emilia also worked in the office with her husband and sister-in-law.

Dr. Cusanelli serving his country in Korea.

(Photo Courtesy of Emilia Cusanelli)

Gabe's hobbies included reading, listening to the opera, and staying current on world affairs and politics. He was an enthusiastic Yale football fan and a member of the Yale Club of New Haven along with the Yale Football Association. When his children were young, Gabe and Emilia took them to every home game and many away games.

In 1994, Dr. Cusanelli retired from medicine to spend more time with his family. He passed away on September 3, 2013.

Dr. James La Femina

From the challenging years of the Great Depression to Redevelopment, Wooster Square was a densely populated residential area. This time period was exemplified by extended families living within walking distance of one another. In the Italian American community, priests and physicians were neighborhood heroes. Doctors such as Dr. Conte, Dr. Bove, and the La Femina's knew their patients by their first names and all the other members of their families. These medical professionals were more interested in curing their patients than enjoying a luxurious life. As a result, they were treated with "old world" kindness and respect.

James La Femina was born on January 4, 1904, on Wooster Street. His parents, Alfonso and Anna Colloso La Femina, had eight children. The origins of the clan can be traced back to Castellammare. Anna's father Joseph was a prominent physician in New York.

Dr. La Femina in the front and center.

(Photo Courtesy of Patti Ilnicki)

James excelled at New Haven Collegiate Predatory School, Fordham University, and the University of Pennsylvania. In 1936, he graduated from Tufts Dental School in Boston. In that same year, James began his career as a dentist in New Haven establishing a practice at 548 Chapel Street. Later, he had offices in Wallingford and Cheshire.

In 1937, James married Marie Ann Cavallo. The couple had two children Ann Judith and James Jr. The family resided at 30 Rochford Avenue in Hamden.

Dr. La Femina, a giving person and a great family man, retired to Florida. While in his eighties, he returned to Connecticut to live with his granddaughter Patti in Cheshire. He passed away on October 30, 1995.

James had a brother named Nicholas who was also a physician. Nicholas was born on March 13, 1903. He graduated from high school in 1919 and Fordham in 1921. Four years later, Nicholas successfully completed his degree at Long Island College Hospital. Following medical school, Dr. La Femina interned at New Britain General Hospital.

La Femina began his private practice as an obstetrician in 1926. On February 2, 1935, Nicholas married the former Mary Boylan of New Haven. They had two daughters and a son. Later, Nicholas was on the staff at Grace New Haven Hospital and he resided at 60 Dawes Avenue in Hamden.

Dr. Anthony Piccirillo

Tony Piccirillo was born as one of two sons to Luigi and Raffelina Piccirillo on November 12, 1928. Tony was raised on Brown Street and later his family moved to 110 Franklin Street in the Berardesca Building. The Berardesca family had a pastry shop on the ground level and rented flats.

Luigi and his wife worked for over forty years at Sargent. Tony was a pleasant kid who was very serious about school. In the mid 1940's, the Piccirillo's moved to East Haven. He graduated at the top of his class at East Haven High School and then Yale University in 1950. Anthony continued his studies at Oxford University on a Fellowship and he graduated from Yale School of Medicine in 1954. "Dr. Pic" also served two years in the Army Medical Corps.

Anthony served in many capacities during his long and distinguished career. He completed his residency in Pediatrics at Yale New Haven Hospital and St. Raphael's. Later, Dr. Piccirillo treated patients suffering from allegeries and asthma.

In 1953, Anthony married Jeanne Pieroway of Gloucester, Massachusetts. The couple had four children, including two who later became physicians. The well liked doctor never forgot the lessons of his youth in Wooster Square. He was kind and caring with his patients.

Anthony was a man of many talents and hobbies. He was an exceptional cook, mastering the lessons that he learned from his parents. He also had an ear for classical music and the opera and he was a historian. Anthony passed away on April 4, 2015.

Martin Piccirillo (Anthony's brother) was also a successful individual. He was a high honor student at East Haven High School before graduating in 1951. As a collegiate student, he earned a double doctorate degree. A lifelong educator, Martin taught at Fordham University and Gettysburg College. He also served as the head librarian at Quinnipiac College and the principal at St. Bernadette School in Morris Cove. Martin passed away on March 29, 2016.

532 Chapel Street-2012

Office of Dentists Dr. Joseph D'Ascanio and Dr. Mark Petchick.

Politicians

Antonio Vannacori was elected as Alderman in 1895. Vannacori, who lived on Wooster Street, became a voice in the city political machine, as thousands of his countrymen were arriving to the Elm City and settling in Wooster Square and the Hill section.

There were many caring Italian American politicians who followed Vannacori. These men and women passionately represented the people in their wards. Politicians such as Mike DePalma and Luisa DeLauro had street corners named in their honor. Biagio DiLieto and Rosa DeLauro represented the next generation and became household names in the Italian American community.

Rosa DeLauro on Wooster Street-July of 2015.

(Photo Courtesy of Joann Buccetti)

Tony Ciarlone

Banquet in New Haven.

(Left to Right) Yogi Berra, Vin Aitro, Tony Ciarlone, and Phil Rizzuto.

(Aitro Collection)

Tony Ciarlone was a part of the rich tradition of Italian American Aldermen serving in the Wooster Square area. Along with Lou Ragozzino (R), Louie Izzo (R), Jimmy Lamberti (D), and Paul Falcigno (D), Ciarlone served with distinction for the people of his close knit community.

Gaetano and Carmella Ciarlone had two children named Tony and Eleanor. Tony was born on May 8, 1929, at 257 Greene Street. Gaetano worked as a scissor grinder servicing the garment industry and the local restaurants. During World War II, he was employed at High Standard Rifle on Dixwell Avenue. After the war, Gaetano earned a living as a tile contractor. Carmella was a seamstress at Sunbeam Dress Shop on Wallace Street.

In 1941, Gaetano purchased the home at 236 St. John Street. Tony attended Eaton and Columbus Schools. In his free time, he was involved with the Boys Club and he participated in CYO basketball at St. Michael Church. While attending Hillhouse High School, Ciarlone was a high honors student, along with neighborhood pals Larry Iannotti and Dante Rosselli. Tony graduated in 1947 and the following year he enrolled at Junior College of Commerce. He completed his course work from that institution in 1949.

In the early 1950's, Tony went to work for A.J. Mongillo Plumbing on Olive Street. After a few years of gaining valuable experience, he established Mechanical Plumbing Contractors located at 81 Olive Street.

Eighth Ward Chairman Jimmy Lamberti encouraged Tony to run for Alderman. Ciarlone, a Democrat, ran and lost to Carmella Scopetta (R) from Olive Street. Disappointed, he challenged the incumbent and defeated her two years later. Ciarlone served for three terms before resigning to win a seat as a State Representative. Powerful New Haven politician, Arthur Barbieri (D) backed Ciarlone in his successful bid as a State Senator. In total, Tony spent sixteen years in Hartford as a State Representative and Senator.

Tony married his first wife Jeanne who was from West Haven. The couple had four daughters and seven grand-children. Sadly, Jeanne passed away and years later he married the former Jane Milano. Jane had a daughter from a previous marriage.

Today, in his late eighties, Ciarlone is working in real estate for Guadioso Realtors in East Haven. Tony is proud to have served as the past president of the Alpha Club. At the time of his presidency, the club had one hundred and twenty members. Ciarlone was also a longtime trustee for St. Michael Church.

Luisa DeLauro

Luisa DeLauro has resided in Wooster Square for nearly a century. Her parents, Cesare Canestri and Luisella Coppola Canestri were originally from Amalfi. They immigrated to America and were married at St. Michael Church. Like hundreds of Italian Americans in Wooster Square, Cesare worked at Sargent. In 1910, the couple established Canestri's Pastry Shop on Wooster street. Quickly, Canestri's became a local favorite known for its fine cannoli and as a place where family and friends could converse.

In 1918, Cesare died of the Spanish Flu. Sadly, he left behind Luisella who was pregnant and their five children. With the support of her extended family who resided on Olive Street, Luisella was able to run the business for years.

Luisa married her husband Tito "Ted" DeLauro on November 17, 1938, at St. Michael Church. Ted was the son of a carpenter who originated from Scafati. At an early age, Ted's mother Rosa died of tuberculosis. Her husband Nicolo immigrated to Fair Street in 1913 along with Ted and his sister Philomena.

A kind and well-liked individual, Ted was self-educated. A victim of discrimination, he quit school in the 7th grade after a teacher insulted his intelligence. Nevertheless, he became well spoken and was respected in the Wooster Square community. In fact, he earned the moniker "Mister Wooster Square."

Luisa and her husband were both active in the political arena. Ted served as an Alderman in the late 1950's. In time, Luisa followed his lead and she was elected to the Board of Alderman in 1965. Remarkably, she served under six mayors over the course of thirty-five years.

As an elected official, Luisa was the driving force in getting legislation approved that designated Wooster Square as the first historical district in the Elm City. A devout Catholic, she is also a proud parishioner of St. Michael Church and she was instrumental in the founding of the Cherry Blossom Festival.

On August 6, 2011, the corner of Academy and Chapel Streets was officially designated as "Alderwoman Luisa DeLauro Corner." At the ceremony attended by over two hundred people, Rosa DeLauro paid homage to her mother by saying, "my mother was a fierce member of the Democratic Party. She fought the system for her neighborhood and she enjoyed a good fight. This park (Columbus Park) she considered to be hers. When Conte School did not have crossing guards, she was there before school early in the morning helping the kids."

Luisa and Rosa DeLauro-June 2011 on Wooster Street.

On December 24, 2013, Luisa became a centenarian. A gala party with over one hundred family and friends was held at Consiglio's Restaurant.

DeLauro Family Table

On Sunday October 22, 2011, over three hundred people gathered in Columbus Park to celebrate the unveiling of the DeLauro Family Table. The four piece granite structure (a bench, table, and two chairs) cost $25,000 and was financed by private contributions. The monument represented Ted and Luisa DeLauro's home where Wooster Square residents were welcomed to discuss their concerns.

The weeks leading up to the celebrated event were filled with controversy. Over one hundred local residents signed a petition against the monument. The protestors argued that the table would violate the historical integrity of the park. Ralph Buccetti, whose family has resided on Warren Street for over seventy years, wrote an editorial in the New Haven Register emphasizing the contributions of the DeLauro family in Little Italy for the last seventy-five years.

Mayor John DeStefano, stated "as mayor, I proudly accept this table, in this place, the right place, and the right park." The first three people to sit at the monument were Kathy DeStefano, Ginger Miller, and nine year old Nicholas Miller.

The ceremony lasted over an hour and was followed by coffee and pastries at Conte School. Rosa DeLauro, the last speaker, was very emotional. She concluded by stating, "my parents, Ted and Luisa, made sure that I received every possible lesson from piano and dance to French lessons and horseback riding and a Catholic education. Imagine, an Italian riding a horse. Above all, my parents did not want me to work in a sweatshop. Imagine, what my parents would have accomplished with the education that they gave me."

Rosa and Luisa DeLauro

Rosa DeLauro

St. Patrick's Parish Neighborhood Reunion Honoree
Rosa DeLauro with Chairman John Ragozzino on
October 5, 2014.

"The neighborhood is the neighborhood because of the people who lived in Wooster Square and brought it alive. Every single person helped to make a difference in somebody's life. You know where my heart is, it is here."

Rosa speaking at the ceremony to dedicate the statue of St. Maria Maddalena on Wooster Street in July of 2015.

Rosa DeLauro was born on March 2, 1943. Her parents Ted and Luisa were Wooster Square icons advocating for the needs of the Italian people as long serving Alderman and Alderwoman. Her parents taught Rosa many life lessons including the importance of education and giving back to the community.

Rosa graduated from Lauralton Hall and then went on to earn her B.A. from Marymount College in 1964. On the post graduate level, she obtained a M.A. in International Politics from Columbia and she studied at the London School of Economics.

Rosa along with Mayor John DeStefano on Wooster Street in the summer of 1996. Rosa's mother is second from the right.

(SSMM Archives)

On November 6, 1990, Rosa was first elected to Congress in the 3rd District. For decades, she has served in that capacity while earning the adoration of members of both parties on all levels of government. While in office, the popular DeLauro has been a strong supporter of health care reform and women causes.

In 1978, Rosa married Stanley Greenberg, who is the President of Greenberg, Quinlan, Rosner, a research firm. The couple has three children named Anna, Kathryn, and Jonathan, as well, as four grandchildren.

Throughout her distinguished career, Rosa has been honored a number of times. In 2014, she was honored by the St. Patrick's Parish Area Neighborhood Reunion and she has been inducted into the Connecticut Women's Hall of Fame.

Never forgetting her roots, Rosa has been a presence in the Wooster Square area. Revered by the Italian American community, she has attended countless affairs of the St. Andrew and St. Maria Maddalena Societies.

Rosa (left), Tony Vitolo, Luisa, and Joe Amarone (right) on Wooster Street in the summer of 2003.

(SSMM Archives)

Mike DePalma

The Wooster Square area has had a deep and enriching tradition of men and women who fought for their neighbors to improve all aspects of life. Beloved leaders such as Antonio Vannacori, the DeLauro's, Tony Paolillo, and Mike DePalma were idolized by Italian Americans because of their fairness and willingness to confront the political establishment.

Lorenzo DiPalma (his surname was changed) and his wife Rosa DiLieto DePalma arrived to America on July 28, 1893.* The young couple completed the arduous transatlantic voyage aboard "The Hesterly." In New Haven, they had eight children.

Michael DePalma was born on September 19, 1903, at 15 Collis Street. A smart individual with a great sense of humor, he was forced to withdraw from school at the age of eleven to go to work. He found employment in the lumber industry. Initially, Mike worked in the yard and later as a truck driver for DeForest and Hotchkiss located on Water Street. Eventually, he was transferred inside because of his ability to communicate in Italian to the carpenters. Later in life, DePalma was employed by Batter Lumber and West Haven Lumber.

Mike and Luisa on their 50th wedding anniversary at the Dante Club in January of 1973.

(Photo Courtesy of Vera Santacroce)

Mike married the former Luisa Scarpellino DePalma. Luisa was a fascinating woman. A leader in her own right, she inherited from her father Giuseppe, the buildings at 61, 67, 71, and 75 Warren Street. The four buildings housed twelve apartments which were occupied by members of the Scarpellino family.

The couple had four children named Rosemary, Vera, Larry, and Joseph. Rosemary became a physical education teacher and Larry a teacher and a administrator at Wilbur Cross High School. Joseph earned a living as a police officer. Larry was an accomplished athlete. He was a standout in basketball and baseball at Hillhouse High School. As a collegiate athlete at Providence College, he participated in baseball and he signed a minor league contract with the Braves.

Alderman DePalma was known by his friends as "Uncle Mike." A Republican, he served twenty-two years on the Board of Alderman, eighteen years on the Fire Commission, and ten years on the Police Commission. Luisa DeLauro led the movement to have a street in the neighborhood named in his honor. In September of 1989, (Mike passed away on June 29, 1987) the city dedicated DePalma Court to pay homage to the dapper man who led with dignity and honor.

*Interview. Vera Santacroce. July 24, 2012.

Biagio DiLieto

Biagio DiLieto was born as one of seven boys and six girls on November 23, 1922. His parents, Angelo and Olympia, traced their roots back to Amalfi and Atrani. The large family resided on Wooster Street and later Brown Street as Angelo worked at Sargent. In 1935, Angelo moved his family to Wolcott Street in Fair Haven. A brother named Frank was a good boxer while serving his country during World War II.

Ben was an academic and an avid reader. Upon graduation from Commercial High School, he became the first person in his family to achieve that honor. DiLieto went on to earn a two year degree from the University of New Haven. Years later, while on the police force, he participated in a three month course at the FBI Academy and he took a course in police administration at the University of Southern California.

With the desire to help others, DiLieto became a police officer. On his first day, November 23, 1949, the city was plagued by a major snow storm. In total, he served twenty-nine years. As police chief, in the 1970's, he was very popular with the men and women in uniform.

The charismatic DiLieto became the 47th mayor of the city when he defeated Frank Logue. Ben went on to serve from 1980 to 1989. As mayor, he revitalized the arts district and his administration improved the city's ties with Yale University. His strong friendship with Yale President Bart Giamatti enabled that to take place.

On November 23, 1980, a 6.89 earthquake on the Richter Scale struck southern Italy. Close to three thousand people died and three hundred thousand were left homeless. DiLieto helped to raise millions of dollars for the victims. Ben and his wife traveled to Italy to personally hand the check to the mayor of a village that was decimated. His son Robert paid homage to his father by stating, "my father was motivated by his dad who was ambitious. My dad was a man of the people and he never forgot where he came from. Because, he grew up poor in a tight knit neighborhood, he was always kind and considerate to the people of the city." * On May 13, 1994, City Hall was dedicated in his honor.

In his personal life, Ben married his wife Rose (she grew up on St. John Street) at St. Donato's Church in Fair Haven. The couple had four sons named Robert, Ben, Edward, and Anthony. In his free time, Ben enjoyed reading books (his favorite was *Old Man of the Sea* by Ernest Hemingway), fishing and cooking Italian food. He was very proud of catching a eight hundred pound tuna off of the coast of Gloucester, Massachusetts.

*Interview. Robert DiLieto. July 24, 2011.

Ben passed away on November 8, 1999. His services were held at St. Bernadette's Church in Morris Cove and Iovanne Funeral Home.

Luisa DeLauro and Ben DiLieto (third from the left) meeting with a delegation from southern Italy.

(Photo Courtesy of Robert and Michelle DiLieto)

Mike Freda

Columbus Day Wreath Cermony-2012.

Columbus Green

Energetic, approachable, popular, and visible are a few words that best describe Mike Freda as the First Selectman of North Haven, Connecticut.

Mike was born as one of two sons to Michael Sr. and Mary Palumbo Freda. Michael Sr. was raised in the Hamilton and Wallace Street area. He served his country in the Navy. Mary was born in Derby in 1928, but grew up in New Haven. The couple raised Mike and his brother James in West Haven.

Mike graduated from Notre Dame of West Haven. He enrolled at Southern Connecticut State University and took courses in sociology and public speaking. Prior to office, he was a business leader working with Fortune 500 companies. His skills in public speaking, business development, and corporate management have guided him as a First Selectman.

In 2009, Freda was elected as First Selectman. His charisma and talents have led North Haven through challenging economic times. While in office, the town has renovated the fire houses and the school system and completed other projects to improve the infrastructure of the town. Today, North Haven is considered one of the most desirable places to live in New England.

Despite a demanding schedule, Mike is a presence throughout the greater New Haven area including Wooster Square. Annually, Freda participates in the Columbus Day festivities as well as the St. Maria Maddalena and St. Andrew Societies processions. Mike and his late father have been honored at the St. Patrick's Parish Area Neighborhood Reunion. In his private life, Mike and his wife Shirley have three children.

St. Patrick's Parish Area Neighborhood Reunion-October 5, 2014.

(Photo Courtesy of Jo-Ann Buccetti)

Mary Freda worked as a crossing guard for thirty-five years at the Seth G. Haley Elementary School in West Haven. After a brief illness, Mary passed away on August 14, 2013.

Tony Paolillo

Tony Paolillo was born on April 19, 1891, in Amalfi. His parents, Luigi and Maria arrived in America with their young family in 1895. The Paolillo's took up residency at 15 Collis Street.

Ironically, a future confidant and political ally, Mike DePalma was born at the same address in 1903. Both men became influential Republicans and members of the Board of Alderman.

Tall and dapper, Tony served in the United States Army during World War I. In 1918, he was stationed in France. Professionally, Paolillo worked in the insurance and real estate professions. Tony never obtained a driver's license, thus he walked throughout the city. Years later, Abe DePalma, a former prizefighter served as his driver.

ANTHONY J. PAOLILLO

Tony Paolillo

(Photo Courtesy of Ant Paolillo)

On March 9, 1933, Tony's father Luigi passed away. Luigi was one of the founding members of the St. Andrew Society. Tony inherited his leadership skills from his father. Proudly, he served as the president of the Flavio Gioia Society. From 1948 to 1954, Paolillo was the Director of Public Works. For fourteen years, he was the Alderman for the Tenth Ward.

In athletics, Tony managed football and baseball teams at the Nutmeg Athletic Club. He was also a premier boxing promoter organizing cards at the New Haven Arena. The Arena, which was located on Grove Street, had a seating capacity of four thousand spectators. Paolillo frequently filled the house with amateur and professional boxing matches.

New Haven Arena

(Photo Courtesy of Egisto Filipelli)

As a result of his contributions, Tony was honored on many occasions. A few of these events were:

Testimonial Dinner
Hotel Taft
January 28, 1940

Connecticut Boxing Alliance
March 30, 1942

Testimonial Dinner
Towne House Restaurant
April 12, 1948

Dante Club
Co-Recipient Wayne Candella
May 21, 1962

In 1964, Tony collapsed on East Street. The affable Paolillo was taken to Grace New Haven Hospital where he passed away.

Their Stories in Wooster Square

Marie Cangiano

Alphonse "Shorty" Florenzano

Andrea Colavolpe

Marie Cangiano-was born at 151 Wooster Street to Bonventuro and Carolina DeLandra. Marie married her husband Andrew at St. Michael Church in 1951. The couple lived in England while Andrew served in the Air Force. After the service, they returned to New Haven. Andrew worked for the water company until his retirement. The couple had two children.

Alphonse "Shorty" Florenzano-was born as one of ten children to Anthony and Rose Florenzano. Anthony worked at Sargent for a quarter of a century. The family lived at 82 Wooster Street. That building was owned by Antonio and Anna Galardi who lived on the second floor. In this photo, "Shorty" is sitting in Columbus Park after Hurricane Irene in 2011. He recalled the Hurricane of 1938 stating, "at 1:00 P.M. they released us from Columbus School. I remember being blown by the wind across Academy Street."

Andrea Colavolpe-emigrated from Amalfi to Collis Street in 1947. His parents raised their five children in New Haven. Andrea and his wife had children named Anthony and Lucille. Andrea worked for the State of Connecticut. He has been an active member of the St. Andrew society for over fifty years.

Images From Little Italy

Scarpellino Building, Warren Street-November of 2015.

Inside Muro Macaroni Factory-1930's.

(Photo Courtesy of John Migliaro)

Saint Andrew Ladies Society-Early 1970's.

(Teresa Falcigno Collection)

Campania Athletic Club

515 Chapel Street, New Haven

Founded-March 14, 1914

2016 President-Carl "Chip" Murano

2016 Memebership-108 Members

The Campania Athletic Club was founded by Don Raffaele Marcarelli on March 14, 1914. Raffaele emigrated at an older age from a small village named Vitulano. Initially, Marcarelli settled on County Street and the club was located in a vacant storefront at 65 County Street. The original name of the organization was Circolo Educativo Campania. Raffaele and the other founders, firmly believed that education and Italian language lessons needed to be provided to the immigrants and their children.

Founding Members of Campania Club-1930.

(Photo Courtesy of Julius Marcarelli)

Don Raffaele Marcarelli

(Photo Courtesy of Julius Marcarelli)

In 1929, the Campania Club had over one hundred proud members. In that same year, the club began to sponsor football and baseball teams. By the mid-1930's, the baseball team was competing in national tournaments in Cleveland and Dayton, Ohio. The squad also played in Ossining, New York against the Sing Sing Prison team. Packy DeFonso and Joseph DeGale managed the teams.

In time, the club relocated from County Street to 44 Hudson Street and then to Goffe and Orchard, followed by Goffe and Webster. In 1939, the clubhouse moved again to 91 Whalley Avenue.

Joseph DeGale

Joseph DeGale was born in the Elm City on January 20, 1900. He was a popular individual and a sports enthusiast. Joseph passed away on January 17, 1949. On June 17, 1957, the city paid homage to his contributions to the community with the dedication of the Joseph DeGale Memorial Field in Beaver Pond Park. For a number of years, the Campania Club honored an outstanding Italian American athlete from the area. That young man was the recipient on the DeGale Award.

Partial Listing of the DeGale Award Recipients

1949-Phil Ragozzino-Commercial

1950-Frank Sasso-Hillhouse

1951-Charles Avallone-Wilbur Cross

1952-Anthony Barbaro-Wilbur Cross

1953-Santo Listro-Hillhouse

1954-John Esposito-Wilbur Cross

1955-Nick Pietrosante-Notre Dame

1956-Anthony Ruotolo-Wilbur Cross

1957-Ronald Carbone-Wilbur Cross

1958-Tony Aceto-Hamden

1959-Ray Ciarleglio-Notre Dame

1960-Roger Milici-Hamden

1961-Louis Aceto-Hamden

1962-Joe Tonelli-Notre Dame

1963-N/A

1964-Jim Guercia-Wilbur Cross

1965-Tony Barone-Hillhouse

In 1945, the men glowed with pride when longtime member William Celentano became the mayor. William, the proprietor of Celentano Funeral Home, was a kind man and he was in office for eight years.

In 1950, a Ladies Auxiliary was added to the club. At its peak, there were over one hundred female members. In 1958, the organization added a bowling team and bocce league for its members. Throughout the decade, the Campania Club held musical comedies that took place at Fair Haven and Troop Junior High Schools.

Ray Ciarleglio-DeGale Award Honoree-March 15, 1959.

(Photo Courtesy of Julius Marcarelli)

DeGale Monument-Late 1950's.

(Photo Courtesy of Julius Marcarelli)

For the duration of the 1960's, the Campania Club continued to prosper. Annually, the group held a banquet which attracted hundreds of people. In 1964, Jimmy Guercia of Wilbur Cross received the DeGale Award. The event was held at Settentrionale Society Hall located at 239 Boulevard. The 1970's and 1980's, brought trepidation as the founders and their children began to pass away. Furthermore, younger Italian Americans were not interested in joining clubs or they were simply too busy to participate. By the mid-1980's, the club had a dozen members and was in jeopardy of being disbanded.

In the late 1980's, Chip Murano succeeded Sonny Melotti as club president. Chip, whose parents Carl and Eleanor originated from Wooster Square, was faced with the insurmountable task of increasing the membership. With a clear vision for the future, he returned the club to the long standing tradition of sponsoring softball and bowling teams. The players represented an influx of younger members eager to partake in the club affairs.

Founders (1914-1929)

Don Raffaele Marcarelli

Giulio Marcarelli

Domenico Marcarelli

Edmondo Marcarelli

Giovanni Fuggi

Domenico Cusano

Pasquale DeMennato

Antonio Fuggi

Adam Goglia

Fillippo Goglia

Severio Fuggi

Antonio Vertone

Gerimio Fusco

Pasquale Goglia

Nicolo Pesticci

Giovanni Ocone

Luigi Revillini

Mariano DeGennaro

Domenico Revillini

Cosimo Ocone

Louis Fusco

Nicolo Mastrocinque

Mayor Celentano presenting Phil Ragozzino the DeGale Trophy in March of 1949.

(Photo Courtesy of Julius Marcarelli)

Past Presidents

Don Raffaele Marcarelli

Guilio Marcarelli

William Celentano

Ralph Marcarelli

Louis Leopold

Rocco Girasuolo

Vito "Lefty" DeFrancisco

Carmen "Sonny" Melotti

Today, the Campania Club is situated in the St. Andrew Society building on Chapel Street. The two organizations peacefully coexist and engage in many joint activities such as a summer outing and Christmas Party. Carl "Chip" Murano, and his vice president Bobby Alberino, along with Chef Tommy Tuscano, and the board members, work feverishly to keep the club active and financially strong. With one hundred and eight dedicated members, the Campania Club is primed to be a vibrant organization for decades to come.

President Carl "Chip" Murano at the 2011 Columbus Day Wreath Ceremony.

Board Members in Clubhouse-1955.

(Photo Courtesy of Julius Marcarelli)

Campania Athletic Club Banquet-1957.

(Photo Courtesy of Julius Marcarelli)

Santo Listro, Hillhouse High School, receiving the DeGale Award from William Celentano-1953.

(Photo Courtesy of Julius Marcarelli)

25th Annual

Carnevale Celebration

Saint Michael Church Hall

Wooster Square

Southern Italy Religious Societies

In 1987, the Wooster Square Religious Societies united to form the Southern Italy Religious Societies (S.I.R.S.). We celebrated our Twenty-Fifth Anniversary in 2012.

We, whose ancestors inspired us to the devotions and traditions of our Patron Saints, wish to thank God for the wisdom to follow in their footsteps. We pray that this unification will continue for many years to promote our heritage and customs and sponsor an annual activity to benefit the Church of Saint Michael, where our Patron Saints are prominently displayed in a lovely chapel. The Church of Saint Michael, founded in 1889, is the oldest Italian church in Connecticut.

Thank you, most sincerely for your support and cooperation and for being with us this afternoon. May Almighty God, Lord Jesus, and all of our Saints continue to bless you and your family.

The 24th Carnevale Celebration

Front Row (L to R)-Alphonse "Shorty" Florenzano and Bobby Goglietino
Back Row (L to R)-Joey Possidento, Anthony Paolillo, and Rich Biondi

2012-Society Presidents

Saint Maria Maddalena (Founded 1898)	Andrew Consiglio
Saint Andrew Apostle (Founded 1900)	Frank Gargano
Saint Catello (Founded 1901)	Irene Cuticello Flynn
Saint Maria Delle Vergini (Founded 1906)	Ruby Proto
Saint Trofimena (Founded 1908)	Julia Nicefaro
Saint Andrews Ladies (Founded 1923)	Theresa Argento
Saint Maria Maddalena Ladies (founded 1925)	Rheta DeBenedet

Entertainment

Neapolitan Songs by-Richard DiPalma
Special Guest Performers-Ralph Nicefaro, Bill Iovanne, and Tom Tuscano
Music Director-Jeff Briglia
Invocation-Rev. Ralph Colicchio

Ralph Nicefaro, performing as Frank Sinatra.

Santa Maria Maddalena Members

Nicola Incarnato (L) and Joey Possidento (R)

Chestnut Lodge

Fred Ferrie grew up at 165 St. John Street. His great grandfather arrived to America from Benevento in 1865 and founded a construction company at 136 Greene Street. Fred's father, Fred Sr., also created a company named V. Ferrie and Brothers Construction. Fred Sr.'s wife, Eleanor, worked at the New Haven Clock Shop.

As a child, Fred was an active member of the Boys Club. While in his late teens and into his twenties, Ferrie was a member of the Chestnut Lodge. A group of "knock around" guys from Chestnut, St. John, and Chapel Streets hung out at their clubhouse on Chestnut Street. The members played cards and pool and hung out at Savin Rock. Simultaneously, the Greene Lodge and Crimson Lodge were situated on St. John Street.

The Chestnut Lodge also sponsored football and basketball teams. In 1969, the Fairmont A.C. captured the city and state championships. Looking back a half a century later, Ferrie reminisced, " we had tightness in the group. We hung around with guys that we grew up with. A group of us are still friends and we see each other over fifty years later."*

*Interview. Fred Ferrie. July, 20, 2015.

Members of the Chestnut Lodge 1958-1963

Vinny "Hawk" Amarante

Frank "Dickie Nunz" Annunziato

Frank "Frost" Annunziato

Frank "Frav" Avallone

Neil "Oink" Avallone

Mike "Buzz" Bizzario

Louis "Jumbo" Cacace

Ralph "Garloo" Capiello

Roger "Terrible Touhy" Czuchra

Lou "Rub" Ciampini

Charlie "O'Tool" Consiglio

Johnny "Boy" Coppola

Bob DeAngelo

Fred "Ham" DelVecchio

Pat "Rems" DelVecchio

Arthur "Butch" DiAdamo

Jerry "The Jet" Esposito

Fred "Shit Hands" Ferrie

Egisto "Flip" Fillipelli

Pete "Sweats" Gibbons

"Baby" Jake Grasso

Vinny "Baca" Guarnieri

Louis "Tumbleweed" Maselli

Jack "The Back" Massari

Bob "Baron" Mercurio

Puzzy "Sheets" Persico

Al "Fat Butch" Piombino

"Crazy" Ralph Proto

Anthony "Rance" Ranciato

Bob "Rap" Rapuano

Frank "Fly Paper" Scapetta

Ralph "Meatball Pinch" Solli

Al "Fonz" Spardaro

John "Squirrels" Squeglia

John "Vein Head" Tortora

Steve "Dirty Pierre" Vuolo

Tony "Fat Ass" Vuolo

George Waldron

Richie Biondi

Frank Fronte

Dom Onofrio

Committee-Fred DelVecchio, Pat DelVecchio, Arthur DiAdamo, Jerry Esposito, Fred Ferrie, John Tortora, and Tony Vuolo.

Members of the Chestnut Lodge at a Wedding-1970's.

(Photo Courtesy of Bob Mercurio)

Rich Biondi (Left) and Bob Mercurio

on Wooster Street in August of 2011.

Circolo St. Michael

234 Greene Street

Circolo San Michele

(Source-*La Colonia Italiana di New Haven*-Antonio Cannelli)

The Circolo San Michele was in existence as early as 1921 when Antonio Cannelli wrote his book *La Colonia Italiana di New Haven*. The Aitro twins, Vincent and Carmen, grew up at 205 Greene Street. They walked to the clubhouse and eagerly participated in the activities of the organization. These functions included the summer outing and playing on the baseball team.

Carmen Aitro

(Source-Aitro Collection)

Commonwealth Athletic Club

Collis Street-Circa 1920's

Commonwealth Athletic Club

(Photo Courtesy of Al Lauro)

Dante Club

Dante Club Members on Fairmont Avenue.

(Photo Courtesy of Al Lauro)

The Dante Club was established on Chapel Street under President Mike Coppola. In time, the club moved to Wooster Street before settling at 104 Fairmont Avenue. The majority of the membership came from Wooster Square.

The members enjoyed playing cards, and the weekly Friday night dinners. They also participated in parades and held dances. The hall was rented out for private functions. According to Al Lauro, the club closed its doors in the 1970's to the disappointment of the loyal members.

Dante Club-Ladies Auxiliary

Josephine Esposito

Peter and Josephine Esposito on their wedding day.

(Photo Courtesy of Patti-Jo Esposito)

During the early 1960's, the Dante Club was flourishing. The male members were active and loyal to the organization. In 1963, Josephine Esposito established the ladies auxiliary. Eagerly, she wrote the bylaws, set the annual dues at $5.00, and selected the board. The Board of Directors were Rose Marie Panzo (her husband Joe was the president of the Dante Club), as well as her sister-in-law Rose Panzo and Dorothy Del Conte.

The female members assisted the men in organizing dances, the Christmas and New Year's Eve parties, Bingo, and other functions. Al Lauro and Sal Pace catered the events. The annual Harvest Dance was popular and attracted over three hundred people at the club hall.

At its pinnacle, there were fifty female members of the auxiliary. In the mid-1970's, the Dante Club was disbanded.

Josephine Pettola Esposito was delivered on March 19, 1934, by Dr. Gentile at 76 Chestnut Street. Her parents, Luigi and Elizabeth, married on September 30, 1929, at the Church of St. Michael. The couple had two other children named Andrew and Elizabeth.

Josephine enjoyed a cheerful childhood. "As kids we played in Columbus Green. The children had bikes that were bought on Oak Street in the flea market. We played stickball. Our parents made a ball out of tape and newspapers. We also played hide and seek and hop scotch," commented Josephine.*

Josephine attended St. Michael School from the 5th through 8th grades. She graduated from Sacred Heart High School in 1952. While in high school, she was employed at Clark's Dairy on State Street. After graduation, she worked at a trucking firm on Dixwell Avenue.

During the Korean War era, Peter Esposito served his country in the Marine Corps. Through a friend, Peter met Josephine on the eve of Palm Sunday in 1952. The couple married on April 30, 1955, at the Church of St. Michael. Twelve years later, their daughter Patti- Jo was born. Peter worked as a truck driver and later dispatcher and then co-owner of New Haven Transport. He was a loving husband and father. Peter was strongly involved in the Italian American, Wooster Square community including the Church of St. Michael and grammar school. Furthermore, he was an active member of the St. Andrew the Apostle Society serving as the co-chairman of the feast for fifteen years. Peter passed away on May 15, 2001, at the age of sixty-seven.

After the passing of her husband, Josephine returned to work at Kohl's in Branford until 2008. She then began working and has continued to work for the City of New Haven Food Service at Wilbur Cross High School. Josephine enjoys her "Cross Kids" as she affectionately calls them.

*Interview. Josephine Esposito. March 17, 2016.

Soul mates and best friends.

(Photo Courtesy of Patti-Jo Esposito)

Peter and Josephine at Church of St. Michael.

(Photo Courtesy of Patti-Jo Esposito)

2015 Columbus Day Parade

Josephine and Patti-Jo

(Photo Courtesy of Patti-Jo Esposito)

First Independent Club

112 Wooster Street

The location of the F.I.C. Club at 112 Wooster Street was originally a two family home. Years later, the Nutmeg Athletic Club moved into the building before it became a car parts store. At its peak, the club had two hundred members. After a series of legal troubles, the club re-opened in the Spring of 2010 under the leadership of President Fran Limone. A few years later, the building was sold to a private owner.

First Independent Club-Summer of 2005.

The F.I.C. Club was originally located at 231 Chapel Street.

(Photo Courtesy of Harry DeBenedet)

Rocco DiBianco was born on Frank Street in the Hill section. In 1942, he joined the Navy and became a Seabee in the Pacific Theater. He helped to build airfields from Guadalcanal to Okinawa.

Rocky married the former Marie Visconti and they had four children. To provide for his family, Rocky drove a truck for Bilkays Trucking Company. He passed away on February 13, 2014.

Nutmeg Athletic Club Basketball Team-1932-1933.

(Photo Courtesy of John Acampora)

2009 F.I.C. "Men of the Year"

Mike Coppola (Left) and Felix DelGuidice at Anthony's Oceanview.

League of Abruzzi

Pasquale Taddei

771 Grand Avenue

Pasquale Taddei was born in 1898 in Abruzzi, Italy. His parents had three sons and a daughter. During the pinnacle of immigration to America, Pasquale arrived to Ellis Island and settled in an Italian enclave in Philadelphia.

At the outbreak of the Great War, he was summoned back to Italy to serve in the Army. His unit was deployed to the Italian Front in the Eastern Alps. While in combat, Taddei was wounded in the leg and he was taken as a prisoner of war. When the conflict ended in November of 1918, he was in an Austrian Hungarian prisoner of war camp.

In time, Pasquale healed and for the second time he completed the transatlantic voyage to America. Pasquale and his wife Massimma, settled in New Haven. The adoring couple had four sons and resided on Lyon Street.

Pasquale was the proprietor of several shoe repair businesses in New Haven. His profitable shops were located first on State and Trumbull and later on Grand and Hamilton. In the early 1960's, Taddei purchased North Haven Shoe Repair located at 4 Linsley Street. Daily, he took a city bus from Grand Avenue to North Haven. Upon his retirement in the mid-1960's, the business was sold to Ed Caso and it is still in operation in 2016. Interestingly, Pasquale's brothers Andrew and Anthony had shoe repair businesses.

Lega of Abruzzi President

(Photo Courtesy of Pat Taddei)

Pasquale was a stylish dresser and a well-spoken man. He enjoyed being around people and he was a masterful bocce player. For a dozen years, he was the President of the League of Abruzzi. The clubhouse was located at 771 Grand Avenue above and Italian grocery. To be a member, the individual had to have had roots from that region in Italy. During Taddei's reign, there were well over one hundred members.

Saturday night dinners at the clubhouse were well participated functions. The members skillfully cooked and the atmosphere was set by the performance of a three piece band. Men and women, as well as local politicians, were frequent attendees.

Pasquale passed away in 1970.

Adrianna's Restaurant, located at 771 Grand Avenue, in the winter of 2009.

Albert Annunziata

Attorney at Law

President of Melebus Club-137 Water Street

Albert Annunziata was delivered by a mid-wife on January 1, 1930, at 138 Wooster Street. His parents, Joseph and Gelsomina Cavallaro Annunziata traced their linage back to the village of Scafati, Italy.

In 1900, Joseph arrived to New Haven and fourteen years later his future wife completed the transatlantic voyage. During World War I, Joseph served in the U.S Navy. Shortly after his return to the Elm City, he married Gelsomina at St. Anthony Church. To provide for his three daughters and three sons, Joseph managed Prete's Furniture located at 138 Wooster Street. In addition to running the household, Gelsomina worked in the garment industry.

Al enjoyed an enriching childhood. He spent many days at Waterside Park playing baseball, football, and kickball with friends from the neighborhood, including Peter and Betty Nazario, Emiddio and Silvio Cavaliere, and Larry DePalma.

At the age of eight, Al began to earn money by selling newspapers on the corner of Church and Chapel Streets. Without his mother's consent, he also "bar hopped" on Saturday evenings to shine shoes into the early morning. Gelsomina, fearing for her son's safety, would not have supported his profitable occupation. Therefore, Al hid his shoe shine box at the Nazario home on Warren Street.

As a result of hard work, Joseph was able to purchase the property at 520 Chapel Street. The Annunziata's lived above the storefront. In the early 1940's, a butcher occupied the ground floor. Often the butcher complained about having difficulty making the rent. Al, at the age of twelve, convinced his father to evict the butcher, so that, he could establish a bike rental business. The young entrepreneur regularly made ten dollars a weekend renting bikes to children who rode in the neighborhood and in Columbus Park. The leadership and managerial skills that Al acquired in childhood, helped him throughout his legal career.

Scholastically, Al attended Dante and Columbus Schools. For the 9th grade he was enrolled at Troop Junior High and he graduated from Hillhouse in 1947. Al was an accomplished student and he was very popular with his classmates. What differentiated Al from his peers was that while in high school he was the proprietor of yet another successful business.

At the age of sixteen, Al was working for a Jewish man named Pat Zolot selling ice cream. He pushed a cart throughout the city selling the product. Al came to realize that he had the experience and desire to go off on his own and make a sizable profit. Eventually, he bought ice cream trucks, and he worked the shoreline from New Haven to Old Saybrook. Financially, Annunziata did so well selling ice cream that he paid for his college tuition as well as the tuition of his two brothers. In fact, he was still in the business after passing the Connecticut Bar exam.

Upon his graduation from high school at the age of seventeen (he skipped a grade), Al enrolled in an eleven month accounting program at Bryant College. By the age of twenty, he was a certified public accountant working for his cousin Joe Annunziata. Al found the profession to be tedious. Despite being good with numbers, he left the profession and attended Fairfield University graduating in 1953. By the time of his graduation he decided that he wanted to become an attorney. He attended law school, at Boston College, graduating from the prestigious institution in 1956.

Robert Woodruff, who had a thriving practice at 109 Church Street, hired Al. Woodruff was in ill health and within a year, Annunziata was directing the firm. For six decades, Al worked in the legal profession establishing himself as one of the revered attorneys in the city. His practice, Albert Annunziata P.C. and Associates, employed four other attorneys plus a support staff. Al also had the distinction of being sworn in as a judge on the state supreme court for the landmark case of Griswold v. Connecticut. Al retired from law at the age of eighty-two leaving his firm in the capable hands of his son Albert A. Annunziata.

During his remarkable life, Al also was involved in city politics and he was a leader in the Italian American community. In the early 1960's, influential Italian Americans including Arthur Barbieri, Bill Celentano and Al founded the Melebus Club. The organization which was located on Water Street, was comprised of notable members of the medicine, legal and business communities.

The Melebus Club, at its peak had hundreds of male members and a ladies auxiliary. Arthur Barbieri, Al and Jimmy Celotto were the only three men to serve as president. Popular events included, the Sunday night dances. Paul Florentino was the chef and a band provided entertainment. The club also had a profitable bar, and in the later years a workout facility. The club held bingo games, hosted conferences, baby showers and weddings. On special occasion, the club was the venue for amateur and professional boxing cards. Legendary Italian American comedian Pat Cooper performed in front of a boisterous crowd.

Arthur Barbieri was a close friend of Al's. Barbieri, a Democrat, had tremendous power on the local and state levels. To earn a living, he sold insurance and did real estate at an office at 109 Church Street. Arthur convinced Al to run for Democratic Ward Chairman. Al won the seat and the two men were instrumental in getting Bill Clinton to visit the Melebus Club. For a variety of reasons, the Melebus Club closed in the mid-1980's.

In 1970, Al met Karen Vitello of Derby. Karen and her sister Diane, and Diane's husband Frank Toro were going out for dinner. Boldly, Al invited himself along. For Al it was, "love at first sight." The couple married at St. Mary's Church in Derby in 1971. Al and Karen have four children named Albert A., Elizabeth, Joseph, and Karen.

Now in his retirement, Al enjoys spending time with his family. His hobbies include reading, bowling and shooting pool.

(Photo Courtesy of Karen Annunziata)

Mendillo Post

297 St. John Street

In September of 1938, a destructive hurricane hit New England. The Hurricane of 1938 leveled over fifty thousand homes and killed hundreds of people. At 297 St. John Street, stood a church rectory, that was decimated by the category three storm. For the next decade, the location remained an open lot. In 1949, the Mendillo Post was constructed. Named after a veteran of World War I from the area, the hall was utilized for parties and weddings. Emily Cocco had her wedding shower at the Mendillo Post before she married Michael Balzano who hailed from Warren Street. Men who lived in the vicinity also played Italian card games at the post. Today, the brick edifice consists of condominiums.

Bobby Goglietino, who lived at 325 St. John Street in the "Ragazzino Building," remembered the Mendillo Post as an active and popular place. Bobby's grandfather Pasquale Ragazzino owned the building which consisted of six railroad flats. All of the apartments were occupied by members of his family.

The former Mendillo Post-2012.

Mendillo Post

On August 27, 1949, the Frank Mendillo Post was dedicated at 297 St. John Street. The hall was named after Frank Mendillo who was a soldier during World War I. Private donors raised $20,000 for the purchase of the building. The trustees for the organization were Sam Marco, Romano Ianotti, James Papa, and Vincent DiMassa.

Opening Ceremonies

(Photo Courtesy of Mark Petonito)

The Master of Ceremonies for the grand opening was Mayor William Celentano. Also in attendance was Dr. Frank Anastasio. Previously, Dr. Anastasio had unsuccessfully run for mayor against Celentano. Despite his defeat, Anastasio had a significant career. In 1941, he was elected State Treasurer. Anastasio served as a private in the First World War. During World War II, he achieved the rank of a major and he was stationed in Iceland and Africa. Dr. Anastasio was a past commander of the Mendillo Faugno Post Hall and the State Federation of Italian Democratic Clubs. Proud of his heritage, he also served as the Chairman of the Columbus Day Parade. Dr. Anastasio died in August of 1966 at the Veterans Hospital. He was sixty-eight years old.

Dr. Frank Anastasio

Salvatore Petonito (R) at the opening ceremonies.

(Photo Courtesy of Mark Petonito)

Neighborhood Athletic Club

"I remember as a kid going to the Neighborhood Athletic Club with my relatives. There were seven or eight Scarpellino's in the club. It was right down the street from where we lived. Joe "Ducks" and Joe "the Tiger" Scarpellino were members as were Junie, Hank and Danny Scarpellino. From the area, Mel DeLieto, Dickie Gambardella, and Sal and Tony Midola were also members. It was a place to go. We had a television, and a pool and card tables. The club also had basketball and softball teams. We were a very tight group of friends."

Philip "Skippy" Scarpellino

The Neighborhood A.C. was situated on the corner of Warren and Wooster Streets. The members, young men from the neighborhood would assemble to socialize, play cards, and to shoot pool.

During the 1950's, there were roughly fifty active members. Later, the club relocated to Forbes Avenue.

In 1965, the Aitro twins were honored as "Men of the Year."

Men of the Year

(Aitro Collection)

Pietro Angelo Frigente Society

San Valentino Torio is a small village in the northern region of Salerno, Italy. The town is located near Mt. Vesuvius and contains fertile soil. The primary occupation of the area is farming.

Procession Circa-1930's.

(Photo Courtesy of John Migliaro)

At the turn of the 20th Century, the San Valenesse began to depart Italy for America. In New Haven, the immigrants established the Pietro Angelo Frigente Society. Antonio Muro, the brother of macaroni factory owner Genoroso, brought the statue from his hometown to the Elm City. The Our Lady of Consolation statue is housed at St. Michael Church.

Antonio Muro

(Photo Courtesy of John Migliaro)

Societa di Sant' Andrea Apostolo

515 Chapel Street

Founded-November 1, 1900

Female Society Founded-July 1, 1923

2016 Male President-Frank Gargano

2016 Female President-Theresa Argento

Male Membership-Over 200

Past Male Presidents
Salvatore Benissimo
Mariano Anastasio
Alfonso Longo
Gaetano Palo
Alfonso Nastri
Salvatore Ruoppolo
Salvatore Orio
Gennaro Aliberto
Raffaele Freccia
Salvatore Amici
Matteo Carrano
Giovanni Volpicelli
Andrea DeCusati
Andrea Sacco
Andrea Cimmino
Andrea Diotavito
Domenico Erba
Frank Sacco
Matthew Ruoppolo
Michael Savo
Frank Carrano
Andrew R. Iovine
Salvatore Savo Jr.
Anthony M. Colavolpe
Alfonse Abbagnaro

Presidente Onorario Perpetuo

Salvatore Benissimo

Societa San. Andrea Apostolo

Soci Fondatori

November 1, 1900

Gennaro Alberti	Salvatore Amendola
Mariano Anastasio	Alfonso Proto
Lazzaro Gambardella	Francesco Prete
Alfonso Gambardella	Andrea Bonito
Antonio Milano	Vincenzo Carrano
Salvatore Ruoppolo	Andrea Vallombroso
Vincenzo Pacileo	Andrea Prete
Matteo Ruoppolo	Domenico Proto
Andrea Benissimo	Francesco Gambardella
Francesco Lucibello	Antonio Bellini
Francesco Carrano	Salvatore Milano
Antonio Cuttiere	Cleto Arabo
Salvatore Cretella	Andrea Damiano
Salvatore Del Prete	Giuseppe Scarpellino
Luigi Paolillo	Antonio Cretella
Crescenzo Salatino	Andrea Cretella
Luigi Pinto	Gennaro Esposito
Orlando Bruno	Giuseppe Alfone
Gaetano Bruno	Antonio Savo
Matteo Carrano Di Francesco	Matteo Carrano Fu Giuseppe

Amalfi in the Summer of 2011.

(Photo Courtesy of Frank Bisceglie)

Columbus Day Parade-2012.

Columbus Day Parade-2014.

Mary Florenzano and her family gathering before the 2011 Procession.

Procession in front of St. Michael Church on June 25, 2011.

Presidents Frank Gargano and Theresa Argento-2011 Procession.

Presidential Profile

Frank Gargano

Elected President-1997

<u>Born</u>-Frank Gargano was born as one of two sons to Andrew and Josephine Berretto Gargano. Andrew grew up at 12 Franklin Street and his wife in Fair Haven. Later, Josephine lived in the Aitro Building on Greene Street. To provide for his family, Andrew and his brothers Gabriel and Bonaventuro were fishermen. Their boat was named "Two Brothers" and it was docked in Long Island Sound near Waterside Park. In the 1960's, Andrew left the difficult life of commercial fishing.

<u>Education</u>-Frank graduated from St. Michael School in 1963 and Notre Dame High School in 1967. For two years, he studied Italian at Southern Connecticut State College. In 1970, Gargano graduated from American Academy McAllister Institute of Funeral Service.

<u>Career</u>-For the past forty-five years, he has been a licensed embalmer and funeral director in the Greater New Haven area. Frank is a lifelong parishioner at St. Michael Church where he serves as a lector. He is also the head of the finance committee.

<u>Family</u>-Frank and his wife Mary have two daughters and three grandchildren.

St. Ann Society

2016 President-Valerie LaRose Souza

The St. Ann Society is comprised of roughly forty-five females under the direction of President Valerie Souza. The society is dedicated to the welfare of St. Michael Church. Additionally, the group conducts fundraisers and donates the proceeds to the parish.

Annually, from July 24 to the 26, the members celebrate a novena in honor of St. Ann. Their other marquee events are a Fall Harvest Dinner and participation in the Cherry Blossom Festival. Past President, Gail Parillo commented, "the St. Ann Society is a very strong and active group. We meet on the second Tuesday of the month and the ladies take great pride in assisting the church. I was the president for two years and I enjoyed that time."*

Wooster Square icon, Theresa Argento added, "my mother was a member of the Mother Cabrini Society. When I was a child in the 1930's, she took me to the meetings at St. Michael Church. The St. Ann Society came a little later and I have been a member for decades. We do a lot of good for the church."**

*Interview. Gail Parillo. January 4, 2016.   **Interview. Theresa Argento. January 4, 2016.

St. Ann Society-April of 2016.

St. Catello Society

Founded-November 3, 1901

2016 President-Paul Criscuolo

Membership-190 men and women

The Saint Catello Society was founded on November 3, 1901, by male immigrants from Castellammare di Stabia. Immigrants from this region of southern Italy settled in the Wallace Street area. Their clubhouse, "Circolo Stabiese" was located on Wallace Street. The mission of the society was to assist recently arrived immigrants and to practice their regional culture.

During the 1960's, the St. Catello Society was in the state of decline. Louis Longobardi and his sister Phyllis led the resurgence of the organization by recruiting dozens of members. Their father, Dominico hailed from Castellammare di Stabia and he was a founding member. Dominico's wife, the former Giuseppina Laudano, originated from Amalfi.

During the Second World War, Louis served his country in the Army. He was stationed in the Philippines Islands. Upon his return to the Elm City, he began his half century career as a funeral director. For decades, he was a leader in the Wooster Square community serving on the Redevelopment Committee and he was a member of the Wooster Square Business Association. Longobardi was also an usher at St. Michael Church and he belong to the Holy Name and St. Andrew Societies.

Longobardi married the former Lena Cofrancesco and the couple had two daughters. In September of 2002, Louis stepped down as president. The amiable Irene Cuticello Flynn succeeded him.

2014

Columbus Day Parade

Today, the St. Catello Society is thriving with a loyal membership and multiple activities. The society celebrates mass on the third Sunday in January and their beautiful statue is on display at St. Michael Church.

St. Catello Society Gallery

(Photos courtesy of Ed Flynn)

Saint Catello Society members line up for a group photo at Saint Michael Church following a meeting on Ju 18, 2002. 1st row l-r:Pat Longobardi, Phil Amore, Ann Fluter, Betty Amore, Robert Esposito, Vandy & Gabriel Esposito, Connie Carlson, Luisa Martucci, Bruna DeMartino, Mary Scillia, Carmel Donarumo, and Vincer Afasano. 2nd row: Theresa Savenelli, Mary Florenzano, Philip Esposito, Dolores Esposito, Treasurer Iren Flynn, Rosalie Merola, Norma Bailey, Ann Mei, Frank Merola, Charles Costanzo, and Ed Flynn. 3rd row: Lou Savenelli, Nicholas Onofrio, Joseph Amore, Frances Amore, Mario Turcio, Louis Turcio, Archie Iovanne, Ralp DeMartino, Paul Criscuolo, Josephine Longobardi, Dan Fluter, Vincent Brillante, Agnes Brillante, Macl Costanzo, and President Louis Longobardi.

Saint Catello Society of New Haven on the steps of Saint Michael Church New Haven, CT USA (1930's)

Directors and Officers for 1928

Giovanni Turcio-President
Alfonso LaFemine-Vice President
Catello Celotto-Corresponding Secretary
Giovanni Amore-Financial Secretary
Alberto Celotto-Treasurer
Editors-Giuseppe Turcio and Luigi Esposito

Domenico DiPalma-Sergeant At Arms

Counselors

Mariano Raffone
Francesco Grazioso
Aniello Longobardi
Francescopaollo Esposito
Tommaso Turcio

Columbus Day Parade-2015.

Presidential Profile

Paul Criscuolo

Elected President-2015

Born-Paul was born as one of four children to Michael and Charlotte Criscuolo. His great grandfather, Michael, came to America from Castellammare di Stabia in 1892. Michael originally lived on Hamilton Street and he was very proud of his roots. Michael taught his children, grandchildren and great grandchildren to cherish their heritage and family history.

Education-Paul attended grade school in Guilford. He enrolled at Notre Dame as a freshman before transferring to Branford High School the following year. He graduated in 1967. Criscuolo played football and basketball for the Hornets. As a student athlete at Bryant College, Paul played third base. He was also the sports editor for the university newspaper "The Archway." Paul graduated in 1971 with a B.S. in Business Administration.

Paul Criscuolo-Grand Marshall Columbus Day Parade-2013.

<u>Career</u>-Paul has been employed in sales, advertising and promotions. A tireless and charitable man, he has dedicated his adult life to volunteerism. Paul has served on a myriad of committees and boards. Included in this list are:

National Football Foundation
New Haven Gridiron Club
Chairman of Branford Park and Recreation Commission
Branford Italian American Club
Public address announcer for Branford High School football and basketball games
President of the Columbus Day Committee of Greater New Haven

<u>Family</u>-Paul married his high school sweetheart Dorothy "Dody" Blackstone. Dody was an all-state athlete at Branford High School participating in field hockey, basketball, and track. She later coached at her alma mater. Both Paul and his wife are inducted into the Branford Sports Hall of Fame. The Criscuolo's have two children named Brian and Julie and two granddaughters named Prudence and Beatrice.

As president, Paul would like to recruit younger members to join the society that their grandparents and great grandparents helped to build. He stated, "I have great respect for S.I.R.S. and the other societies of Wooster Square. All of the societies are working for the greater good of the Italian American culture. I am proud to be a part of that."*

*Interview. Paul Criscuolo. December 16, 2015.

East Haven Columbus Day
Parade-2015.

Presidential Profile

Irene Cuticello Flynn

President-2002-2014

Born-Irene Cuticello Flynn was born on November 23, 1940. Her father James and mother Lillian had two daughters and a son. At a young age, Irene's family moved from Fair Haven to 683 Woodward Avenue. Her grandfather Catello Cuticello, who arrived from Castellammare di Stabia in 1897, owned the three family home.

James supported his family by working as a butcher at the A&P Store, first on Grand Avenue, and later in the Hill. James was affectionately known as "the singing butcher." He loved to serenade his customers by singing Italian melodies.

Education-Irene attended Woodward Avenue School and Fair Haven Junior High School. She graduated from Wilbur Cross High School in 1958.

Career-At the age of eighteen, Irene went to work at New Haven Bank (NBA) in New Haven. While employed there, she met her future husband Ed. The couple married on November 23, 1961, at St. Vincent de Paul Church. Irene left the workforce to stay at home to raise her children. Years later, she was approached by Father John Georgia of St. Bernadette Church to work as the parish secretary. Skillfully, she worked in that capacity for fifteen years. Irene also worked at St. Elizabeth Church in Branford for three years.

Family-Irene and Ed have two children. Edward III. was born in 1964, and his sister Kathleen in 1973.

Ed grew up in the Goatville section of the Elm City. After serving his country in the Army (1959-1961), he was appointed to the New Haven Fire Department in March of 1962. During his prestigious career, Flynn served as the Director of Planning and Information. Ed retired after thirty-seven years in the department as a Battalion Chief. In 2005, he co-authored a book entitled "*New Haven Firefighters*." The publication was well received within the fire fighter community and the general public.

For twelve years, Irene enthusiastically guided the St. Catello Society. Through her diligence, the membership rose from 65 to 190. As president, Irene took great pride in her role of preserving the culture of Castellammare di Stabia.

President Irene Cuticello Flynn holding a letter of accomplishment.

(Photo Courtesy of Ed Flynn)

Societa Santa Maria Maddalena di Mutto Socorso

123 Wooster Street-Little Italy

Founded May 1, 1898

(The oldest fraternal organization in the State of Connecticut)

2016 Male President-Andrew Consiglio

Active Male Membership-165

Santa Maria Maddalena Ladies Society-Founded 1925

2016 Female Society President-Rheta DeBenedet

Past Male Presidents	Past Female Presidents
Luigi Pellegrino	Grace Bosse
Ralph Pisani	Ida Zingarella
Cosmo Perrelli	Lillian Libero
Nick Carrozza	Nonnie Fronte
Biagio Fronte	
Pat Zingarella	
Michael Fimiani	
Dominic J. Savo	
Anthony Vitolo	
Alphonse Lauro	
Frank Fronte	
Joe Amarone	
Paul Pagliaro	

Atrani-Summer of 2011.

(Photo Courtesy of Frank Bisceglie)

Luigi Pellegrino arrived to the United States from Atrani around 1895. Eventually, his three brothers and a sister joined him in New Haven. Luigi was literate and he acquired property on Collis Street. Unfortunately, like millions of other Americans, he lost his real estate during the Depression. Luigi remained in New Haven before passing away at an early age.

SSMM Building-1951.

Columbus Day-2013.

Friday Night Dinner-September 2011.

Tony Vitolo, (L) Frank Fronte, Frank Bisceglie and President Andrew Consiglio (R).

The Maria Maddalena Building in the Winter of 2011. Over two hundred years ago, Eli Whitney developed a patent model of his cotton gin in the building located at the northeast corner of Wooster and Chestnut Streets. His factory operated at that location for years. The society was founded in 1898. The peak membership was five hundred in 1905.

(Photo Courtesy of Frank Bisceglie)

Corner dedication-July 21, 1998.

Presidential Profile

Andrew Consiglio

Elected President-2006

Born-Andrew was born as one of six children to Andrew Sr. and Louise Consiglio at 85 Hamilton Street. Andrew Sr. worked on the docks and his wife was employed at a shirt factory.

Education-Andrew attended Hamilton Street School, Fair Haven Junior High, and Wilbur Cross High School.

Career-Andrew joined the City of New Haven Police Department in 1966. He retired as a Captain in 1999.

Family-Andrew and his wife, the former Carol Ann Gambardella (Carol Ann passed away in 1997) had two sons a daughter. Today, Andy resides in North Haven.

President Andrew Consiglio

(Photo courtesy of John Varone)

Presidential Profile

Rheta DeBenedet

Elected President-1986

Born-Rheta was born on Wallace Street as one of six children to Eugene Lenzi and Henrietta Civitello Lenzi. The family moved to 186 Hamilton Street and later 11 Wooster Place. Eugene served in the Navy and worked in construction. His wife was a waitress at Joe's Luncheonette on Grand Avenue.

Education-Rheta attended Hamilton Street School, Fair Haven Junior High, and Wilbur Cross High School.

Career-Rheta has worked in sales (Morrison's Clothing Store), as a secretary at an attorney's office, and as an assistant manager at a credit bureau in the loan department.

Family-Rheta married Harry on October 29, 1966, at St. Michael Church. The couple have two sons, Michael and Joseph.

Rheta during the SSMM Procession in 2012.

Saint Trofimena Di Minori Society

St. Trofimena Society-Early 2000's.

(Photo Courtesy of Julia Nicefaro)

On December 20, 1908, forty-six Minoresi assembled in a house on Wooster Street. The recently arrived immigrants collaborated to create a society to assist their fellow countrymen. The society had a clubhouse on Wooster Street.

Mr. Antonio Esposito, who was not Minoresi, paid for the statue of the patron saint to be shipped to America. Antonio married Raffaele DePonte who hailed from Minori, a small village along the stunning Amalfi coast. The feast day of the society is celebrated on July 13th.

In 1958, the society celebrated its fiftieth anniversary with hundreds of members attending a gala banquet. At that time, Gennaro Ruocco served as president. By 1980, the society had only a dozen members and was ready to be dissolved. Anthony D'Amato and his sister Frances D'Amato Crisci worked faithfully to reorganize and rebuild the organization.

25th Anniversary Banquet

(Photo Courtesy of Julia Nicefaro)

Since 2008, Julia Nicefaro has served as the president. As a result of her diligence, the St. Trofimena Society continues to be an active force in the Italian American community in the greater New Haven area.

Presidential Profile

Julia Nicefaro

Elected President-2008

Born-Julia was born as one of eight children to Ralph Velleca and his wife Francis D'Amato Velleca on the corner of Wooster and Chestnut Streets. Ralph worked as a pants presser in a factory on Hamilton Street. Ralph also operated a dry goods store on Wooster Street. Francis worked as a seamstress in a sweat shop.

Education-Julia attended Dante School. As a teenager, her family moved to Newhallville. She graduated from Hillhouse in 1949. She earned a degree in education from New Haven State Teacher's College.

Career-During her career in education, Julia taught at Winchester School, Lincoln Bassett, and Sheridan Junior High School. She retired as a librarian at Hillhouse in 1994.

Family-Julia married Ralph Nicefaro who hailed from Wallace Street. He attended St. Patrick's Church. Before Redevelopment, Ralph moved to Morris Cove. He worked as a printer. The couple has two sons. They are employed in education and as a correctional officer.

Columbus Day Parade-2011.

(Ralph and Julia are on the left)

Santa Maria Della Vergini Society

Founded-1906

2015-President Rubina Proto

Santa Maria Delle Vergini Society in front of St. Michael Church-Mid 1980's.

(All photos are courtesy of Ruby Proto)

The Santa Maria Della Vergini Society was founded by immigrants from Scafati in 1906. The society gave assistance to immigrants who settled in New Haven. At one time, there were hundreds of members. In 2015, the society had a handful of members under longtime President Ruby Proto.

Rubina was born as one of eight girls to Domenic Berretto and his wife Constance. To support his family, Domenic worked on the railroad and the family resided on Greene Street. As a child, Ruby attended Greene Street and Columbus Schools. She went to Commercial High School for three years before going to work. Ruby and her sisters Joan and Louise walked to work at the Robby Len Bathing Suit Company on State Street. She was employed there for forty-one years.

Both Ruby and her husband Serefino (Bob) served as President of the Santa Maria Delle Vergini Society. Ruby passed away on March 6, 2015.

Procession in July of 1985.

Ruby and Robert Proto-Mid 1980's.

Southern Italian Religious Societies (S.I.R.S.)

The first celebration of S.I.R.S. took place on September 13, 1987, at Sante's Manor in Milford. For decades, the societies that are a part of S.I.R.S. have worked hard to retain and promote the Italian culture. The center of the organization is at the Church of St. Michael.

Columbus Day Parade

2012

Societa Operaia di Mutuo Soccorso

Prof. Luigi Palmieri

37 Wooster Place

STATUTO E REGOLAMENTO
DELLA
Societa' Operaia
di Mutuo Soccorso
Prof. LUIGI PALMIERI

Stamperia Corriere del Connecticut
37 Wooster Place
New Haven. Connecticut

Luigi Palmieri, was a physicist and meteorologist who was born in Faicchio, Benevento on April 22, 1807. Luigi earned a degree in architecture from the University of Naples. After college, he taught in secondary schools in Salerno, Campobasso, and Avellino.

In 1845, Luigi became a Professor of Physics at the Royal Naval School in Naples. Two years later, he was appointed the chairman of physics at the prestigious university. By the 1850's, Palmieri was serving as the Director of the Vesuvius Observatory. His body of work as director was extensive and impressive. He modified sensitive equipment that was used to detect seismic activity. Through his efforts, scientists were more capable of predicting volcanic eruptions.

Luigi Palmieri died on September 9, 1896, in Naples, Italy.

<u>Constitution Article One</u>-On the 11th day of February 1927, a society was formed in New Haven, Connecticut for the purpose of extending mutual aid to those entitled to such benefits and this society was given the name of Societa Operaia di Mutuo Soccorso Professor Luigi Palmieri.

37 Wooster Place-2012.

To be a member, the person had to be male and at least sixteen years old, but not over, the age of forty-five. All members had to pay $1.oo at each monthly meeting. On the death of a member, the Society sent a floral piece costing $10.00 and hired an automobile for the funeral procession.

Elenco Dei Soci Fondatori

Giovanni Di Meo	Arcangelo Izzo	Antonio Merola
Domenico Siclari	Giuseppe Derrico	Andrea Grolioso
Domenico DiCenzo	Pietro Derrico	Francesco Onofrio
Nicola Domenico	Pasquale Morelli	Giuseppe Olivieri
Marcellino Giusto	Marco DiPalma	Enrico Ciarlo
Antonio Marenna	Francesco Perillo	Giovanni Tatto
Pasquale Tatto	Antimo Damiano	Francesco Petrelli

Ignazio Imparato | Giuseppe Esposito | Leone Franco
Filomino Biondi | Francesco Di Gioia | Alessandro Riccio
Pasquale Di Donato | Gaetano Cappelletti | Giovanni Ilianello
Michele Iannatuono | Raffaele Iannotti | Vincenzo Antonuccio
Antonio Petrelli | Donato Magista | Pasquale Rubino
Vincenzo Rubino | Cristoforo Villano | Giuseppe Tartaglione
Angelo Iannone | Pasquale Rapuano | Giovanni Dinorci
Giovanni Botto | Antonio Perillo | Giuseppe Posato
Giuseppe Nastri | Antonio Di Palma | Giuseppe Riccio
Angelo Coppola | Geremia Moscatello | Luigi Cavallaro
Pasquale Mongillo | Pasquale Porto | Giuseppe Borrelli
Michele Onofrio | Giustino Dellapella | Antonio Tondo
Raffaele Lombardi | Geremia Rapuano | Antonio Forte
Giuseppe Di Francesco | Pietro Gogliettino | Gaetano Mazziotti
Michele Mattei | Raffaele Biondi | Giuseppe Russo
Francesco Filippelli | Attanesio Brio | Nicola Ferrara
Luigi Villano | Generoso Achille | Andrea D'Ambrosio
Raffaele DiNello | Giuseppe Villano |

ANNO............				NUM............				
Elenco dei Versamenti fatti alla Cassa Sociale								
DATA		MESI Pagati	Causale del Versamento					FIRMA del COLLETTORE
Giorno	Mese		Ammissione	Mensile	Assic. Vitale	Diverse	TOTALE	
....	....	Genn.	.....	..	...	....	....	....
....	....	Febbr.	.....	...	...	....	....	....
....	....	Marzo	.....	..	...	....	....	....
....	....	Aprile	.....	..	...	....	....	....
....	....	Magg.	....	...	...	....	....	....
....	....	Giug.	....	..	...	....	....	.. ..
....	....	Luglio	....	....	...	....	....	....
....	....	Agosto	....	..	...	....	....	....
....	....	Sett.	....	..	...	....	....	....
....	....	Ottob.	....	..	...	....	....	....
....	....	Nov.	....	..	...	....	....	....
....	....	Dic.	....	..	...	....	....	....

Palmieri Society Monthly Dues Book.

(Courtesy of Joe Derrico)

Victorian Club

The Victorian Club was established in 1942. The members were mostly young men who eventually went off to war. The club was located in the basement of a business at 62 Wooster Street.

(Photo Courtesy of Andrew DePalma)

Melebus Club-1980's

The Melebus Club was located at 137 Water Street.

(SSMM Archives)

Procession of St. Maria Maddalena-2004.

Bill Iovanne (L), Egisto Filipelli (C) and Kessler Bailey (R)

(SSMM Archives)

Italian American Fraternal Societies-Circa 1920

Source-*La Colonia Italiana di New Haven*

(Antonio Cannelli)

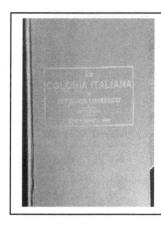

Organization	President
Societa Fratellanza Italia	F. Marra
Giuseppe Garibaldi	M. Leggieri
St. Antonio di Padova	D. Romano
Marineria Italiana	L. Costanzo
Cristoforo Colombo	L. Spignesi
Nord Italia	Avv. P. Trenchi
Arti e Mestieri	C. Mazzacane
Mandam di Caiazzo	G. Golia
Cusanese	M. Cassella
Provincia Avellino	M. Mignone
Regionale Marchigiana	G. Bacchiocchi
St. Catello	V. Esposito
Italia	Pietro Diana
Torquato Tasso	D. Spignesi
St. Clemente Martire	F. DeLucia
Gioia Sannitica	Pietro Ferrucci
St. Stefano	G. Popolizio
St. Andrea Apostolo	S. Orio
M. SS della Consolazione	M. Paparella
St. Lorenzo Martire	L. Mattei
Mand. Piedimonte d Alifie	F. Grande

Circolo San Carlino-Founded October 1897.

220 Wallace Street

St. Maria Maddalena Society Building

Early 1900's.

St. Maria Maddalena Society	L. Pellegrino
Vittorio Emanuele III.	P. D'Andrea
St. Leone Magno	G. Golia
St. Trofimena	N. DeRosa
Amorosi	C. Calandrella
Castelpagno	G. Lupo
St. Antonio Abate	S. Brancato
Prov. Basilicata	D. Campagna
Societa Acernese	A. DeFeo
St. Francesco di Paola	R. Rizzuti
Tripoli Italiana	V. Virgulto
Operaia Casalidi Falcchio	F. Porto
Cerreto Sannita	A. DeNardo
M.S. Dante Alighieri	D. Morcaldi
St. Maria Delle Vergini	N. DiLauro
Operaia Italiana	A. Cosenza
Flavio Gioia	A. DiPino
Fabio Massimo	M. Mattei
Cittadina Italiana	O. Balzano
Caiatina	G. Della Valle

Circolo Del Sannino-314 Oak Street-The Hill.

Founded November 27, 1897

Incorporated January 21, 1907

Circolo Gaiatino

Wooster Square Clubs and Societies-1935

(Source-www.library.yale.edu)

Organization	Meeting Place
Alpha Club	855 Grand Avenue
Aversano Protective Loan Assn.	173 Wallace Street
B and F Boys Club	36 William Street
Beavers Athletic Club	129 Franklin Street
Cappuano Pietro Club	28 Franklin Street
Circolo Fratellanza Minoresi	143 Wooster Street
Circolo Gabriele D'Annunzio Democratic Club	115 Hamilton Street
Circolo Italo Balbo	220 Hamilton Street

Gabriele D'Annunzio Democratic Club-Circa 1940. The club was founded in July of 1908.

(Photo Courtesy of John Ragozzino)

Circolo Stabiese	**205 Wallace Street**
Columbus Alliance	**144 Wooster Street**
Cooperative Cesar Battiste Inc.	**24 Hamilton Street**
Cosmopolitan Social Club	**123 Chestnut Street**
Dino Grandi Social Club	**182 Hamilton Street**
Di San Guilliano M.A. Club	**693 Grand Avenue**
Eleventh Ward Democratic Club	**176 Chestnut Street**
Flavio Gioia Association	**78 Wooster Street**
Franklin Athletic Club	**777 Grand Avenue**
Gioia Flavio Club	**19 Hamilton Street**
Hamilton Republican Club	**175 Hamilton Street**
Italian American Independent Club	**206 Wallace Street**

St. Catello Society 1949

(Photo Courtesy of Ed Flynn)

#1   #2   #3
Identified in the picture are Angelo Squillo, Domenico DePalma, Albert Germanese

Italian Provident Association	**127 Wallace Street**
Panthers Athletic Club	**295 Wallace Street**
Political Independent Club	**206 Wallace Street**
Progressive Circle Club	**178 Wooster Street**
Rail Social Club	**45 St. John Street**
Red Hawks Athletic Club	**100 Wallace Street**
Renaissance Dramatic Club Inc.	**188 Wooster Street**
Rinascente Gioventu Minorese Club	**100 Wooster Street**
Societa Santa Trofimena	**53 Collis Street**
Sons of Italy Grand Lodge of Ct.	**23 Wooster Place**
Sports Enterprise	**855 Grand Avenue**

Tenth Ward Citizens Club	188 Wooster Street
Tenth Ward Young Men's Democratic Club	174 Wooster Street
Valentino Rudolph Club	132 St. John Street
Verdi Sport Club	80 Wallace Street
Virtus Social Club	483 Chapel Street
Walnut Boys Club	256 Wallace Street
Waterside Athletic Club	87 Water Street
White Eagles Athletic Club	190 Franklin Street
New Haven Boys Club	31 Jefferson Street
Wooster Boys Club	53 Wooster Street
Campania Athletic Club	137 Geoffe Street

SSMM Archives-Festa 1950.

Wooster Square Clubs and Societies-1950

(Source-www.library.yale.edu)

Organization	Meeting Place
Alpha Club	855 Grand Avenue
Alpha Club	23 Wooster Place
Amerigo Vespucci Club	61 Wooster Street
Boys Club Association	31 Jefferson Street
Cape Verdian Social Club	229 Hamilton Street
Cesare Battista Club	24 Hamilton Street
Circolo Costtiera Amalfitana	483 Chapel Street
Circolo Flavio Gioia	62 Wooster Street
Circolo Pietro Badoglio	206 Wallace Street
Circolo St. Andrea Apostolo	141 Chestnut Street
Circolo Stabiese	182 Wallace Street
Circolo Vesuviano	148.50 Franklin Street
Clover Athletic Club	123 Wooster Street
Columbus Alliance	144 Wooster Street
Comitato Soccorsi Pro Atrani Italia	123 Wooster Street
Commonwealth A.C	138.50 East Street
D'Annunzio Gabriele Democratic Club	147 Wallace Street
Darin Lodge	79 Wooster Street
Dino Grandi Social Club	654 Grand Avenue
Di San Guiliano M.A Club	695 Grand Avenue

Flavio Gioia Inc.	62 Wooster Street
Independent Club	234 Chapel Street
Frank Mendillo Post	941 Grand Avenue
Lega Abruzzese	771 Grand Avenue
Lincoln Club	184 Wallace Street
Marco Polo Club	42 Collis Street
Minorese Fratellanzo Circolo	159 Wooster Street
Nutmeg Athletic Club	722 Grand Avenue

St. Michael Club Outing-Circa 1930.

(Aitro Collection)

Red Hawks Athletic Club	131 Wallace Street
St. Michael Club	234 Greene Street
St. Trofimena Minoresi Athletic Club	17 Hamilton Street
Shangra-la Athletic Social Club	53-57 Wooster Street
Sons of Italy Grand Lodge	21 Wooster Place
Tenth Ward Citizens Club	176 Wooster Street
Valentino Rudolph Club	126 St. John Street
William Verdi Sport Club	78 Wallace Street

Procession on Wooster Street in 1981.

(SSMM Archives)

Clubs and Societies

Their Reflections

"I am a Catholic and this (St. Maria Maddalena Society) is a Catholic organization. There are a lot of nice guys here. I really enjoy myself when I come to the club."

Tony Capone

" I have very strong ties to the Italian American societies of New Haven. My mother's family is from Amalfi and my father's family is from Atrani. With that being said, I have loyalties to St. Andrew and St. Maria Maddalena. I first started walking with my grandmother Nicoletta Gatto Esposito to honor Maria Maddalena. My father Pete "Doc" Esposito was the chairman of the Feast of St. Andrew the Apostle, for fifteen years until his death in 2001.

I do this because I have always said that you cannot go forward without knowing where you came from. We are, who we are, because of our heritage and traditions and without that we are lost. I only hope to keep making people aware of our heritage so that it is not lost."

Patti-Jo Esposito

"The St. Catello Society gives me a continued attachment to my grandparents, Catello and Rosalie, who were born in Castellammare di Stabia, Italy. They formed the foundation of my family."

Irene Cuticello Flynn

"When I took over from Carmen "Sonny" Melotti, in the late 1980's, the Campania Club had fifteen members. Today, there are well over a hundred and we just celebrated our 100th Anniversary. There is tremendous camaraderie. We have been members, and friends, for well over forty years. On a Friday night, when the guys are eating and playing cards, I look over the room and get very emotional. Other than my family, being the President of the club, is the most gratifying experience of my life."

Chip Murano

"I enjoy coming to Wooster Square because I belong to the three societies (Campania Club, St. Andrew, and St. Maria Maddalena). It is a chance to socialize, talk about old times and to be with friends."

Tony Paolillo

Their Stories in Wooster Square

Andrew and Anita DePalma   Junie and Lorraine Scarpellino   Paul and Agnes Falcigno

Andrew DePalma-married his wife Anita in 1969 at Our Lady of Fatima Parish in Wallingford. To earn a living, Andrew was employed as a carpenter for Local 24. Anita worked at Yale. The couple has two sons. Their son Michael is a Dectective for the Hamden Police Department. His brother Andrew Jr. is the Director of Technology at Eastern Connecticut State University.

Junie and Lorraine Scarpellino-Junie was delivered by Dr. Conte at 71 Warren Street on May 27, 1933. Amazingly, over eight decades later, he still sleeps in the same bedroom. In 1953, he was drafted into the Army. Junie served until 1955 as a Mess Hall Sergeant. After the military, he entered the restaurant and catering business. Scarpellino married the former Lorraine Spino, who came from the Farnham House Projects on Hamilton Street. The couple had five sons.

Paul and Agnes Falcigno-arrived to New Haven from Gioia Sannitica, Campania in the late 1890's. They lived at 104 Wallace Street with their five sons and two daughters. Paul worked at Sargent, and through frugal living, he was able to purchase his building. Three of his sons, Vincent, Anthony, and Michael resided at 104 Wallace Street. Another son Carl, lived nearby on Wallace Street.

Images From Little Italy

Dante Club-Columbus Day Parade on Chapel Street-1960's.

(Photo Courtesy of Al Lauro)

Frank Gargano (Left) with his parents and Bishop Peter A. Rosazza on Wooster Street in 1996.

(SSMM Archives)

Societa Santa Maria Maddalena 1958

Wooster Street Festival-1926.

St. Trofimena Society-Early 2000's.

(Photo Courtesy of Julia Nicefaro)

Joe Maiorano, owner of
Tre Scalini and his grand -
daughter on Wooster Street
in July of 2015.

SSMM Lady Board-
1970.

President Grace Bosse

(SSMM Archives)

Giovanni Volpicelli
Past President
St. Andrew Society

Vincenza Esposito Volpicelli
Founder
St. Andrew Ladies Society

(SSAA Archives)

Flavio Gioia Society of Wooster Street-1920's.

(St. Catello Society Archives)

Feast of SSMM-1926

Wooster Street

(Photo Courtesy of Biagio Fronte Jr.)

Feast of Maria Maddalena on Wooster Street in July of 1988.

(Photo Courtesy of Ruby Proto)

Dante Club

25th Anniversary Committee

(Photo Courtesy of Al Lauro)

1936

Columbus School Officers

Michael Mattei, Anita DeLieto, President Salvatore Petonito, Gertrude Aiello (L to R)

(Photo Courtesy of Mark Petonito)

Graduation Program

❖

SALUTE TO THE FLAG }
ODE TO THE FLAG } . . . *Class*

MUSIC . . . . . *Class*
"GREETING SONG"

ADDRESS OF WELCOME . *Rose Mary Sommers*

PIANO SOLO . . . *Eva Bertha Bloom*
"DER SCHARPENTANZ"

ESSAY . . . *Luisa De Martino*
"HISTORY OF OUR FLAG"

MUSIC . . . . . *Class*
"THE SOLDIER'S LIFE"

ORATION . . . *Salvatore Anastasio*
"THE FLAGMAKERS"

DUET—Violin and Piano *Abraham Yale Levine*
"SOUVENIR"

RECITATION . . . *Elena Celentano*
"WHO FOLLOW THE FLAG"

MUSIC . . . . . *Class*
"DANCE OF THE FAIRIES"

ORATION . . . *Dominico Zito*
"THE MEANING OF THE FLAG"

RECITATION . . . *Assunta Cavaliere*
"OLD GLORY"

MUSIC . . . . *Girls' Chorus*
"MOON RISE"

Graduation Program

❖

RECITATION . . . *Carmela Anastasio*
"A SONG FOR OUR FLAG"

MUSIC . . . . . *Class*
"THERE IS A PERFUME"

ORATION . . . *Moses Cooperstack*
"THE AMERICAN FLAG"

PRESENTATION OF CLASS GIFT
Francesco Orlando Prostamo

AWARDING OF DIPLOMAS

MUSIC . . . . . *Class*
"FAREWELL SONG"

❖

Graduates
Boys

Abramo Agostino Albelli	Luigi Gambardella
George Patrick Allen	Nicola Fiorillo
Antonio Aitra	Tommaso Guarini
Salvatore Anastasio	Nicola LaFemino
Andrea Amici	Abraham Yale Levine
Giovanni Borelli	Gennaro Lupoli
Guiseppe Cappetta	Giovanni Mele
Charles William Caron	Salvatore Malgonico
George Bernard Carroll	Howard Elmer Moerseburg
Moses Cooperstack	Giovanni Pomarico
Tommaso Cottiero	Andrea Pontecorvo
Antonio DeFala	Francesco Orlando Prostamo
Pasquale Di Lella	Clarence Edward Rogan
Francesco Durso	Terrence Francis Smith
Nicola Gimmino	Fidele Trotta
Francesco Gogliettino	Vincenzo Zito
	Dominico Zito

1915 Greene Street School Graduation Program.

(Photo's Courtesy of Teresa Falcigno)

The majority of the Italian immigrants that settled in Wooster Square originated from the *Mezzogiorno* or southern Italy. Back home, the southern Italians were faced with poverty, natural disasters, debt, and a distrust of the school system which after the unification of Italy, was controlled by the north. Education was not viewed as a priority, and in most cases, children left school at the age of fourteen (as dictated by the law) and went to work. As a result, in 1900, seventy percent of southern Italians were illiterate* (Sowell, *Ethnic America,* pp. 103).

The Wooster Square area had a handful of public schools within the district. They included; Columbus, Dante, Eaton, Fair Street School, Greene Street School, Hamilton Street School, Wallace Street School, and Wooster Street School. The Hamilton Street School was a rarity because the teaching staff was made up of nuns from St. Patrick's Church.

Three parochial schools were also located in the vicinity. In 1889, St. Louis French Catholic Church was established. In 1925, this parish celebrated the opening of its school. On August 29, 1960, a fire destroyed the church which was located on the corner of Chestnut and Chapel Streets. The parish relocated to 89 Bull Hill Lane in West Haven. In 1989, the parish closed the school.

The Polish immigrants celebrated their first mass at St. Boniface Geremia Hall on September 16, 1900. Ironically, the hall was located on Wooster Street. A few years later, St. Stanislaus Church was built on State and Eld Streets. In 1921, the parish established a parochial school. Fifteen years later, a short distance away, St. Michael School was opened. For six decades, the two schools flourished. In 1993, declining enrollment forced the schools to merge. In 1995, St. Stanislaus School closed.

2010
The former St. Stanislaus School.

The children of immigrants faced insurmountable obstacles at school, including a language barrier. In many cases, when the children began school they could not read, write or speak English. The lack of these skills humiliated the Italian students and greatly hampered their progress.

At home, parents spoke regional dialects to their children which often were vastly different and confusing. Parents stressed to their children that the family was the only institution that Italians could count on. Furthermore, most Italian families needed every able hand to work to earn money to help the family not get ahead, but simply to survive. As a result, smart and motivated students like Teresa Falcigno left school. Others such as Ted DeLauro, withdrew from school because he could no longer tolerate discrimination from his teachers. There were exceptions such as Charles Bove who was encouraged by his parents to stay in school and to excel. Later, Charles became a very popular dentist in the neighborhood.

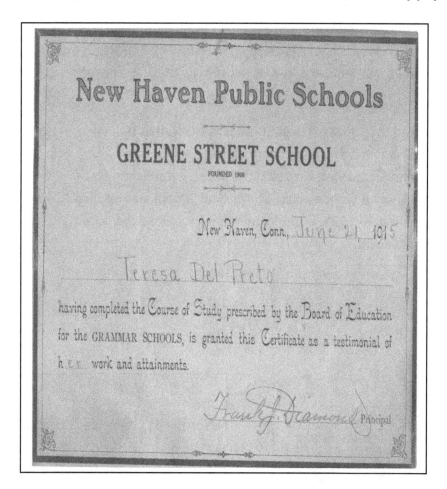

Teresa Del Preto's certificate from Greene Street School in 1915.

(Photo Courtesy of Paul Falcigno)

The attitude towards schooling improved with each succeeding generation. Italian Americans were becoming assimilated and education was no longer viewed as a threat to the sovereignty of the family. Post World War II, Italian Americans were beginning to marry non-

Italians. Furthermore, the victory overseas and the G.I. Bill of Rights paved the way for young Italian Americans to attend college.

The Teachers

From the early to mid-decades of the 20th Century, teachers in New Haven experienced numerous difficulties within their chosen profession. At that time, teachers were overworked and grossly underpaid. For many, they were "married to their jobs" simply because the demands of their occupation did not leave ample time to devote to marriage or a family.

There were many public and parochial schools within the Wooster Square district. The majority of the teachers were non-Italian, female, and single. This put the educators in an awkward position because their Italian students were taught at home to be fiercely proud and protective of their family and culture. Nevertheless, the teachers were given great respect and authority by parents, most of which did not graduate from high school either in Italy or in the states.

Marie DeLandra Cangiano (graduate-Hillhouse High School 1946) fondly remembers her teachers that she had at Dante School. Three in particular stand out over seventy-five years later. Ms. Ashton, Ms. Burton, and Ms. Reagon would walk together to school which was located on Chestnut Street. Marie stated "my family lived above our fish market at 151 Wooster Street. My mother would often ask the teachers to go to our flat for cookies and coffee."

Ann Derrico Norman (graduate-St. John High School 1956) attended St. Michael School. The majority of the staff were nuns. An exception was Ms. Cottage who was her 3rd grade teacher. Ms. Cottage and her colleagues taught all subjects and even took part in non instructional activities such as recess. Ann proclaimed, "my 5th grade teacher, Sister David played kickball with us in the yard. She was in full garb and she was a good player. I asked her how she could kick the ball so hard, and she replied, that she grew up with four brothers."

Sister Eugenia-St. Michael School 1952.

Front Row-Jerry Appicella, Ralph Del Santo, John Coppola, Barry Trasacco, and Anthony Cimino

Back Row-John Borello, Joe Colello, Sister Eugenia, John Pascale, William Coppola, and Tom Giamo

(Photo Courtesy of Ann Norman)

Vera DePalma Santacroce (graduate-St. John High School 1940) grew up on Warren Street. She walked a few blocks north to attend Fair Street School from Kindergarten to 6th grade. Vera passed by the banana companies to go to the dilapidated school. "Ms. McKiernan was my favorite teacher. She was especially sweet to her students."

Another antiquated school, Eaton School was located in what is now Lenzi Park. Mike Ferraro of Lyon Street had Ms. Pascale and Mr. Tuttle as his principals when he attended the school in the 1930's. Eighty years later, he recalled Ms. Kennedy, "she had a fish bowl in her classroom. I can still see her in the hallway cleaning out the bowl in the sink."

Discipline

The majority of the children who attended schools in Wooster Square were from working class families. At home, their parents were firm and taught them to respect authority. Parents often viewed an unruly child as an embarrassment to the family. In the classroom, teachers had complete sovereignty and in some cases were heavy handed when disciplining their students.

Vera DePalma Santacroce was well behaved and a stellar student throughout her academic career. Her father, Mike DePalma became a City Alderman despite only having an 8th grade education. Performing well in school was strongly encouraged in the DePalma household. Vera recalled, "never in a million years would my parents have sided with me over my teachers. I had a lot of respect for my teachers and I never had a long tongue. My mother would have killed me."

Michelina Afeltra (graduate-Commercial High School 1946) her father owned Giro's Barber Shop at 208 Wooster Street. Michelina did well in school and she never got into trouble with her teachers. She elaborated, "at Columbus School, Ms. Christian was tough. She wore a big ring on her hand. If you misbehaved, she would hit you in the back of the head. As a kid, I was protected at home. If I went home and told my parents that the teacher was upset, my parents would be upset."

Bobby Goglietino (graduate-Wilbur Cross High School 1953) grew up at 325 St. John Street. He attended Eaton School. Looking back, he described the school as old and he vividly remembers the wooden stairs going to the second floor swaying in the middle.

A fun loving kid, Bobby never experienced a trip to the principal's office. His father John would never had tolerated poor behavior. "I never wanted to get into trouble because you could get hit across the knuckles. Then when you got home, you would get a smack from your parents," said Goglietino.

Anthony "Rabbit" Giordano (graduate-Commercial High School 1951) grew up in the projects at 197 Franklin Street. He attended Eaton School and St. Michael. In both schools, the teachers were strict. "In the 3rd grade, I had Sister Marie Paul. She was very strict and some of the nuns had straps to hit the kids," claimed Giordano.

St. Michael School Yard

1950's

Far Left-Mary Ann Landino, Anne Minichino, and Phyllis Criscuolo.

(Photo courtesy of Ann Norman)

   <u>Mike Novella (graduate-Wilbur Cross 1952)</u> was born as one of five children to Michele and Rosina and they lived at 71 Water Street. Life was rigorous for the Novella family. Michele needed his children to work to augment the family income. Mike's sister Antoinette pushed him to graduate from high school. Novella explained, "Columbus School was fun. I went to school with all neighborhood kids and we joked around all the time. However, if you crossed the line, you could get the ruler or the teacher would put her fingernail in your chin. I graduated from high school, but I had to work. My parents had pride. They would never take handouts or welfare. Their kids had to work."

Memories of School

Up until the 1970's, it was common for many students to leave school for a hour and go home for lunch. Mike Novella can recall that a few of his classmates stayed in school for lunch. "Some kids would brown bag it. They would bring their lunch to school. Many times you could see the oil seeping out of their bag."

While in the 7th grade at Columbus School, Michelina Afeltra had additional daytime duties. In the morning, her mother would start to make soup for her father and uncles. While on her lunch break, Michelina would finish the meal by adding macaroni. After eating, she would return to school.

Ann Derrico Norman (Left) and Rosalie Cocco in Columbus Park in the 1950's. Notice Columbus School in the background.

(Photo courtesy of Ann Norman)

John Ragozzino lived at 135-137 Wallace Street. While attending Hamilton Street School, he had a job working at Candee Alley, a bowling alley on East Street. His job was to reset the pins. It was a job that he enjoyed, but his parents wanted more for John. "My parents were working people. My dad was a wall paper hanger and my mother worked at a dress factory. The day of the Franklin Street Fire, she did not go to work. That could have saved her life. Even so, they wanted their boys to succeed in school. My brother Anthony and I did graduate from high school," stated Ragozzino.

Vera DePalma graduated from St. John High School on Davenport Avenue at the age of sixteen. She walked miles every day from Warren Street to school. At that time, the long walk to school or work was common. Vera stated, "I walked to school and never took a bus. There were no crossing guards. Not once was I tardy school. After a big snow storm we would climb on the snow banks and go to school."

Marie DeLandra Cangiano concluded, "after school, I would go home and light the oil stove. I would sit in front of the stove and eat un-pitted olives as I did my homework. Those were fun times."

Graduating Class of 1954-St. Michael.

(Photo courtesy of Ann Norman)

Going to Work

<u>Marie Esposito Naclerio (graduate-Commercial High School 1946)</u> was born at home on Water Street. At Fair Street School, Marie and Frank Santacroce were selected by their

teachers to be monitors. At 2:00 P.M., they were in charge of handing out milk and graham crackers to their classmates.

Marie went on to become the only member of her family to graduate from high school. Her other six siblings had to go to work. Nacelerio stated, "we had supportive parents. Our home life was healthy. We had nothing, but we never felt that we were poor."

Fair Haven Junior High 1952.

Back Row (L to R) unidentified, Mike Balzano, Tommy Scalzo, Ralph Anastasia, Carmen Fappiano

Front Row-unidentified, Ed Candella, Art Lenzi, John Liberti, Jerry Silvestri

(Photo courtesy of Mike Balzano)

Peter Gatto grew up at 119 Water Street. His parents, Philip and Rose had three children. Peter attended Dante and Columbus Schools. In the 9th grade, he decided that he wanted to go to work which upset his parents. He began to work at Yale Neck Tie Company for seventy-five cents an hour. Philip kept part of his salary and gave his son spending money. A few years later, Gatto began his long career as a truck driver.

Rosalie Cocco (Left) and Arlene Vauiso at Columbus School-1950's.

(Photo courtesy of Ann Norman)

Eaton School-1943.

(Photo Courtesy of Mike LaBonia)

Columbus School-Class of 1948

Teachers

Ruth Christenan
Mary E. Coleman
Rose Connor
Rose Horowitz
Julia Kelleher
Ester Narden
Carl Palluotto
Margaret Ruig
Florence Saffner
Florence B. Tower

Students

Joseph Aloi
Maureen Braccia
Richard Branacchio
Mary Ann Bucci
Jerry Cimmino
Gloria Civitello
James Cretella
Paul Curto
Raymond DeCrescenzo
Theresa DeLio
Rocco DeLandra
Sue Carol Downing
James Ferrara
Nancy Frey
Joseph Gargano
Danny Holland
Cassie Inge
B. MacDonald
M. Mercurio
David Morse
James Nelson
Mike Novella
Anthony Petrarca
D. Petrelli
Anthony Pisanelli
Dominic Proto
Louis Proto
Lillian Ragozzino
Phyllis Rosato
Alphonse Ruocco
Nancy Sacco
Judy Santamauro
Marie Sarno
Celeste Vanacore
Joe Vanacore
Rose Verderame

Marie Sarno (Right) with her grandmother and her cousin Marie (Left) on the day of their Holy Communion. Notice the grapes in their back yard on Wooster Street.

(Photo Courtesy of Marie Sarno Branacchio)

Columbus School - 1948

COLUMBUS
1935

Columbus School Class of 1937

COLUMBUS
1956

Dante School-Circa 1920.

(SSMM Archives)

During the early 1900's, children in New Haven attended schools in their neighborhoods. As a result, the schools were ethnically homogeneous. By 1930, the public school system was comprised of fifty-four elementary schools, four junior high schools, as well as, Commercial and Hillhouse High Schools. Dante School was situated in Wooster Square. At that time, eighty-four percent of the population living in Wooster Square were Italian.*

* Stephen Lassonde, *Learning to Forget* (New Haven, 2005), pp. 20.

Sacred Heart Academy

Excelsior-Impelled by Christ's Love

295 Greene Street

"The love of the church and self-respect and respect for others is evident and present in our school."

Sister Rita Petrarca

Sacred Heart Academy opened its doors on September 9, 1946. The school was established with the objective of preparing young ladies for college.

Sister Antonine Signorelli and her staff provided a rigorous curriculum to the seventeen students enrolled in that first year. In just a few years, the school's enrollment expanded exponentially.

In 1953, Sacred Heart moved to the one hundred and twenty-five acre property of the United States Provincialate of the Apostles on Benham Street in Hamden. The spacious and tranquil property is home to the Caritas Christi Center, Clelian Adult Center, and Sacred Heart Manor.

Sacred Heart Academy on Greene Street.

(Permission Granted SHA)

Today, Sacred Heart Academy is considered to be a top educational institution. The traditions of the school, such as the Enthronement of the Sacred Heart and the May Crowning are passionately carried on by the students and the alumnae. The school participates in fourteen varsity sports as a member of the Southern Connecticut Conference.

(Permission Granted by Sacred Heart Academy)

Sister Antonine Signorelli

"Sister Antonine was a good speaker and she was very good at fundraising. She was a saint and she made the school special."*

*Josephine Esposito-Class of 1952.

Sister Antonine Signorelli was born in Missouri in 1915. As a young woman, she served as the principal of St. Joseph School in New York City. In the mid-1940's, she was recruited to become the principal of a newly established school. Sacred Heart Academy, located at 295 Greene Street, opened its doors on September 9, 1946. From the school's inception until her death, Sister Signorelli was a role model for thousands of teenagers and a symbol of educational leadership.

Sister Antonine Signorelli

(Permission Granted Sacred Heart)

Sister Rita Petrarca knew Sister Signorelli as a teacher and later as a colleague. She commented, " Sister Signorelli was a warm and dignified person. As a principal, she set high standards and understood how to motivate her students. As a leader, she was charismatic. As an administrator, she displayed love of the church and respect for others."**

Sister Antonine Signorelli served as principal of Sacred Heart Academy until her death. She was called home by God on Friday night May 19, 1967. She was only fifty-one years old. Today, the Sister Signorelli scholarship is awarded to the incoming freshman who achieved the highest grade on the admission examination.

**Interview. Sister Rita Petrarca. January 13, 2016.

Sister Rita Petrarca

Rita Petrarca was born on August 31, 1940. Dr. Capacelatro delivered her at Grace-New Haven Hospital. Rita's parents Armand and Rose Manna Petrarca had three children and resided at 13 Brown Street. Armand worked first at the Sargent Factory and then at American Steel and Wire. Rose was employed at Brewster Shirt Factory on Franklin Street.

Rita attended Dante School for Kindergarten and 1st grade. Before the start of the 2nd grade, her parents enrolled her at St. Michael School. This change had a profound and lasting impact on her life.

Initially, Rita struggled academically. Patiently, Sister Mary Pia took her under her tutelage, guiding her through the transition, and helping her catch up with the subject matter. Immediately, she enjoyed the parochial school atmosphere, the connection to the church, and the camaraderie between the staff and students. When Rita was eleven, Armand moved his family to 3 Hughes Street in East Haven.

In 1954, Rita entered Sacred Heart Academy located at 295 Greene Street. She thrived at the school academically and socially. Often, Rita stayed after school to interact with her friends and the Sisters. By her Junior year, Rita knew she wanted to serve God and become a nun. In the fall of 1957, Sacred Heart relocated to a spacious campus on Benham Street in Hamden. Daily, she took public transportation to school.

Rita graduated in June of 1958. On September 1, 1958, she entered the Congregation of Apostles of Sacred Heart of Jesus. In 1961, Rita took her first vows and five years later, vows for life.

Sister Rita's first assignment was to teach in the Hill Section in St. Louis, Missouri. The neighborhood was overwhelmingly Italian and traditional. During her long and distinguished career, Sister Rita taught or served as a principal in Pittsburgh, New Castle, and Butler Pennsylvania, Johnston, Rhode Island and Bridgeport, Connecticut. In total, she was an administrator for over two decades. She also enjoyed a year on sabbatical (1981) to study in Rome. Furthermore, Sister Rita worked as pastoral associate in parishes in Providence, Rhode Island, as well as, Meriden and Shelton, Connecticut.

Currently, Sister Rita is serving as the Archivist for the United States Province of the Apostles of the Sacred Heart. For a half century, she has made an impact on the lives of countless children and adults. A reflective Sister Rita commented on her years as principal, "what I had was a personal relationship with the students and their families. Today, in education, the administrators spend too much time filling out paperwork or fundraising. When I was teaching, there was a trust between the teacher and the parents and their children."*

*Interview. Sister Rita Petrarca. January 13, 2016.

1954.

Alphonse Proto, the leading historian of the Wallace Street area, has written extensively on his old neighborhood. According to Proto, at one time, the Hamilton Street School had an enrollment of seventeen hundred students. A destructive fire occurred on May 5, 1958, and the building was closed a month later.

(Photo Courtesy of John Ragozzino)

St. Michael School

The Final Years

St. Michael School was established in 1936. From its inception until Redevelopment, the school had a healthy enrollment and was thriving. Mayor Lee's urban renewal program had a devastating impact on the parish and the parochial school. Hundreds of Italian American families were displaced to East Shore or suburban communities. Initially, dedicated families continued to enroll their children in the school. However, by the mid-1970's and into the 1980's, the enrollment declined.

Legacy Children

Angelo Ciaburro (Class of 1960) attended St. Michael School from Kindergarten to 6th grade. While in the 7th grade, his family moved to California, only to return in time for the start of the 8th grade. Angelo participated on the basketball and baseball teams coached by his father, Fred "Bang Up" Ciaburro, and Joe Scarpellino. At that time, the rival of St. Michael was St. Donato. Angelo stated, "I have good memories of the school. We had fun with the nuns. Of course, they would whack us with a ruler and we could not tell our parents. I was with all of my friends. Neighborhood guys like Tommy Consiglio, Joe Sansone, Phil "Do" Scarpellino, and Pat Vissicchio. We had great times."

Angelo and his wife Therese enrolled their four children at St. Michael School. The Ciaburro's were friendly with the majority of the parents and had known them for years. As parents, they were determined to have their children experience the traditions of the school. Their daughter Kellie Ciaburro Guth graduated from St. Michael in 1984. Daily, she walked from the Columbus Mall, to the school with classmates Jimmy Romano, Dom Scarpellino, Kim Mineo, Dawn Bentley, and Christine Baer.

In the classroom, Kellie did very well. Her favorite teacher was Sister Donna Marie, who was young and had a good rapport with her students. Kellie was involved in extra-curricular activities as a cheerleader. After the basketball games, the players, cheerleaders, and parents went to Sally's Apizza. Kellie and the majority of her friends attended Catholic high schools. She graduated from Sacred Heart in 1988 and later Quinnipiac with a degree in Science and Radiology. Kellie reminisced, "looking back, the atmosphere of the school was very close. Everyone knew one another from church. St. Michael prepared us for high school. It was a great way to grow up."

Phil "Do" Scarpellino's (Class of 1960) parents Joseph and Adrianne insisted that their children attend St. Michael School. Joseph, a carpenter by trade, paid six dollars a month per child for tuition. Phil "Do" had Sister Michael for 1st, 6th and 8th grades. The students stayed in the same room the duration of the day and the teachers rotated to their different rooms. At 11:30 A.M., Scarpellino walked home to Warren Street for lunch as did most of his classmates. For the students who commuted, they "brown backed it." Phil "Do" was a talented baseball player. He played for his dad who was the coach. To raise funds for equipment, the players held newspaper drives. Decades later, Phil "Do" and his wife sent their children Hope, Jane, Phil, and Joey to St. Michael School.

Classmates

John Basta grew up in a brownstone at 36-38 Lyon Street. The building was purchased by his great grandfather. During the 1980's, every unit was occupied by a member of John's family. As a child, John often walked to church with his grandmother and to Lucibello's with his grandfather.

At that time, the families on Lyon, St. John, and William Streets were close. John had many close friends including Pasquale Pisano, and Angela, Ralph, Lenny, Vito, and Robert Bonanno. This group of friends walked to St. Michael School together. In the summer time, the children played Wiffle ball on Lyon Street or went over to the Bonanno's since they were the only family in the area that had a swimming pool.

John had Sister Helen Francis for the 1st grade and Sister Barbara the following year. Having nuns for teachers also had an impact on the weekend. If John did not attend mass, he would have heard about it on Monday morning. "St. Michael was a special school. There was no pressure to make friends. All of our parents knew each other. The parents grew up together. Everyone watched out for each other. The school was closely tied to the church. Values were installed in us. We had to keep our noses clean. We did not know anything else. I considerate it a privilege to have known everyone in my class. Kids like Anna Saracco, Lenny Lupoli, Patti-Jo Esposito, Pasquale Pisano, and Cosmo Amoritti. I have fond memories of the church carnival. My grandmother would bake a cake or cookies to sell. The money went to the school," concluded Basta.

Lenny Lupoli's mother taught at St. Michael School for thirty-eight years. Mrs. Lupoli was the first female lay teacher at St. Michael. She was a very popular history teacher. Lenny grew up in Morris Cove. However, he spent a great deal of time at his grandparent's home located at 17 Lyon Street.

At the time of Lupoli's enrollment, the bottom floor of the school was for grades 1-4 and upstairs for grades 5-8. The Kindergarten children were in a separate building. Remarkably, Lenny had thirty-five classmates in his class, and the students remained in the same room the entire day. The teachers rotated throughout the building. During recess, the younger students went first, followed by the older pupils.

Lenny participated in the drama club under the tutelage of Sister Barbara. He also played baseball and basketball. Andrew Salzo, a mailman, coached basketball and Benny Minichino was the baseball coach. The athletic teams from St. Michael held their end of the season banquets at Amarante's.

Following high school, Lenny attended Hamden Hall and Milford Academy. He continued his education at Pace University and American Academy McAllister of Funeral Services. In 2015, Lenny and his wife Gina re-opened Lupoli Funeral Home located at 80 Circular Avenue in Hamden. Now in his late forties, Lenny still has vivid memories of the school. He reminisced, " we were very close. There were no video games. The students grew up together. We went to school, church, athletic games, and midnight mass together. The majority of the teachers were nuns. We were so afraid of the nuns, there was no disrespect for our teachers and we treated the janitor just like we treated the principal. It was sad when the school closed. I am still in contact with many classmates on Facebook."

Anna Saracco Festa's parents arrived to New Haven from Benevenuto in the mid-1950's. Raymond Saracco, a butcher by trade, and his wife Ermelinda DiPaolo Saracco had four children. To earn a living, Raymond established a hair salon as his wife worked in a dress shop on Hamilton Street. Within the Saracco home, Italian was the primary language and Raymond insisted that his children attend a Italian, Catholic school.

While in Kindergarten, Anna had Sister Ludovico. Sister Ludovico was energetic and she put forth a great deal of time and effort for the graduation of her students. For their graduation, the Kindergarteners performed in front of a packed crowd in the gym.

Anna particularly enjoyed her 3rd grade teacher, Mrs. Longo, who was a nurturing woman who had a great rapport with her students. While enrolled at St. Michael, Anna took part in drama and the musicals including "Wedding of Jack and Jill." She graduated from the school in 1981 and St. Mary High School in 1985. Anna continued her education earning a degree from a community college in Radiology and MRI Technology.

In 2016, Anna is serving as the Alderwoman of the 10th Ward. She earnestly believes that as an elected official, she must represent the voice of her constituents. Anna and her husband Christian (an Italian immigrant), have three sons. Anna feels that her father and her education at St. Michael School gave her a foundation for public office. She stated, "the education that I received from my father has helped me as an Alder. St. Michael School gave me a foundation of hope, integrity, and faith. My father, an immigrant, taught me that I have a voice in America. At the school, my classmates came from a similar background. The majority were Italian and Catholic. The school was a community. The bonds that were formed there were brotherly and sisterly. Only the people who attended the school can understand and appreciate it."

Family Affair-The Esposito's

Josephine Pettola Esposito was born at 76 Chestnut Street in March of 1934. She attended St. Michael School from 5th through 8th grades graduating in 1948. Almost seventy years later, she vividly recalls the many warm memories of her teachers, and classmates. For example, on the first Friday of the month, the students attended mass before school. Afterwards, the parents provided the children with chocolate milk and doughnuts. In high school, Josephine attended Sacred Heart Academy graduating in 1952.

Peter Esposito grew up on Warren Street. Peter and Josephine were introduced by mutual friends. They married at the Church of St. Michael on April 30, 1955. The Esposito's had a daughter named Patti-Jo.

For Kindergarten, Patti-Jo attended public school. In the 1st grade she transferred to St. Michael and had Sister Francis. Initially, the transition to a parochial school was a difficult adjustment. Academically, she was a little behind her classmates. Sister Francis, a patient and devoted educator, worked with Patti-Jo every day after school. By the end of the year, Esposito achieved honors. In the 6th grade, she had Mrs. Lupoli. In that class were thirty-three children.

Patti-Jo was involved in many activities including student council, volleyball, and cheerleading. The cheerleading coaches were Anne Salzo and Patti-Jo's mother. Josephine was also a teacher's aide. Peter was also involved in the St. Michael community as the head of the P.T.A. and he organized the St. Michael Carnival.

Decades later, Patti-Jo and her mother are still actively involved in the Wooster Square community as members of the St. Andrew Society and the church. The memories of the school resonate with Patti-Jo including the father versus son basketball games, the picnics at Mountain Side Park and pizza at Sally's or Pepe's after the games. She concluded, "I cannot put into words how close and how strong the bonds were at St. Michael School. The Class of 1981 is still very close. Most of my classmates are still in touch."

Lunch Mothers-1980's.

(Photo Courtesy of Therese Incarnato)

Faculty Member

Therese Incarnato

Therese Incarnato was born in Wooster Square and her family has deep roots in the area. Therese's sister, Mary Florenzano and her husband Frank owned the popular Frank and Mary's Sub Shop at 102 Wooster Street. Her brother, Joseph Maiorano, is the owner of Tre Scalini Ristorante located at 100 Wooster Street.

As a child, Therese attended Dante and Columbus Schools, and Fair Haven Jr. High, before graduating from Wilbur Cross. She attended Southern Connecticut Teachers College earning a degree (K-8) in education. Incarnato worked six years in the North Branford school system and she taught at St. Brennan Catholic School. From 1990-1993, Therese taught at St. Michael School. By 1990, the school was on life support. The majority of the pupils were from Morris Cove, East Haven, and West Haven. The staff and parents worked diligently conducting fundraisers. Furthermore, in 1990, the nuns from Apostles of Sacred Heart left the school causing a ripple effect. As a result, many parents simply withdrew their children from the school. At that point, the fate of the school was sealed. For a short period of time, St. Michael and St. Stanislaus Schools merged before closing. After her career in education, Therese worked at the Knights of Columbus. She retired from that organization in the summer of 2016.

An emotional Therese added, "I loved the camaraderie between the teachers. I was from the neighborhood. The church and the school meant a lot to me. The parents and the children were wonderful. The last day was very emotional. The teachers, parents, and children were crying. I still think about the school today. It was a terrific school and I loved it and would have never left."

Mrs. Incarnato's-Class 1990.

(Photo Courtesy of Therese Incarnato)

New Haven Public Schools

HAMILTON SCHOOL

FOUNDED 1868

New Haven, Conn., *June 28, 1940*

Michael Anthony Freda

having completed the Course of Study prescribed by the Board of Education for the **Grammar Schools** is granted this Certificate as a testimonial of his work and attainments.

S. Maria Rose Murphy Principal

Graduation From Hamilton Street School-June 28, 1940.

Michael Anthony Freda

(Photo Courtesy of First Selectman, North Haven-Michael Freda)

St. Michael School

Their Reflections

" St. Michael was a neighborhood school. I went to school with my good friends. I had Sister Nina Marie for the 7th and 8th grades. I played basketball and we had good teams. Our coach was Mel DiLieto."

Anthony Aitro Class of 1950

"Everyone was Italian and from the neighborhood. We walked to school with our classmates. We would go home for lunch. We were more than classmates, we were family. All of our parents were friends."

Josephine Esposito Class of 1948

"When the alumni reflect on our memories of St. Michael Grammar School, there really is no word that can explain the school for those who did not go there. It is a feeling that you get when you remember the school, sisters, teachers, the parents, and the events. It was family. It did not matter if you were in the 4th or 8th grades, the students felt supported and safe. You made memories and friends for a lifetime. I may not see all of my former classmates all the time, but with Facebook, I can communicate with them. I was very lucky to have made some of my best friends for life."

Patti-Jo Esposito   Class of 1981

"I did very well at St. Michael School and I was an honor roll student for each grade. I had Sister Antonio for four grades. She was a good teacher. I am still in contact with Annette Florio and Silvio Sagnella who were my classmates."

Antoinette Salvo   Class of 1945

"Not too many people know that Tony Vitolo's first coaching job was at St. Michael. Tony went on to be a legend at Hillhouse. Tony was a good coach and he taught the fundamentals. In fact, we won the championship that year. In the 8th grade, I had Sister Antonio. She was a wonderful teacher. I graduated with my buddies Dom Aitro, Bill Iovanne, and Phil "Junie" Scarpellino."

Salvatore Savo Class of 1947

Image From Little Italy

Wooster Street-October 2, 2016.

Acknowledgements

I would like to thank Marie Cangiano, Al Lauro, and Ann Derrico Norman. These three proud individuals spent countless hours providing me with family histories, photographs, and stories from the Little Italy neighborhood. Large portions of this book were based on their recollections of the families and businesses that once existed before Redevelopment.

I would like to thank the members of the St. Maria Maddalena Society, St. Andrew Society, St. Catello Society, and the Campania Club. I formally and informally interviewed hundreds of members over the past two decades. Sal Zarra, a math teacher at Branford High School, was of great assistance with the graphics and layout of the project. I cannot thank Sal enough for the hundreds of hours that he devoted to the book.

I would like to thank the parishioners of St. Michael Church. Lastly, I would like to thank my wife Ramona, who has always supported me in my projects associated with the Italian American culture.

If you would like to speak with me or share your family history please contact me at:

Richard D. Biondi

rdbiondi@snet.net

Grazie mille

Front Cover (Photograph Courtesy of Marie Cangiano.)

(Left to Right) Bonaventuro DeLandra, Frank Pepe, a Pepe family relative from Brazil, Sal Alba, and Frank Pepe's granddaughter Genevieve. The photo was taken in 1956 on Wooster Street.

About the Author

Richard Biondi is a Social Studies teacher at Branford High School in Branford, Connecticut. For the past thirty years, he has coached Cross Country, Indoor, and Outdoor Track.

Richard is involved with various Italian American organizations in the greater New Haven area including the Santa Maria Maddalena Society on Wooster Street, the St. Andrew and St. Catello Societies, and the Campania Club. Biondi serves on the board of directors for the Santa Maria Maddalena Society, the St. Patrick's Neighborhood Reunion, and the Civil War Round Top of Southeast Connecticut. He has authored two books on boxing and he has written articles for boxing publications. Richard resides in North Haven Connecticut with his wife Ramona who is a teacher in New Canaan Connecticut.

Also by Richard Biondi:

Pugilistic Paisani

Elm City Italians

If you would like to contact Richard Biondi
rdbiondi@snet.net

Salvatore Zarra and Richard Biondi have taught in the Horizons Alternative Education Program since the mid-1990's. For twenty years, they have served as Co-Chairmen for the Veteran's Appreciation Day at Branford High School. Currently, Salvatore serves as a Volunteer Firefighter in Cheshire, Connecticut and he is the Youth Basketball Commissioner.

-

Appendixes

Marker in Columbus Park.

1989 New Haven Register Photo.

The Italians in New Haven-Historical Timeline

(Source: The Ethnic Heritage Center of SCSU)

1717-William Diodati, from Genoa, the first Italian in the Elm City.

1873-Anthony DeMatty opened the first Italian shoe store on Grand Avenue.

1874-Paolo Russo established the first Italian grocery store on the corner of Congress Avenue and Oak Street.

1884-La Fratellanza and La Marineria Societies were formed to help Italians make the transition to America.

1885-Paolo Russo opened an Italian bank.

1888-The Italian population in New Haven reached 2,000.

1890's-Italian immigrants pour into the Hill section and Wooster Square.

1896-The newspaper *Corriere Del Connecticut* was established.

1897-Santa Maria Maddalena Benevolent Society is formed.

1900-Population of St. Michael Church reaches 10,000.

Societa di Sant Andrea Apostolo is formed by immigrants from Amalfi.

1904-St. Anthony Church becomes a place of worship in the Hill.

1909-Marchegian Club is founded in the Hill.

1914-New Haven Register in an article referred to Wooster Square as "Little Naples."
     Campania Athletic Club is formed.

1915-St. Donato Church in Fair Haven becomes the third Italian parish in the city.

1925-Pepe's Apizza established by Frank Pepe.

1936-Amity Club is formed.

1938-Sally's Apizza opened on Wooster Street.

1945-William Celentano becomes the first Italian American mayor of New Haven.

1949-September 20-Fair Haven resident Eddie Compo lost to Willie Pep in a world
     championship boxing match in Waterbury.

1954-Richard Lee is elected as mayor. His Redevelopment program changed the
     landscape of the city.

1957-January 25-Franklin Street fire erupted in a garment factory. It is the deadliest fire in the
     history of the city.

1958-Robert Giamo is elected to Congress.

1970-Bart Guida is elected as mayor and Bart Giametti becomes the President of Yale
     University.

1980-Biagio DiLieto becomes the mayor. The Italian American Historical Society is founded.
     Philip Paolella was the first president.

1990-Rosa DeLauro is elected into the House of Representatives. She would go on to serve for
     three decades.

1994-John DeStefano Jr. is elected into office for the city of New Haven.

Foreign Born Italians in the Elm City

(Source-The Ethnic Heritage Center)

Decade	City Population	Italians
1850	20,345	3
1860	39,267	10
1870	50,840	10
1880	62,882	102
1890	81,298	1,876
1900	108,027	5,262
1910	133,605	13,159
1920	162,537	15,084
1930	162,655	14,510
1940	160,605	12,652
1950	164,443	9,843
1960	164,443	2,515
1970	126,109	2,499
1980	126,109	2,499
1990	130,474	956

2000 Census-Ancestry Report

13,038 Italian Americans in New Haven

New Haven Ethnic Groups-1930

Italians-50,000

Irish 35,000

Jews 25,000

British Americans 20,000

Germans 19,000

Polish 6,000

African Americans 5,300

Scandinavians 3,500

(Source-*New Haven From Puritanism to the Age of Terrorism*-Page 115)

Staff at Muro Macaroni Factory-Circa 1930's.

(Photo Courtesy of Matthew Lupoli and John Migliaro)

La Colonia Italiana di New Haven

Antonio Cannelli-April, 1921

Advertised Businesses in Wooster Square

Wooster Street

Alfonso Afragola Importing 81 Wooster Street

Alfredo Palmiero Tailor 124 Wooster Street

Amendola Brothers Music 164 Wooster Street

Canestri Sons Pasticceria 227 Wooster Street

La France Ice Cream Parlor 95 Wooster Street

Odone Astolfi Dry Goods Store 178 Wooster Street

P.M Perrilli and Maresca Italian Importing 153 Wooster Street

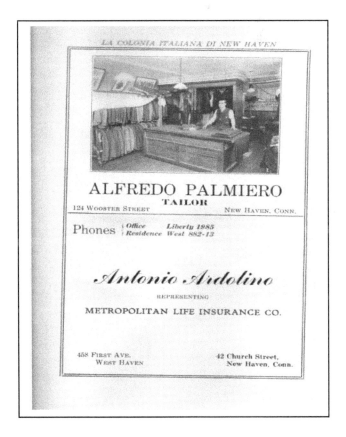

Academy Street

Donato Vece Real Estate 30 Academy Street

Brown Street

Vincent Scaramella Painter 13 Brown Street

Chapel Street

Avvocato Paolo Russo Banchiere 539 Chapel Street

C. Cusanelli Second Hand Furniture 691 Chapel Street

College Tailor Shop-Michael Giaquinto 597 Chapel Street

Fiore Studio 625 Chapel Street

Gagliardi Brothers Funeral Home 514 Chapel Street

Henry Giamarino M.D 532 Chapel Street

Ufficio Laboratorio Di Giuseppe Terranova Dentiere 627 Chapel Street

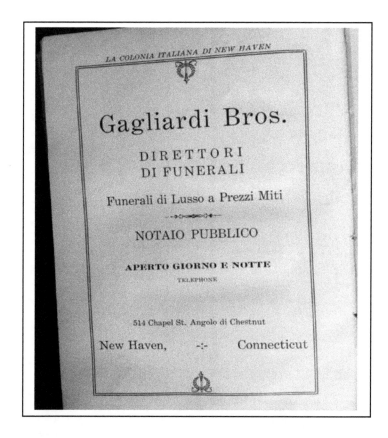

East Street

Vincenzo Virgulto Groceries and Meats 597 East Street

Franklin Street

Angelo Battista Leather and Shoes 192 Franklin Street

Berardesca Pasticceria Napoletana 112 Franklin Street

Frank Taglialatela Carpenter 137 Franklin Street

Papa Brothers General Contractors 165 Franklin Street

Grand Avenue

Alfonso Fasano Photo's 582 Grand Avenue

Antonio Pollio Cheese 708 Grand Avenue

Banca Frank DeLuca 555-559 Grand Avenue

DeVita and DeVita Investments 847 Grand Avenue

Ernest Del Monico Hats 950 Grand Avenue

Farmacia Volpe 609 Grand Avenue

Giovanni Fasano Jewelry 602 Grand Avenue

Little Paris Shop Millinery-Owner Rosina Coppola 629 Grand Avenue

Louis D'Ambrosio Merchant Tailor 613 Grand Avenue

Luigi Battista Fine Shoes 600 Grand Avenue

S.G Grillo Hardware 652 Grand Avenue

Hamilton Street

Alfonso Lavorante Importer Grocer 43 Hamilton Street

Gennaro Cestaro Plumbing 194 Hamilton Street

Giuseppe DeLucia Supplies 200 Hamilton Street

Papagoda Brothers Soda Water 91 Hamilton Street

Sofia Gentile Dry Good Store 182 Hamilton Street

Olive Street

Giuseppe DeFelise and Son Importing 38 Olive Street

Wallace Street

Frank Amato Electrical Contractors 223 Wallace Street

Orazio Flacco Sartoria Italia 176 Wallace Street

Salvatore Apuzzo Italia American Dealer Houseware 192 Wallace Street

Water Street

Angelo Porto and Figli Banco 285 Water Street

Paolo Riccio Shoe Repair 249 Water Street

Italian American Mayors of New Haven

The first mayor of New Haven was Roger Sherman. He was the only man to sign all four State Papers (Continental Association, Declaration of Independence, the Articles of Confederation, and the Constitution). Sherman was in office from 1789 to 1791.

The Elm City has had four Italian American mayors. The first, William C. Celentano, was born in 1904 on Howe Street. His father was an immigrant who peddled fruit. As a teenager, Celentano worked at his dad's store which was located across the street from a funeral home. This was his initial introduction into the profession. In 1924, he graduated from Renouard Training School for Embalmers which is located in New York City.

In 1929, Celentano became the Republican Alderman for the 21st Ward. He performed in this capacity until 1945. From 1945 to 1953, he served as mayor of the Elm City. After his term, he continued to operate his business until passing away in 1972. Celentano was a proud member of the Amity Club.

Source-www.celentanofuneralhome.com

Bartholomew Guida was born on July 8, 1914. A kind man, he was an Alderman from 1948 to 1969. Guida succeeded Mayor Lee and he was in office for three terms from 1970 to 1975. He passed away on April 26, 1978.

Mayor Guida

Wooster Street-July of 1973.

(SSMM Archives)

Biagio DiLieto was born on November 25, 1922. Immensely popular, DiLieto was the police chief from 1970 to 1976. In 1977, he lost the Democratic Primary to Frank Logue. Two years later, he won the race for mayor. DiLieto served five terms. Ben and his wife, the former Rose Greco, had four sons. He passed away on November 8, 1999.

John DeStefano was born on May 11, 1955. While attending UCONN, he met his future wife Kathy who was a career educator in West Haven. In 1989, DeStefano was defeated by John Daniels in the primary. Two years later, he was victorious and John was sworn in on January 6, 1994. A Democrat, John was the mayor until January 1, 2014 making him the longest serving mayor in the history of New Haven.

The DeStefano's have two sons and he is currently working in banking.

Mayor John DeStefano on Wooster Street-1995.

(SSMM Archives)

Sixty Years of History From the Old School

Presented by Cavaliere's Grocery

1934 to 1994

Researched By:
Angelo Cavaliere, Emiddio Cavaliere, Silvio Cavaliere,
Joe Amore, Alfonso Carrano, Ralph Pisani,
Al Lauro, and Chris DeAngelo

Revised by Al Lauro March, 2012

80 G'S John DeMilo	Babe Amendola	Brooks Lucibello
Abe Argento	Babe Proto	Bubbelhead Gargano
Abe DePalma	Babs Amendola	Bucky Boccamiello
Ace Duce Sarno	Baby Bear Simione	Bucky Sinatra Consiglio
Ah Frange Bonito	Baby Doll Joe Digolo	Bum Steer Amendola
Ah Padella Stiano	Baby Jim Consiglio	Burtski Gambardella
Ah Palome DeVito	Baby Jim Gambardella	Buster Giamo
Ah Sard Appi	Bago Esposito	Butch Proto
Al Klaw Klaw Gambardella	Al Bananas Lauro	Ca Set Socks Crisantemi
Al Blonde Cocoon D'Amato	Bang Up Ciaburro	Calabrese Maiorano
Al Di Di Nazario	Beasel DeMartino	Carbone Barbaro
Al Tim McKoy Consiglio	Ben Swish Amarone	Carmel O Panatera Midolo
Alabama Albano	Benny Burns Vitola	Carmenuch D'Amore
Albert GiGi Barlett Cellio	Benny Goodman Criscuolo	Casa Moosh DeRosa
Alphonse Mingo D'Agostino	Bert Burpsy Notarino	Chappy DePalma
Alphonse BarBierd Cavaliere	Bingo Riccuti	Chappy Salemme
Alphonse Shorty Florenzano	Black Ace DeCato	Charles Carlo DeLieto
Andrea Palone Amarone	Blondie Amendola	Charley The Gangster DePino
Andrew Champ Proto	Blubberhead Esposito	Cheech Amen Amendola
Andrew Gus Notarino	Blues Haggerty	Chicken Hand Casanova
Andrew Gute DePalma	Bob The Boob Montagna	Chico Erba
Andrew Muzie Proto	BoBo Gambardella	Chico Midolo
Andrew PaBuch Criscuolo	BoB Palumbo	Chief D'Ambrosio
Andy The Captain Consiglio	Bockmon Tortora	Chirp Canestri

Angelo Gears Papa	Bogash Maselli	Chuck Gambardella
Angelo Julie Cavaliere	Bonehead DeFillio	Clackers Vetri
Anthony Beaver Ascenzio	Bonehead Mele	Pat Copperhead Amarone
Anthony Professor Perrelli	Boots Florio	Lou Corchi Fronte
Art Artooch Palumbo	Bow Wow Sansone	Vinny Crabs Lucibello
BaBa Barbara	Broadway Aielio	Tony Crickets Amendola
George Crime Doctor Visconti	Frank Joe Louis Bonito	Jimmy Bella Lagosi Sarno
Pat D.A DePalma	Frank Monty Montagna	Jimmy Boy Brangi
Tony Danuch Crissi	Frank Poppy Vincent	Jimmy Dogs Elefante
Richard Desert Red Magnotti	Frank Small Chief Abbrosio	Jimmy Pop Monaco
Dewey Maiorino	Frank T Rod DiAuito	Jimmy Rogers DeLeito
Doc Tortora	Frankie Lee DePalma	Jimmy The Apple Consiglio
Dom Boo-Zock Brangi	Frankie Long Gambardella	Jimmy The Chicken Della Sola
Dom Poli Taud Galardi	Fred Chip Ciapuro	Joe Bat Sansone
Dom Red Savo	Freddie Beans Colosso	Joe Bra Bra Buccitti
Dom Slats Marangelli	Mike Frenchy Bonito	Joe Cook Abbanante
Dom The Beak DeAngelis	Fuzzy Brangi	Joe Duck Scarpellino
Don Andrea Proto	Gary Colibardi Gambardella	Joe Flash Falengo
Dondi Dondi Cozzolino	George Washington Nazario	Joe Gas Anastasio
Mike Drink A Beer Novella	Larry Geronimo Amendola	Joe Hop Montagna
Andrew Ducky Duck Amendola	Gi Ta Morth Gambardella	Joe Jo Jo Catatza
Duke Buccitti	Giacamo Chick Esposito	Joe Jr. Gulie Gogliettino
Dykes Zito	Gilardi D Albis	Joe Puck Raiola
Eddie E.R Roberts	Gilly Alfred DeRosa	Joe Stump Ascenzio
Eddie Rye Riolino	Gip Capone	John Pony Shit Ascenzio
Eli Carradine	Greasy Dan Scarpellino	John Vicious Midolo
Emiddio Fat Cavaliere	Hank Cappella	John Zi Zi Brangi
Andy Escarole Masto	Harry James Accurso	Johnny Ann Brangi
Benny Fasuillo Amendola	Joe Hatchet Panzo	Johnny Buck Buck Cimmino
Fat Jimmy Conforte	Hobo Notarino	Johnny Mac Libertti
Fat Joe Vissechio	Hook Fraulo	Vinny Jr. Roe Rosarbo
Fat John Vissechio	Horse Acenzia	Al Judge Gambardella
Andrew Fats Gargano	Sal Hot Lips Vissechio	Jumbo Bonito
Fats Oronzo	Howdy Doody Simino	Vinny Junky Jim Farace
Feminella Gambardella	Sal I. E Pace	Kelly Raiola
Ralph Fi Fi Fish Aquarulo	Joe Ice Man Durso	Killer Amendola
Al Fonzi Carrano	Joe Ingin Criscuolo	Kite Gogliettino
Foot Crisantemi	Johnny Boy Coppola	Lamb Scasino

Foote Dellamora	Jams Gambardella	Phillip Lefty Burke Scarpellino
Al Fow Faw Ignato	Paul Jap Giangeoria	Legs Grazio
Frank Fox Volpe	Jerry Dirt Redenti	Lou Candy Man Nastri
Frank The Barber Del Vecchio	Jerry The Rat Paolillo	Lou Lu Lu Brangi
Frank Butch Savo	Jeruselum Oronzo	Lou Milk Man Genovese
Frank F. G Gambardella	Diamond Jim Amore	Lou O Babia Somma
Frank Futz Celio	Jim Blue Jay Vitagliano	Lou Sneze Riccuti

Corner of Chestnut and Wooster Streets-July, 1987.

Standing (Left to Right)-Al Lauro, Frankie Florenzano and Corchi Fronte

Sitting (Left to Right)-John Vessichio and Benny D'Agostino

July 2004-Dolly Dogolo (L) and Babe Acampora (R).

Lou Squirksie Redenti
Louis Lutch Conforte
Louis O Sproola Rosarbo
Louis Red Brangi
Louis The Milkman Mele
Luigi Ay Melone Gambardella
Mac Dermit Gargano
Maddalena A Fach Tagatilia Manz
Manhatten Camera
Manax Scapetta
Manga A Patano Bonito
Manny The Jew Simons
Mark Bull Head Scarpellino
Matches Amici
Max Bear Boccamiello
John Meatballs Papero
Mel Allen Gargano
Mickey Dolan Grazio
Mickey Williams Landino
Midge Renault Annunziato
Dom Midgique Fronte
Mike Nazone Gargano
Mike Oak Street Materese
Mike R.I Red Lambert
Mike Spike Cedro
Mingo Minichino
Tom Mix Vederamne
Moe Maselli
Lou Moe Oronzo
Tony Moonhead Gambardella
Moto Celio
Mousie Plano
Ralph Murmur Latarocco
Murphy Maiorino
Mush Amendola
Nash Barbaro
Nick Nateski Amarone

Andy The Blast Amarone
Nick The Crow Alberino
Nick The Sport Forte
Nicky Nock Passariello
Nuch Crisantemi
Pete Nunz Nazario
O General Bonito
O Lattari DeBenidetto
O Mola A Forbigia Ricutti
Sal O Morte Savo
O Papone Gambardella
O Pasqualone Fish Bonito
O Pep Williams
O Pie Doll Lombardi
O Rock Williams
O Spatatore Gargano
O Storte Siano
O Tool Proto
Ogrose Barbaro
One Eye Buff Corvino
One Eye Pete Brasile
Papa Pat Consiglio
John Papash Durso
Paper Lover Acenzio
Pat Hoche Cohse Aquaro
Pat Nerves Esposito
Patty Football Fico
Peach Ferriaoilo
Pen Rod Coppola
Pete Gulie Gogliettino
Pete Sardines Notarino
Pete The Tramp Amendola
Petro Gambardella
Petrozine Gambardella
Red Pidgon Shit Capucci
Pinkey Albano
Pip Libro

Pip Scarpellino
Plaw Plaw Montagne
Polock Aquarulo
Pop Amendola
Pop Grazio
Pop Johnson Ferraro
Popcorn DeMartino
Porkey Russo
Portovala Amici
Andy Potato Esposito
Provolone Consiglio
Jack Pussy Pisani
R.D DeMartino
Radio Esposito
Radio Mike Ferro
Ralph Carne Carrano
Ralph Finil Bucchetti
Ralph The Barber Amendola
Rancho Riccuti
Rasio Esposito
Raymond Lemons Maresca
Red Aurora
Red Nazario
Red Russo
Red Sonny Purficato
Red The Rug Graziano
Richard The Chair Santomassino
Rip Gargano
Saint John Villano
Sal Cally Florenzano

Fire escape tomato garden above Russo Park in the Summer of 2009.

Sal Flying Fortress Carrano
Sal O Italian Bonito
Sal The Whale Amore
Sally Boy Gambardella
Sally Oil Anastasio
Sarduzza Oronzo
John Sausage Ferraro
School Boy Roe Calandra
Scotty Ruggiero
Paul Swegurt Corvino
Senza O Cuore Perrelli
Shanks Amendola
Shellhorn Capucci
Hawk Shinny Eyes Scarpellino
Shoes Scarpone
Shorty Crisamtemi
Shorty Gambardella
Shotgun Scapetta
Sid Barbaro
Skippy Castalione
Onofrio Skippy O Surpe Masto
Slim Casanova
Small Change Mosca
Smokey Gambardella
Soap Savo
Nick Soapy Suds Carrano
Sonny Mack Chieppo
Sonny Sausage Quartiano
Spad Me Bith Farace
Square Head Camera

Steak Sansone
Steak Santori
Stormy Weather Vitola
Sweeney DePonte
T-Rod DiAudo
Ta-Da Esposito
Tappy Balzano
Tarzan Camera
Al Taw-Taw Langello
Teeth Celio
Jim The Apple Consiglio
Giro The Diaper Man Torre
The Hand De Albis
Nick The Hat Corvi
Tom The Lord Consiglio
Thomas Big Daddy Aquaro
Three Finger Joe DePino
Tibby DeVito
Tibby Vermiglio
Tick Tock Amendola
Tiger Ray DePonte
Tony Tiny Tim D'Amato
Tiny Tim Gambardella
Tips Oronzo
Tom Mix Carrano
Tom The Greek Kledaras
Anthony Tondo Coppola
Anthony Tony Blues Carrano
Tony Hartack
Tony Moe DelMonico

Tony Poop Consiglio
Tony Shorty Notarino
Tony Chicken Man Proto
Tony Florist Rescigno
Totsie Esposito
Totsy Libero
Ventiquatto DePino
Vincenzo Englese Perrelli
Vincenzo O Shema Barletta
Vinny Heart Attack Totora
Vinny Sausage Quartiano
Virginia Ah Mamana
Walther Winchel Capucci
Whitey Tropiano
Wild Bill Maresca
Wild Man Frank Fronte
Wild Man Grasso
Willey Clams DeLandra
Wizz Esposito
Yip Iovine
Yip Ranciato
Zeke Mercurio
Zia Preveda Aquarulo
Zip DeLito
Zip Mele
Zizza A Vacca Benevento

Tony Pisanelli and Corky
Santacroce-July 2012, on Chapel
Street.

Wooster Square Neighborhood Heritage Exchange-Facebook

Benedetto Minichino was born on William Street. During his youth, his family also resided on Chapel and Greene Streets. Minichino's family has deep roots in the Wooster Square area. In 1895, his grandfather Antonio purchased the building at 103 Wooster Street.

Antonio, was a very prominent businessman. Along with a relative, Alphonse Gambardella, they owned the Reliable Fish Company based out of Plymouth, Massachusetts. Nightly, for forty years, Antonio took the train from New Haven to the Fulton Fish Market to sell his product.

Benedetto attend St. Michael School where he served as the class president in 1971. He has many memories of enjoyable times with his classmates Billy Coppola, Kevin DeMartino, and Susan Lombardozzi. Minichino graduated from Wilbur Cross in 1975. While there, Benedetto formed a close bond with Principal Robert Conte. Today, Benedetto is employed at Ferraro's as a food product buyer. He is married to his wife Karen.

In the early 2000's, he created the Wooster Square Neighborhood Heritage Exchange page. Benedetto commented, "I was born and raised in the area. I wanted the Facebook page to be a resource for people to research their family history. I feel like it is my duty to pass on the history of the neighborhood to the next generation. It is heartwarming and gratifying for me to see all the families on the site. Everyone can look back and be nostalgic about Wooster Square."*

*Interview. Benedetto Minichino. March 11, 2016.

Markets in Wooster Square   (1913-1950)

X=No Listing

Address	1913	1923	1935	1950
42 Bradley	Angelo DeMattis	DeMattis	Capuccio	Capuccio
106 Bradley	X	Giorgio	Pietrofesa	X
21 Brown	Andrea Retento	X	X	X
231 Chapel	X	X	Fucci	X
460 Chapel	X	X	X	Carrano
516 Chapel	X	X	X	Amore
595 Chapel	X	Serino	Serino	Serino
21 Chestnut	Biagio Esposito	Esposito	Siena	X
35 Chestnut	Domenico Bardino	Sorvillo	X	X
53 Chestnut	X	X	Lauro	X
81 Chestnut	X	Cappiello	Scopetta	X
174 Chestnut	Antonio Bolognese	Bolognese	Bolognese	X
176 Chestnut	Sal Acampora	Acampora	X	X
5 Collis	X	DeLeone	X	X
7 Collis	X	X	Anastasio	X
13 Collis	X	X	Afragola	Afragola
19 Collis	X	Cirillo	DePonte	X
21 Collis				Esposito
25 Collis	Domenico DeFrancesco	X	X	X
27 Collis	Nicolangelo Afragola	X	X	X
29 Collis	X	Afragola	Afragola	X
36 Collis	Antonio Sacco	Acampora	X	X
45 Collis	G. Amento	Orifice	Ristaino	Ristaino
48 Collis	X	Gambardella	X	X
50 Collis	Bonifacio Santore	X	X	X
51 Collis	X	Bonito	X	X
55 Collis	Michele Coolino	Coolino	Gamberdella	X
47 Court	X	X	X	DiBlasi
53 Court	Andrea DiPino	DiPino	X	X

69 East	Gennaro Maroni	X	X	X
132 East	X	X	X	Mingione
138 East	X	Vietro	Vietro	X
156 East	Francesco	Ruggiero	X	X
174 East	Tomaso Navaretta	Giagrande	X	X
189 East	Enrico Gambardella	X	X	X
266 East	Louisa Perugino	Martone	Martone	X
292 East	Cresceno Manelli	Manelli	X	X
300 East	X	Carforo	X	X
352 East	Saturno	Saturno	X	X
358 East	X	Fiore	X	X
379 East	X	Vollano	X	X
385 East	X	X	DeLise	X
387 East	Anna Miccia	Miccia		
390 East	Antonio DiPoto	X	X	X
395 East	X	Sangiovanni	X	X
398 East	Maria Tomaro	X	X	X
399 East	X	X	X	DeLucia
420 East	X	Pascarelli	Pascarelli	DeLucia
422 East	X	Maggi	X	X
424 East	X	Ambrando	X	X
515 East	X	Pessapane	Pessapane	Landolfi
534 East	X	Perotti	Perotti	X
597 East	X	Virgulto	DellaRocco	X
22 Franklin	Alfonso Criscuolo	Criscuolo	Criscuolo	Criscuolo
31 Franklin	X	Sacco	Capella	X
114 Franklin	X	Anastasio	X	X
117 Franklin	X	Grinberdella	X	X
137 Franklin	X	Pietro	X	X
142 Franklin	X	Persico	X	X
180 Franklin	X	Caporossi	Caporossi	X
187 Franklin	Ernesto Barbuto	X	X	X
194 Franklin	X	Cuomo	Cuomo	Cuomo
210 Franklin	Giuseppe Caparossa	X	X	Giamo
244 Franklin	X	Spignesi	X	X
38 Greene	Pacifico Migliore	X	X	X
50 Greene	Luigi Cretella	X	X	X
51 Greene	Alberto Pelligrino	X	X	X
73 Greene	X	DiGenaro	X	X
81 Greene	X	Landino	Landino	Landino
111 Greene	X	Ruocco	Ruocco	Ruocco

112 Greene	X	Pas	Gaetano	X
126 Greene	X	LaValle	X	X
142 Greene	X	X	Papagoda	X
179 Greene	X	Papagoda	X	X
210 Greene	X	Scala	X	X
223 Greene	X	Amarante	Amarante	Micarelli
231 Greene	X	X	X	Gamberdella
19 Hamilton	Mary Mele	DePalma	X	X
78 Hamilton	X	Piscatelli	X	X
87 Hamilton	X	X	X	Ciaburro
107 Hamilton	X	Nuo	X	X
108 Hamilton	Francisco Palumbo	Morro	DiBrino	DiBrino
113 Hamilton	X	Rubino	X	X
115 Hamilton	Christine Nucolo	X	X	X
120 Hamilton	X	X	X	Pescitello
132 Hamilton	X	Papa	Papa	X
154 Hamilton	X	Migliaro	X	X
181 Hamilton	X	X	Cipolla	Cipolla
184 Hamilton	Gennaro DeStefano	DeStefano	X	X
187 Hamilton	Alfonso Pavone	X	X	X
197 Hamilton	Cattelo Vergutto	Capone	Capone	Hamilton
208 Hamilton	X	Pallicio	X	X
212 Hamilton	X	Altieri	X	X
216 Hamilton	Alessandro	Ferruillo	Ognibene	X
218 Hamilton	Rasimo Matrisciano	X	X	X
220 Hamilton	X	DeNello	X	X
227 Hamilton	X	X	X	Bonito
229 Hamilton	X	Matrisciano	X	
242 Hamilton	Rascati	Rascati	Pagliaro	x
243 Hamilton	Antonio Altieri	X	X	X
244 Hamilton	X	X	X	Moscato
259 Hamilton	Vincenzo Apria	Capone	Capone	X
266 Hamilton	X	Aiardo	X	Radecki
17 Olive	X	Nostri	X	X
22 Olive	X	X	Picardi	X
25 Olive	X	Cavallaro	X	X
44 Olive	X	Capucci	X	X
72 Olive	X	X	Bonfiglio	X
106 Olive	X	X	X	Ferro
109 Olive	X	LoSchiavo Adinolfi	X	X
115 Olive	X	X	Gagliardi	X

134 Olive	X	Auroro	X	X
23 St. John	Liborio DeFrancesco	X	X	X
43 St. John	X	Iovanne	X	X
47 St. John	X	Ragonese	X	X
49 St. John	X	X	X	Idone
123 St. John	Antonio Carangelo	X	X	X
155 St. John	X	X	Pomarico	Pomarico
208 St. John	X	X	Carpentieri	Lamberti
275 St. John	X	Fufari	Serratielo	X
8 Wallace	X	X	Pascarello	X
19 Wallace	Rafaele Cirillo	X	X	X
23 Wallace	Vincenzo D'Ambrosio	X	X	X
80 Wallace	Maria Carlino	X	X	X
84 Wallace	Giuseppe D'Onofrio	Fucci	X	X
86 Wallace	X	X	X	DiPino
88 Wallace	Gus Pasariello	Pasariello	X	X
105 Wallace	Antonio Mastore	Avino	X	X
144 Wallace	Domenico Cretella	Cretella	X	X
146 Wallace	Giuseppe Barera	Cretella	Cretella	Cretella
157 Wallace	Pasquale DiLeonardo	Balsamo	Durso	Trotta
163 Wallace	Francesco Coppola	X	X	X
197 Wallace	X	Cangiano	Cangiano	Nuo
210 Wallace	X	DeMartino	X	Mauro
222 Wallace	Michele Fisco	X	X	X
238 Wallace	Carlo Lepoli	Lepoli	X	X
254 Wallace	X	X	X	Maruca
295 Wallace	J. Bruno	X	X	X
312 Wallace	Rocco Triano	X	X	X
28 Warren	X	D'Acata	X	DeCato
52 Warren	X	X	Cimmino	Cimmino
77 Water	Pasquelle Lucibello	X	X	X
87 Water	Amendola	Amendola	Amendola	Amendola
97 Water	X	X	X	Pellino
121 Water	Vincent Esposito	Angiolina	DiLieto	X
274 Water	Rosa Ciaramello	X	X	X
285 Water	X	X	Piccolo	X
303 Water	Antonio DiBrigero	X	X	X
307 Water	Italian Cooperative Store	X	Branchini	X

1 Wooster	X	Apicelli	X	X
57 Wooster	Guiseppe Amatruda	X	X	X
62 Wooster	Francesco Gambardelli	Fico	Bigio	X
79 Wooster	X	X	Donarumo	X
81 Wooster	Alfonso Afragola	Afragola	X	Veteran's
95 Wooster	X	X	X	Torre
102 Wooster	Nicola Amodio	Amodio	X	X
117 Wooster	X	Co-Operative	Perrelli	X
118 Wooster	X	Pacillio	X	X
131 Wooster	X	Stano	X	X
134 Wooster	DiPino	Laudano	Cavaliere	X
140 Wooster	X	X	X	Cavaliere
150 Wooster	Alfonso Lavoreto	Ippolito	Ippolito	Ippolito
157 Wooster	X	X	Durso	X
158 Wooster	X	X	Amore	X
170 Wooster	X	X	Sarno	X
172 Wooster	Raffaele Arcangelo	X	X	X
178 Wooster	Gus Guarini	X	X	X
182 Wooster	X	X	Pano	X
184 Wooster	Andrea Pana	Pana	X	X
187 Wooster	X	X	X	Nastri
227 Wooster	Vincenzo Amarante	DeFelice	X	X
235 Wooster	X	X	Arminio	Esposito
237 Wooster	Gennaro Gimoni	Carpentero	X	Erba
242 Wooster	Antonio Milano	Meno	Procopio	X
260 Wooster	X	Cambardella	X	X
268 Wooster	Francesco Gambardelli	Acampora	Acampora	X
272 Wooster	Gaetano Carbone	DeFillippo	X	X
274 Wooster	X	Carbone	X	X

List Courtesy of
Emiddio Cavaliere

Books

Abucar Mohamed. Italians. Nova Scotia: Four East Publications. 1991.

Alba Richard. Italian American Twilight of Ethnicity. Englewood Cliffs:
    Prentice Hall. 1985.

Amfitheatrof Erik. The Children of Columbus. Boston: Little, Brown and Company. 1973.

Brown Elizabeth Mills. New Haven. A Guide to Architecture and Urban Design.
    New Haven. Yale University Press. 1976.

Cannelli Antonio. La Colonia Italiana di New Haven Connecticut. 1921.

Caplan Colin. Legendary Locals of New Haven. United States: Arcadia Publishing. 2013.

Caplan Colin. Then and Now-New Haven. United States: Arcadia Publishing. 2005.

Carrano Valerie Ann. This is War. United States: Iuniverse. 2014.

Cateura Brandi Linda. Growing Up Italian. New York: William Morrow. 1987.

Ciongoli Kenneth and Parini Jay. Beyond the Godfather. London:
    University Press of New England. 1997.

Cupelli Alberto. Italians of Old New Haven 1847-1900. New Haven:
    Branford Printing Company. 1959.

Daniels Roger. Coming to America. United States: Harper Perennial. 1990.

DiStasi Lawrence. The Big Book of Italian American Culture. California:
    Sanniti Publications. 1996.

Fischetti P.R. The Ethnic Cultures of America. Washington D.C: Educational
    Extension Systems. 1997.

Freedman Russell. Immigrant Kids. New York: Puffin Books. 1995.

Gallo Patrick. Old Bread New Wine. Chicago: Nelson Hall. 1981.

Gambino Richard. Blood of My Blood. Garden City: Doubleday. 1974.

Gans Herbert. The Urban Villagers. New York: The Frees Press. 1962.

Grimaldi Lennie. Greater Bridgeport Italian Style. Bridgeport: Harbor
        Publishing. 1992.

Grimaldi Lennie. Only in Bridgeport 2000. Redding CT: Harbor Communications. 2000.

Grossman Ronald. The Italians in America. Minneapolis: Lerner Publications. 1966.

Handlin Oscar. Immigration. Englewood Cliffs, New Jersey: Prentice Hall. 1959.

Hoobler Dorothy and Thomas. Italian American Family Album. New York:
        Oxford University Press. 1994.

Hommann Mary. Wooster Square Design. New Haven: Redevelopment Agency. 1965.

Jackson Isaacs Mandi. Model City Blues. Philadelphia: Temple Press. 2008.

Kraut M. Alan. The Huddled Masses. Illinois: Harlan Davidson. 1982.

LaSorte Michael. La Merica. Philadelphia: Temple Press. 1985.

Lassonde Stephen Learning to Forget. Yale University Press. 2005.

Lattanzi Robert Dr. Oyster Village. Chester: Pattaconk. 2000.

Lee. Kathleen. Tracing Our Italian Roots. United States: John Muir Publications. 1993.

Leeds Mark. Ethnic New York. Illinois: Passport Books. 1996.

Lehman Eric. Bridgeport The Park City. Charleston: History Press. 2009.

LoPreato Joseph. Italian Americans. New York: Doubleday. 1972.

Mangione Jerre and Ben Morreale. La Storia. United States: Harper Perennial. 1992.

Maynard Preston and Noyes Majorie. <u>Carriages &Clocks, Corsets & Locks</u>. London: University Press on New England. 2004.

Munich Adrienne. <u>New Haven's Outdoors.</u> New Haven: Citizens Park. 1985.

Namias June. <u>First Generation American Immigrants</u>. Boston: Beacon Press. 1978.

Nelli Humbert. <u>From Immigrant to Ethnicity</u>. England: Oxford Press. 1983.

Olmsted Frederick Law and Gilbert Cass. <u>Plan For New Haven</u>. San Antonio Texas: Trinity University Press. 2012.

O'Neal Teresa<u>. Immigration</u>. San Diego: Greenhaven Press. 1992.

Orsi Robert Anthony. <u>The Madonna of 115th Street</u>. New Haven: Yale Press. 1985.

Panico Alfonso. <u>The Italians of the New New Haven</u>. New Haven: Minit Print. 1997.

Pisani Lawrence<u>. The Italian in America</u>. New York: Exposition University Books. 1957.

Rae W. Douglas<u>. City</u>. New Haven: Yale University Press. 2003.

Riccio Anthony V. <u>Farms, Factories, and Families</u>. Albany: State University of New York Press. 2014.

Riccio Anthony V<u>. The Italian American Experience in New Haven</u>. Albany: State University of New York Press. 2006.

Riis Jacob. <u>How The Other Half Lives</u>. New York: Dover Publications. 1971.

Sletcher Michael. <u>New Haven From Puritanism to the Age of Terrorism</u>. South Carolina. Arcadia Publishing. 2004.

Smith B. Sharon<u>. Connecticut's Civil War</u>. Milford: Featherfield Publishing. 2010.

Sowell Thomas. <u>Ethnic America</u>. New York: Basic Books Publishing. 1981.

Sowell Thomas. <u>Migrations and Cultures</u>. New York: Basic Books. 1996.

Stotsky Sandra. <u>The Italian Americans</u>. New York: Chelsea House. 1996.

Suarez Ray. <u>The Old Neighborhood</u>. New York: Free Press. 1999.

Weibust Patricia. <u>The Italians in Connecticut</u>. Storrs: Parousia Press. 1968.

Witkoski Michael. <u>Italian Americans</u>. Florida: Rourke Corporation. 1991.

Citizens Park Council. <u>New Haven Outdoors. A guide to the City's Parks</u>. New Haven:

The New Haven Colony Historical Society. <u>Reshaping the City 1900-1980</u>.
        Arcadia Publishing: 2004.

The New Haven Historic District Commission. <u>Iron Fences of Wooster Square</u>.
        North Haven: John McCrillis. 1970.

The New Haven Preservation Trust. <u>History of Wooster Square Architecture 1825-1880</u>. New
        Haven: James Skerritt. 1969.

<u>Wooster Square Redevelopment and Renewal Plan</u>. June 2, 1958. New Haven.

Interviews

Giuseppe Ferraro February 1, 1992

Theresa Argento March 1, 1992

St. Andrew Lady Society March 18, 1992

Rod McKenzie October 22, 1992

Luisa DeLauro May 31, 1993

Rose Cimmino July 10, 2011

Ralph Macarelli July 10, 2011

Caterina DeMartino July 11, 2011

Lt. John Tiedemann July 12, 2011

Robert DiLieto July 24, 2011

Ruby Proto July 26, 2011

Robert Pellegrino August 1, 2011

Frank MyJack August 7, 2011

Michael Persico August 14, 2011

Emiddio Cavaliere September 4, 2011

Andrew DePalma November 7, 2011

Grace Romandetti December 12, 2011

Angelina Midolo January 29, 2012

Michael Balzano January 30, 2012

Rosalie Cocco DeRicco January 31, 2012

Mike Caprio February 22, 2012

Dominic Galardi February 28, 2012

Joe Libero March 1, 2012

Josephine Longobardi March 7, 2012

Ann Norman March 14, 2012

Father Borino March 24, 2012

Johnny Boy Coppola April 11, 2012

Vincent Aitro April 18, 2012

Mark Migliaro June 18, 2012

Marie Sarno Brancaccio June 21, 2012

Andrew DeLandra June 26, 2012

Mike Daniele July 2, 2012

Al Cimino July 20, 2012

Vera Santacroce July 24, 2012

Neil Rapauano July 29, 2012

Matteo and Marie Naclerio July 31, 2012

Michelina Afeltra August 9, 2012

Edward Taddei September 18, 2012

Nicholas Colavolpe September 27, 2012

Doug Guidone (Salzo) October 7, 2012

Rocco Candela October 14, 2012

Pat Amarone October 15, 2012

William Ruocco October 18, 2012

Theresa Scarpellino October 22, 2012

Philip A. Scarpellino October 30, 2012

Abe DePalma October 31, 2012

Mrs. Joseph Panzo November 1, 2012
Pasquale Consiglio November 2, 2012
Elaine Franco Candela November 3, 2012
Mike Coppola November 11, 2012
Anthony Aitro November 23, 2012
Michael Libero Sr. November 23, 2012
Marilyn Gizzi December 3, 2012
Louis Panzo December 9, 2012
Carmen Lupoli December 17, 2012
Frank Corso December 21, 2012
Paul Falcigno December 26, 2012
Matteo Berardesca January 23,2013
Peter Faggio March 16, 2013
Billy Mascari March 18, 2013
Mrs. Salvatore Verderame June 30, 2013
Gennaro Germe July 1, 2013
Joe and Billy Mascari July 7, 2013
Anna Anastasio July 10, 2013
Dom Perno July 12, 2013
Michael Quiello August 12, 2013
Frank Gargano August 13, 2013
Marie Cipriano DeMusis August 17, 2013
Michael and Pasquale Ferraro August 19,2013
Ralph DeFrancisco August 26, 2013
Al "Fasul" Proto August 30,2013
John Raggozino August 30, 2013
Anthony Ricciuti September 8, 2013
Ralph Proto September 9, 2013
Fred Frese September 17, 2013
Tony Vitolo October 5, 2013
Tony Esposito October 9, 2013
Celia Agnellino October 11, 2013
Rheta DeBenedet October 28, 2013
Beverly Carbonella November 13, 2013
William Iovanne Sr. November 23, 2013
Mrs. Conte November 24, 2013
Steven Falcigno November 25, 2013
Mary Florenzano December 7, 2013
Rae Somma December 14, 2013
Cosmo Perrelli December 19, 2013
Paul Montano December 30, 2013
Teresa McClure February 16, 2014
Caesar Canestri April 3, 2014
Ron Palumbo June 23, 2014
Salvatore Consiglio June 30, 2014
Maria Luciola Santore July 29, 2014
Gennaro Santore Sr. July 29, 2014
Bernard Garibaldi March 2, 2015
Carmen Gambardella March 3, 2015
John Orso March 16, 2015
Carol Mauro March 27, 2015

Andrew Bonetti April 1, 2015
Harry Trotta April 8, 2015
John Oronzo April 15, 2015
Mrs. Salvatore (Libero) Consigilio April 16, 2015
Norma Zito Bailey April 21, 2015
Rose Pane April 23, 2015
Benny Amendola May 3, 2015
John Palo May 13, 2015
Gabe Cognato May 19, 2015
Pat Taddei May 21, 2015
Anthony DiLungo May 27, 2015
Egisto Filipelli June 13, 2014
Martin Piccirillo June 19, 2015
Susie Buccitti Montaneri June 20, 2015
Matthew Lupoli June 22, 2015
Chris Migliaro June 22, 2015
Salvatore Savo June 23, 2015
Beverly McClure June 24, 2015
Francis Malerba Erba July 6, 2015
Anthony Giordano July 12, 2015
Rita Silvestro July 12, 2015
Francis Santacroce July 13, 2015
Fred Ferrie July 19, 2015
Michael LaBonia July 26, 2015
Ciro Buonocore July 26, 2015
Restituta Malaccio July 26, 2015
Anne Potenziani July 28, 2015
Tony Rescigno July 29, 2015
John Cassidento August 11, 2015
John Migliaro August 15, 2015
Larry Pisani August 16, 2015
Ed Mauro August 17, 2015
Joe DeCato August 17, 2015
Pat Vissichio August 21, 2015
Rosemary Cuomo September 8, 2015
Vincent Panterea September 12, 2015
Elizabeth Raccuia September 13, 2015
Emilia Cusanelli September 16, 2015
Eddie Angiollo October 20, 2015
Richard Aitro October 20, 2015
Monsignor Gerard Schmitz November 12, 2015
Frank Carrano November 16, 2015
Julia Nicefaro December 2, 2015
Dan Elliott December 13, 2015
Paul Criscuolo December 16, 2015
Al Maiorino December 20, 2015
Ed Flynn December 27, 2015
Gail Parillo January 4, 2016
Sister Rita Petrarca January 13, 2016
Vincent Donarumo January 14, 2016
Julius Marcarelli January 23, 2016

Rose Marie Lavelle Higgins February 8, 2016
First Selectman Michael Freda February 15, 2016
Theresa Incarnato February 21, 2016
Angelo Ciaburro February 23, 2016
Tony Ciarlone February 27, 2016
Kellie Ciaburro Guth March 1, 2016
Phil "Do" Scarpellino March 8, 2016
Benedetto Minichino March 11, 2016
Josephine Esposito March 17, 2016
Bobby Esposito April 10, 2016
Biaggio Fronte April 26, 2016
John Basta June 8, 2016
Lenny Lupoli June 11, 2016
Patti-Jo Esposito June 29, 2016
Anna Festa July 5, 2016
Antoinette Salvo July 7, 2016
Albert Annunziata July 8, 2016
Constable "Sonny" Quartiano July 17, 2016
Jean Quartiano July 20, 2016
Al Annunziata Jr. July 22, 2016

Oral History

Teresa Falcigno September 27, 1989

Newsletters/Magazines

"New Haven Wooster Square. Yankee Enclave With an Italian Accent." Monique Burns. Lawn&Leisure Magazine. February 1982.

"St. Michaels Church 100th Anniversary." La Storia. Fall 1990.

"Ethnic Pluralism in the Greater Wooster Neighborhood: Circa 1915." Dr. Gene Fappiano. La Storia. Winter/Spring 2001.

"Dominic Galardi. A History." Chris R. Nelson. Fall of 2013.

"A Great Migration. So Italian." David Holahan. New Haven Living. May 2016.

Publications

"A Remembrance of Sr. Antonine." By Sr. Ursula Bongiovanni. 2005.

"A Square Comes Full-Circle." By Michael C. Bingham. September 2013.

"An Ethnic History of New Haven." The Ethnic Heritage Center of New Haven.

"Fair Haven History and Architecture." Yale.edu.

"100th Anniversary Church of St. Michaels." Dr. Lawrence Pisani.

"Souvenir Program." Boys Club Alumni Association. 1949.

"The Italian American Experience in America. 1870-1920." Yale New Haven Teachers Institute.

"There Goes the Neighborhood:Slums, Social Uplift and the Remaking of Wooster Square." Digitalcommons.lawyale.edu.

"New Haven's Hill Neighborhood." Yale New Haven Teachers Institute. Peter Heal Herndon.

Reports

Do You Remember? Hamilton Street School/St. Paticks/The Neighborhood.
    Alphonse Proto.

"History of Italians in Connecticut." Trinity College EDU.

"Italian and Blacks in New Haven: The Establishment of Two Ethnic Communities."
    Alice Mick and Lula White. Yale University Teacher's Institute.

"The Anatomy of the Wooster Square Area From Self Providing Italian Enclave (1890-1950) to
    Multi Ethnic Neighborhood (1960-1993)." Richard D. Biondi. 1993.

"The Immigrant City of New Haven. A Study in Italian Social Mobility (1890-1930)."
    Michael J. Petriccione. University of New Haven. 1979.

2016 Cherry Blossom Festival

Ed Flynn (Left) and Paul Criscuolo (Right)

Newspapers

"A Big Fire in New Haven Pork Packing House of Sperry and Barnes Destroyed."
New York Times. June 17, 1886.

"New Haven Church is a Mass of Ruins." The Day. January 4, 1904.

"Columbus Day Festivities Planned Around the State." A.P. October 12, 1912.

"Salzo Quadruplets." Norwalk Hour. July 12, 1922.

"A Seven Course Dinner in a Sandwich." New Haven Register. December 10, 1950.

"Paul Russo Overcame Poverty to Win Fan." Grace DeMarco. Sunday Herald.
April 27, 1952.

"Singing Baker." New Haven Register. August 10, 1952.

"One Quad Very Alive." Sunday Herald. July 3, 1955.

"Fatal Factory Blaze Shocks City. Death Toll of Nine Now Possible." New Haven Evening
Register. January 25, 1957.

"Four Still Missing in Connecticut Factory Fire." AP. St. Petersburg Times.
January 26, 1957.

"Fire Wreaks Five Story Loft. Damages Church and School." Meriden Record.
August 30, 1960.

"Harry Conte 71, Died of Heart Ailment." Meriden Journal. April 18, 1961.

"From Melting Pot to Historical District." New Haven Register. March 16, 1965.

"Wooster Square Today." Chris Mascari. New Haven Register. May 25, 1969.

"The Neighborhood That Would Not Quit." Hartford Courant. September 29, 1974.

"City Primaries in Connecticut Spurring Wide Voter Interest." Matthew Ward.
New York Times. September 8, 1981.

"Franklin Street Blaze Haunts It's Survivors 25 Years Later." George Cubanski.
New Haven Register. January 24, 1982.

"The Flavor of Franklin Avenue." Linda Giuca. Hartford Courant. November 2, 1983.

"Italians Flourish on Street." Joseph Rodriquez. Hartford Courant. July 2, 1985.

"Martha Stewart Causes Stir at Wooster Street Delicatessen." Patrick Dilger.
New Haven Register. November 23, 1986.

"Mayor of New Haven won't seek Sixth Term." Nick Ravo. New York Times. March 29, 1989.

"Our Town, Near Yale, Grief Over a Big Man off Campus."   Nick Ravo. New York Times.
May 12, 1989.

"City Remembers "Uncle Mike." Pamela McLoughlin. New Haven Register.
September 11, 1989.

"A True Man of the World." Lenn Zonder. Connecticut Post. December 25, 1992.

"Aitro League Brings History to Area." Seth Davis. New Haven Register. May 2, 1994.

"Dinning Out Third Generation in New Haven." Patricia Brooks. New York Times.
February 4, 1996.

"Vitolo Steps Down as Hillhouse Coach." Steve Wilson. New Haven Register. March 21, 1996.

"Three Hundred Firefighters and Friends Attend Mass to Honor Fifteen Workers Killed in 57."
Alaine Griffin. New Haven Register. January 24, 1997.

"On the Neptune, Three Years Under Sail." Alberta Eisenman. New York Times.
March 2, 1997.

"Teaching the Teachers, a Group Effort." Melinda Tuhus. New York Times. March 14, 1999.

"What Makes a Big Airport Hum? Atlanta May do it Best, But Growing Pains Loom."
 Edwin McDowell. New York Times. October 13, 1999.

"Biagio DiLieto, 76 Mayor of New Haven for a Decade." Tina Kelly. New York Times.
 November 12, 1999.

"You Say Sally's, I Say Pepe's. Wooster Street Legends Deliver to Die Hard Crowds."
 Jim Shelton. New Haven Register. July 21, 2002.

"A Lifetime of Commitment." Carolina Harrington. East Haven Courier.
 August 8, 2002.

"Richard C. Lee 86 Mayor Who Revitalized New Haven." Paul Von Zielbauer.
 New York Times. February 4, 2003.

"Wooster Square Priest Resigns Sexual Abuse Allegations Back to 1983 in Boston." Michael
 Gannon. New Haven Register. January 18, 2004.

"Hartford Priest Accused of Sex Abuse in Bay State." Mark Szaniszlo. Boston Herald.
 January 19, 2004.

"Resident Spread Love of Basketball From New Haven to Africa and Beyond."
 Grace O'Connor. Branford Review. September 8, 2004.

"Welcome to the New Franklin Avenue." Andy Hart. Hartford New. May 17, 2006.

"Mass Today in Memory of Factory Workers Caught in Fire." William Kaempffer.
 New Haven Register. January 24, 2007.

"The Day 15 Died." William Kaempffer. New Haven Register. January 24, 2007.

"Storied Cross Basketball Coach Salvatore Red Verderame Dies."
 Joe Morelli. New Haven Register. February 17, 2008.

"Getting Grief Right." Timothy Shriver. Washington Post. February 18, 2008.

"In Life and Basketball, Red Ahead of His Time." David Solomon.
 New Haven Register. February 20, 2008.

"Semper Fi. A Memorial Day Tribute to a Marine Who Fell at Iwo Jima."
     Jim Shelton. New Haven Register. May 25, 2008.

"Santa Maria Maddalena Society Keeps Traditions Alive." Lauren Garrison.
     New Haven Register. July 21, 2008.

"Tradition rules Wooster Square." Nick Scalia. New Haven Register. November 21, 2008.

"They're a Deli Not a Bakery." Stephan Fries. New Haven Register. April 15, 2009.

"SCSU Professor 88 is a Living History Book." Pamela McLoughlin.
     New Haven Register. May 3, 2009.

"St. Andrew Society Celebrates 109 Years of Feasting With Weekend Festival."
     Christina Borger. New Haven Register. June 26, 2009.

"The Old Days: It was the 50's and a Church was the Neighborhood's Anchor."
     Mary O'Leary. New Haven Register. September 27, 2009.

"A Soldier's Story, WW 2 Vet Remains a Neighborhood Guy." Ed Stannard.
     New Haven Register. October 25, 2009.

"Sweet Success:Lucibello's Marks 80 Years in City." Cara Baruzzi. New Haven Register.
     November 1, 2009.

"Babe Touched Many Lives." Dave Solomon. New Haven Register. November 26, 2009.

"Former West Haven Teacher, Coach Loved Sports and Liked to Eat." New Haven Register.
     January 1, 2010.

"Changing Tastes Along Bridgeport Restaurant Row Reflects Demographic Shift."
     John Burgeson. Bridgeport Post. April 14, 2010.

"Former Italian Consulate Back on the Market in New Haven." Eric Gershon.
     Hartford Courant. April 27, 2010.

"That's Italian. Connecticut Gives Other State the Boot. Claims Most Italian State."

Mara Lee. Hartford Courant. February 22, 2011.

"Lifelong Resident of Wooster Square o Have Street Corner Named in his Honor."
William Kaempffer. New Register. May 20, 2011.

"Bridgeport's Little Italy Not the Same." Connecticut Post. July 6, 2011.

"Author of Little Italies Drops by Consiglio's." Stephan Fries. New Haven
Register. June 11, 2011.

"Consiglio's is Serving Up Some Fun on the Patio." New Haven Register. July 13, 2011.

"Great American Bites"New Haven Clam Apizza Smack Down. " Larry Olmsted. USA Today.
August 4, 2011.

"Luisa DeLauro to Call Corner Her Own." Abbie Smith. New Haven Register.
August 4, 2011.

"Prime Market:New Haven's Statewide Meats Takes on New Role as Part of Sysco."
Mary O'Leary. New Haven Register. September 17, 2011.

"That's Amore, Pizza Passion." Jordan Fenster. New Haven Register.
September 23, 2011.

"More Than 100 New Haven Residents Sign Petition Against DeLauro Family Table."
Angela Carter. New Haven Register. October 10, 2011.

"DeLauro Family Table Up in New Haven's Wooster Square Despite Some Objections."
Angela Carter. New Haven Register. October 19, 2011.

"City Dedicates Monument Honoring DeLauro Family." Amanda Pinto.
New Haven Register. October 24, 2011.

"Dedication of Pisani Pavilion." Post Chronicle. November 23, 2011.

"Vinnie's Still Carrying On After a Century of Games and Service." New Haven Register.
Randall Beach. March 25, 2012.

"For Some, Going to War Was in the Family." New Haven Register. Ann DeMatteo.
    May 28, 2012.

"Sally's Matriarch "Flo" Consiglio Dies." William Kaempffer. New Haven
    Register. September 25, 2012.

"Flo Consiglio to Join Sally on Street Sign." Alexandra Sanders. New Haven
    Register. October 4, 2012.

"Aldermen Go With the Flo." Alexandra Sanders. New Haven Register. October 5, 2012.

"Tony Vitolo Became a Household Legend." Joe Morelli. New Haven Register. October 6,
    2012.

"Italian Fest Puts Icing On Parade." Rich Scinto. New Haven Register. October 8, 2012.

"A Day of Reunion and Goodbyes for Former Students of St. Michael School."
    Rich Scinto. New Haven Register. March 23, 2014.

"Former Alder Luisa DeLauro Turns 100." Rich Scinto. New Haven Register. December 23,
    2013.

"Remembering the Days When Movie Theatres Were Downtown." Randall Beach.
    New Haven Register. February 26, 2015.

"When all Hell Broke Loose." Esteban Hernandez. New Haven Register. April 5, 2015.

"A New Haven Street Becomes a Place." Duo Dickinson. New Haven Register. May 2, 2015.

"Century Old Manufacturing Plant Seeks New Life." Mary O'Leary. New Haven Register.
    June 14, 2015.

"The Taste of Success." Mary O'Leary. New Haven Register. June 16, 2015.

" The Mayor of Street is Hanging Up Her Stogies." Randall Beach. New Haven
    Register. June 21, 2015.

"Joe Canzanella to Step Down as New Haven Citywide Athletic Director." Joe Morelli. New Haven Register. September 5, 2015.

"Canzanella's AD Tree Branches Out." Joe Morelli. New Haven Register. September 6, 2015.

"Bid to Sell Sally's a Tangled Saga." Mary O'Leary. New Haven Register. December 6, 2015.

"9 Families Displaced After Building Facade Starts to Crumble." Mary O'Leary. New Haven Register. December 25, 2015.

"Uncertain Future For Pizzeria That Gave New Haven a Special Flavor." Kristin Hussey. New York Times. January 14, 2016.

"For 71 Years, the Fabulous Fab's Brothers Were Like the Family Doctor." Randall Beach. New Haven Register. February 1, 2016.

"Wooster Sq. Transit Setup Weighed." Mary O'Leary. New Haven Register. July 18, 2016.

"Character of Wooster Square Key to Development." Mary O'Leary. New Haven Register. July 19, 2016.

"Longtime Tradition Keeps You Close to Your Roots." Pamela McLoughlin. New Haven Register. July 25, 2016.

"Greene Street Girls Return." Kate Ramunni. New Haven Register. September 9, 2016.

"Party to Benefit Ronald McDonald House." New Haven Register. September 25, 2016. Mary O'Leary.

On Line Articles

"Life in the Model City. Stories of Urban Renewal in New Haven." Sarah Barca.
New Haven Independent. March 9, 2004.

"Sinatra Gets A Stamp." Melissa Bailey. New Haven Independent. June 9, 2008.

"Historic Gambardella Property Foreclosed." Andrew Mangino. New Haven
Independent. June 10, 2008.

"Fire Ravaged Lincoln Flower Shop." Allan Appel. New Haven Independent.
February 10, 2009.

"At 86, St. Andrew's Helper Readies Another Fest." Thomas MacMillan.
New Haven Independent. June 25, 2009.

"Vet's Honored." Allan Appel. New Haven Independent. November 19, 2009.

"Wooster Square Lays a Wreath Ponders the Future." Allan Appel. New Haven
Independent. October 11, 2010.

"St. Andrews Keeps the Faith." Jacob Cohn. New Haven Independent.
June 27, 2011.

"For a Day They Returned to St. Michael." Allan Appel. New Haven Independent.
September 19, 2011.

"DeLauro Family Table Unveiled." Allan Appel. New Haven Independent.
October 23, 2011.

"She Wore a Fuchsia Boa." Peter Webster. New Haven Independent. May 26, 2015.

"A Conversation with Beverly Carbonella." New Haven Museum-Beyond the New Township
Wooster Square.

"The 19th Century New Haven Flexes It's Industrial Muscle." www.conntact.com

Websites

acgilbert.com

ccowles.com

consiglios.com

ct.history.org

historicalwoostersquare.org

foxonpark.com

lucibellospastry.com

newhavenhillcitypoint.com

newhavenpreservationtrust.com

n.i.a.f.org

pepespizzeria.com

sallysapizza.com

sargentlock.com

ssaanewhaven.com

tonyamendola.com

Columbus Park
Hurricane Irene-September of 2011.

CPSIA information can be obtained
at www.ICGtesting.com
Printed in the USA
BVHW02s1952230118
506095BV00007B/51/P